5000 BRILLIANT WEB SITES

in easy steps
.compact

C

GW00706112

in easy steps and **in easy steps.compact** are imprints of Computer Step
Southfield Road . Southam . Warwickshire CV47 OFB . England
Web site: http://www.ineasysteps.com
Email: books@ineasysteps.com

Notice of Liability

Every effort has been made to ensure that this book contains accurate and current information. However, Computer Step and the author shall not be liable for any loss or damage suffered by readers as a result of any information contained herein.

Trademarks

All trademarks are acknowledged as belonging to their respective companies.

Printed and bound in the United Kingdom

ISBN 1-84078-109-2

Contents

Finance *165*

Food & Drink *189*

Government & Politics *209*

Health *215*

Hobbies *231*

Home *255*

ReadMe.first

The Internet is vast beyond comprehension. Over the last few years countless people from all over the world have contributed to it making it a huge source of information to tap into. The trouble is, much of what is out there is either unsuitable or of poor quality, or both.

This book brings together some of the best websites from around the world. The sites have been carefully selected and categorised so it should be easy to find what you want. When you have located the website you're interested in, open your browser (which will most likely be Internet Explorer or Netscape) and type the address exactly as given in this book in the panel labelled 'Address'. When you've entered it, press the Enter key and the website should be displayed.

Enter the address here

What if it doesn't work?

There are over 5000 web addresses in this book and frankly, I wouldn't be surprised if a few do not work by the time you read this. The fact is that the Internet is notoriously transient. A site that exists today, may have vanished from the face of the Earth tomorrow. Many of the sites on the Internet are run by individuals who have been provided with free space to create their own website, but once the novelty has worn off, the sites are abandoned. But even large companies can run into problems. Only a few weeks before finishing this book, *boo.com*, one of the largest Internet sports clothing reseller, ceased trading.

Where possible, websites by individuals have been avoided, as for the sites that no longer work, all I can say is sorry. At the time of writing, all sites referred to in this book work.

Help us to keep you up-to-date

If you find one of the websites listed in this book doesn't work, please let us know. Send an email to Computer Step (*books@ineasysteps.com*) and let us know the page, the name and the address of the website and we will remove it in the next edition. You might also care to suggest Internet sites that should be included in the updated book. Using the same email address, tell us the name of the site, the address and a brief description of what it's about.

Although this book was written by a British author, the majority of the sites should be of use to users across the World.

Art

This three-letter word seems to cover anything you want it to. Here, I've restricted its use to Artists and Artwork, Antiques, Ballet, Opera, Crafts and Literature.

Art Galleries

You don't have to travel the world to visit the top art galleries as most now have their own website enabling you to bring the gallery into your home. Of course, it's not really as good as visiting in person, but many of these site are a close second.

Aberdeen Art Gallery	*http://www.aagm.co.uk/*
American Arts Guild and Gallery	*http://www.aagg.com/*
Art Gallery of New South Wales	*http://www.artgallery.nsw.gov.au/*
Art Republic	*http://www.artrepublic.com/*
Axia Modern Art	*http://axiamodernart.com.au/ index.html*
Courtauld Institute	*http://www.courtauld.ac.uk/*
Hayward Gallery	*http://www.hayward-gallery.org.uk/*
Louvre, The	*http://mistral.culture.fr/louvre*
Metropolitan Museum	*http://www.metmuseum.org*
Museum of Modern Art	*http://www.moma.org*
National Gallery	*http://www.nationalgallery.org.uk/*

Portraits on display

Room 29: The Turn of the Century

| Robert Polhill Bevan | Sir Frank Swettenham | Henry James | Spencer Frederick Gore |

National Museum & Gallery Cardiff *http://www.nmgw.ac.uk/nmgc/ nmghome.html*

National Portrait Gallery *http://www.npg.org.uk/*

Norwich Gallery *http://www.nsad.ac.uk/gallery/*

Online Art Gallery *http://www.artandparcel.com/*

Royal Academy *http://www.royalacademy.org.uk/*

Tate Gallery *http://www.tate.org.uk/*

Tribal Art Directory *http://www.tribalartdirectory.com/ top_nav.htm*

Virtual Art Gallery *http://www.art.net/*

Wallace Collection *http://www.the-wallace-collection .org.uk/*

Artists

When one thinks of an artist, it's invariably one of the so-called 'old-masters', many of which have a website or two about them. But don't forget some of the more modern artists.

Artcyclopedia   *http://www.artcyclopedia.com/*
Allder Phillip   *http://www.allderart.co.uk/*
Brennan Ian   *http://www.iangb.com/*
David F Wilson   *http://www.users.globalnet.co.uk/*
                               ~dfwil/toc.htm

Feast of Leonardo   *http://www.webgod.net/leonardo*
Joyce Rowsell   *http://members.aol.com/rowsellj/*
LS Lowry   *http://195.226.34.58/frameset/ie.html*
Monet's World   *http://events/fleet.com/*
Picasso   *http://www.clubinternet.com/picasso*
Pre-Victorian Artists   *http://www.speel.demon.co.uk/*
                               artist18.htm

Victorian Artists   *http://www.speel.demon.co.uk/*
                               listart.htm

Antiques

Personally I'm not fussed about the age of an item or it's background. I would just as soon have a china teapot from the local discount store than a priceless antique that you daren't use in case it gets chipped. I recognise I'm probably in the minority, so here are a few sites from dealers and galleries.

Alliance Antiques buys, sells and brokers high quality antiques, collectibles, furniture, art and other fine merchandise. Our antique store and warehouse are filled with vintage stoneware, pottery, art, toys, glass, jewelry, textiles, architectural pieces and much more!

Come in and browse the wide variety of antiques and unique merchandise in our online store - you'll be glad you did!

Alliance Antiques	*http://www.alliance-antiques.com/*
Antiques For Everyone	*http://www.sharongarberantiques.com/*
Arminius Gallery	*http://www.antique-shop.net/*
Art-Co French Art Deco	*http://www.antiquites-france.com/*
Conservation and Restoration	*http://restorationlab.com/*
Daltons Antiques	*http://www.daltons.com/*
Decade Art Deco Catalogue	*http://www.decade.co.nz/*

Europe Antiques	*http://www.europe-antiques.com/*
Great Wall	*http://www.greatwallantique.com/*
Indian Oaks Antique Mall	*http://www.indianoaksantiquemall.com/*
J. Hill Antiques	*http://www.jhill.com/*
Kittinger Furniture	*http://www.kittengerfurniture.com/*
Legacy Antiques and Fine Art	*http://legacyantiques.com/index.html*
Mir Antiques Antwerp	*http://www.antiquesantwerp.com/*
Modernism Gallery	*http://www.modernism.com/*
Odyssey Fine Arts Ltd	*http://www.odysseyart.co.uk/*
Old Asia Gallery	*http://www.oldasiagallery.com/*
Old Bear Company	*http://www.flair.co.uk/oldbear*
Old World Art & Treasures	*http://artreasures.com/*
Otford Antiques & Collectors Centre	*http://www.otfordantiques.co.uk/*

P.L. James & Son Antiques	*http://www.plj-antiques.com/*
Past Pleasures Antiques	*http://www.cyberattic.com/~pleasures*

Pieter Hoogendijk	*http://www.artnet.com/phoogendijk.html*
Post Road Gallery	*http://www.postroadgallery.com/*
Rhumba!	*http://www.tace.com/rhumba*
Russki	*http://www.russiansilver.co.uk/*
Vintage Hardware	*http://www.vintagehardware.com/*
Vintage Watches	*http://www.halem-times.com/*
Weston Antiques (UK)	*http://www.antiques-shop.co.uk/*

Ballet

I'd never been to a ballet until I got inspired by some of these websites which give full details of performances. Some even allow you to book online.

American Ballet Theatre   *http://www.abt.org/*

Australian Ballet	*http://www.austballet.telstra.com.au/*
Ballet in Russia	*http://www.zenon.ru/~vladmo/ digest1.html*
Ballet International	*http://www.ballet-tanz.de/*
Ballet.co	*http://www.ballet.co.uk/*
Bolshoi Theater, Ballet and Opera History	*http://www.alincom.com/bolshoi/*
City Ballet of London	*http://freespace.virgin.net/david .browne/cbl.htm*
Classical Ballet Training	*http://www.robxw.demon.co.uk/ teachers.htm*
Continental Ballet Company	*http://www.continentalballet.com/*

The Electric Ballerina

Fouettés Forever

This difficult turn was made famous by 19th-century Russian ballerina Pierina Legnani in the original Imperial Theater version of *Swan Lake*. Legnani, proud of the fact that she had perfected the ability to do as many as 32 *fouettés* in succession -- a feat that would have been impossible for most dancers of the time -- wanted

Electric Ballerina	*http://www.novia.net/~jlw/electric/ electric.html*

English National Ballet

http://www.ballet.org.uk/

Kirov Ballet and Academy

http://www.kirovballet.com/

London Junior Ballet

*http://www.londonjuniorballet
.cwc.net/*

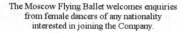

Auditions

The **art**
of **ballet** has reached
a new **height**.

The Moscow Flying Ballet welcomes enquiries
from female dancers of any nationality
interested in joining the Company.

Q & A ★
Auditions ★
Fly With Us ★
Merchandise ★
Contact Us ★

Moscow Flying Ballet

http://www.flying-ballet.com/

National Ballet of Canada

http://www.national.ballet.ca/

New York City Ballet

http://www.nycballet.com/

Royal Ballet School

http://www.royal-ballet-school.org.uk/

Sadler's Wells

http://www.sadlers-wells.com/

Scottish Ballet

http://www.scottishballet.co.uk/

Crafts

I wasn't sure whether to put these sites here or in the section on hobbies. I don't suppose it really matters, but if you like doing something arty/crafty, or would like to learn about a particular craft, there's a good selection here.

Africa Warehouse

http://www.ishop.co.uk/ishop/62

Arts & Crafts Society

http://www.arts-crafts.com/

Art Resources

http://www.artresources.com/

Black Ash Basketry	*http://basketry.miningco.com/library/weekly/aa111698.htm*
Candleshop	*http://www.candleshop.com/*
Candles and Supplies.com	*http://www.candlesandsupplies.com/*
Candle Supply.com	*http://www.candlesupply.com/*
Card Inspirations	*http://www.cardinspirations.co.uk/*
Ceramic Art Space	*http://www.ceramicartspace.com/*
China Painting	*http://www.geocities.com/Paris/3543/*
Clock Movements	*http://www.clockmovements.com/*
Country Seat Inc., The	*http://www.countryseat.com/*

Crafts Etc!	*http://www.craftsetc.com/*

Crafts for Kids	*http://craftsforkids.about.com/kids/ craftsforkids/mbody.htm*
Crochet 'n' More	*http://crochetnmore.com/*
Crochet Musings	*http://crochet.rpmdp.com/*
Crochet	*http://crochet.miningco.com/ index.htm*
Crochet Guild Of America	*http://www.crochet.org/*
Designer Stencil	*http://www.designerstencils.com/*
Dragonfly Glass	*http://www.dragonflyglass.com/*

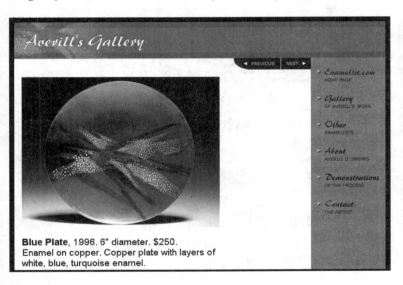

Blue Plate, 1996. 6" diameter. $250.
Enamel on copper. Copper plate with layers of
white, blue, turquoise enamel.

Enamels	*http://www.enamelist.com/*

The Paper Arts

Complete alphabetical listing below - Please follow down *(below the papers and extras)* until you find the Paper Art you are interested in. For links to Paper related sites, visit Paper Pathways. Many of these listings are entire sections dedicated to the particular Paper Art. Choose your favorite and explore. This is a frames website. Please start at Home - otherwise you might miss all the fun things we have!

Papers and Extras (great for all Paper Arts!)

Collage Collections | Washi Quarters *New!* | Paper Collections | Artisan Specialty Papers | Decorative Extras | Even More Embellishments

Fascinating Folds	*http://fascinating-folds.com/*
Glass Art Society	*http://www.glassart.org/*
Glass Craftsman	*http://www.artglassworld.com/*
Glass Museum	*http://www.glass.co.nz/*
Green Dragon	*http://www.greendragon.co.uk/*
Heart Bead	*http://www.heartbead.com/*
Hexaflexagons	*http://www.xnet.com/~aak/hexahexa.html*
Kids Kits Crafts and Projects	*http://www.kidskitscrafts.com/*
Knitting Knook	*http://www.yarnshop.com/*
Knitting & Lace Making	*http://www.tcd.net/~robin/knit.html*
Knitting Now	*http://www.knittingnow.com/*
Knitting Today	*http://www.knittingtoday.com/*

Lace Language	*http://www.touchoflace.com*
Lace Magazine Home Page	*http://www.lacemagazine.com/*
Lacis	*http://www.lacis.com/*
Lampwork Flamework Glass Art	*http://www.mickelsenstudios.com/*
Mad Stencilist	*http://www.madstencilist.com/*

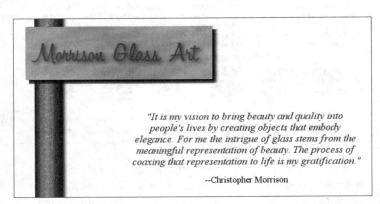

"It is my vision to bring beauty and quality into people's lives by creating objects that embody elegance. For me the intrigue of glass stems from the meaningful representation of beauty. The process of coaxing that representation to life is my gratification."

--Christopher Morrison

Morrison Glass Art	*http://www.eskimo.com/~kmc/MGA.htm*
OrigamiUSA	*http://www.origami-usa.org/*
Painted Fire	*http://www.seattle2000.com/paintedfire/*
Paperfolding.com	*http://www.paperfolding.com/*
Southwest Stencils	*http://www.swstencils.com/*
Stenciling.com	*http://www.stenciling.com/*
Stencil Library	*http://www.stencil-library.com/*
Vogue Knitting	*http://www.vogueknitting.com/*

Wax House, The	*http://www.waxhouse.com/*
Wonderful World of Crochet	*http://www.tallassee.net/~crafts/*
	cro1.htm

Literature

The pen is mightier than the sword and over the years there have been many great men and women who have wealded it to great effect.

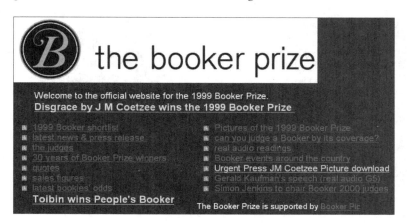

Booker Prize, The	*http://www.bookerprize.co.uk/*
Edward Lear Home Page	*http://www2.pair.com/mgraz/Lear/*
	index.html
George Eliot	*http://www.kirjasto.sci.fi/gelliot.htm*
H.G. Wells	*http://www.geocities.com/Athens/*
	Delphi/8169/index.htm
Jane Austen	*http://www.pemberley.com/janeinfo/*
	janeinfo.html

Jonathan Swift (1667-1745) *http://www.mala.bc.ca/~mcneil/swift.htm*

Kipling Society *http://www.kipling.org.uk/*

the milton-l home page
Devoted to the life, literature and times of John Milton

Home
What's New
About Milton-L
Awards
List Archives
Subscribe!

Chronology
E-texts
  Paradise Lost
Images
Audio
Articles
Book Reviews
Events
Suggest a Site

Milton-L Home Page, The *http://www.urich.edu/~creamer/milton/*

Oscar Wilde *http://www.poetrytodayonline.com/cp.html*

Robert Louis Stevenson *http://www.unibg.it/rls/rls.htm*

Walter Scott, Sir *http://www.camelotintl.com/heritage/walter.html*

William Shakespeare *http://the-tech.mit.edu/shakespeare/works.html*

William Thackeray *http://www.incompetech.com/authors/thackeray/*

Opera

Call me uneducated, but opera is something I cannot get into in a big way. It seems that it's all sung in another language and there are no subtitles. Apparently there is a storyline, but that too, is totally incomprehensible.

Home Page
E N O

Eugene Onegin

Tchaikovsky

Text Shilovsky and Tchaikovsky, after Pushkin

English National Opera	*http://www.eno.org/*
New York City Opera	*http://www.nycopera.com/*
Opera Now	*http://www.rhinegold.co.uk/ rgmgon1.cfm*
Opera Stuff	*http://www.columbia.edu/~km34/ sing.html*
Opera World	*http://www.operaworld.com/*
OperaWeb	*http://www.opera.it/English/ OperaWeb.html*
Royal Opera House	*http://www.royalopera.org/*
Sadler's Wells	*http://www.sadlers-wells.com/*
Sydney Opera House	*http://www.soh.nsw.gov.au/*

Surrounded by water on three sides, at what is known as Bennelong Point, stands one of the most magnificient buildings on one of the most beautiful harbours in the world. The Sydney Opera House, Originally designed by the Danish Architect Joern Utzon, is meant to look like a giant sailing ship.

Sydney Opera House Virtual Tour   *http://www.oznet.net.au/opera*
Virtual Opera House   *http://www.opera.co.za/*

Books

Whatever your taste in reading matter, you'll find it on the Internet.

Bookstores

Whenever I visit a particular high street bookshop (which isn't very often actually) I'm always amazed that the staff allow customers to read the books and papers. Having a quick look at the plot is one thing, but some people actually sit down and read the book and then leave without buying it. The advantage of buying at an online bookshop is that the book you get will be new, unread and unthumbed. The corners won't be 'dog-eared' and the spine won't be broken which means you can give it as a gift without the recipient thinking you've raided your own bookcase.

Absolutely Weird Bookshelf	*http://www.strangewords.com/*
Advanced Book Exchange	*http://www.abebooks.com/*
Alibris	*http://www.alibris.com/*
Alphabet Street	*http://www.alphabetstreet.co.uk/*
Amazon	*http://www.amazon.com/*
Art2Art	*http://www.art2art.com/*
Audio Book Club	*http://www.audiobookclub.com/*
Barnes and Noble	*http://www.barnesandnoble.com/*
B.T.Batsford	*http://www.batsford.com/*
Better Life Books	*http://www.betterlifebooks.com/*

◉ bibliofind

Search Shopping Basket Community Reference Help

Welcome to ◉ bibliofind

More than ten million used and rare books, periodicals and ephemera offered for sale by thousands of booksellers around the world make this the most interesting book-selling site on the Web.

◉ Search for Free!

Author	
Title	
Any other word(s)	
Prices between	and
Books added	at any date ▾
First Editions	□
	Signed/Inscribed □

Search Tips   SEARCH   CLEAR

Bibliofind   *http://www.bibliofind.com/*
Blackstone Press   *http://www.blackstonepress.co.uk/*
Blackwells   *http://bookshop.blackwell.co.uk/*
BOL   *http://www.bol.com/*
Book Garden, The   *http://www.bookgarden.com/*
Book People, The   *http://www.thebookpeople.co.uk/*
Book Pl@ce, The   *http://www.thebookplace.com/*
Booklovers   *http://www.booklovers.co.uk/*
BookNook   *http://www.booknook.com/*
Books A Million   *http://www.booksamillion.com/*

Books are Magic	*http://www.booksaremagic.com/*
Bookstreet, 1	*http://www.1bookstreet.com/*
Chapters	*http://www.chapters.ca/*
Children's Book Centre	*http://www.childrensbookcentre.co.uk/*
Children's Bookshop, The	*http://www.childrensbookshop.com/*
Computer Books Online	*http://www.computerbooksonline.com/*

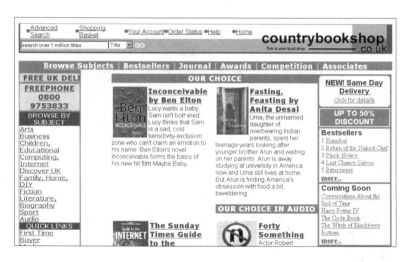

Country Bookshop	*http://www.countrybookshop.co.uk/*
Dymocks	*http://www.dymocks.com.au/*
Edge Book Shop	*http://www.cumbria1st.com/biz/books/*
English Book Centre, The	*http://www.ebcoxford.co.uk/*

Funorama	*http://www.funorama.com/*
Innocom	*http://www.innocom-ltd.com/*
Internet Bookshop	*http://www.bookshop.co.uk/*
James Thin Booksellers	*http://www.jamesthin.co.uk/*
John Smith & Son Bookshops	*http://www.johnsmith.co.uk/*
Lion Publishing	*http://www.lion-publishing.co.uk/*
Long Barn Books	*http://www.longbarnbooks.co.uk/*
Macmillan Computer Books	*http://www.mcp.com/*

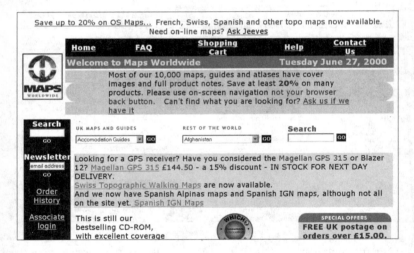

Maps Worldwide	*http://www.mapsworldwide.co.uk/*
Millennium Books	*http://www.meridian-experience.com/*
Mulberry Bush, The	*http://www.mulberrybush.com/*
OK UK Books	*http://www.okukbooks.com/*

Ottakar's *http://www.ottakars.co.uk/*

Oxford University Press Bookshop *http://www.oup.co.uk/*

Pan Macmillan *http://www.panmacmillan.com/*

PC Bookshops	*http://www.pcbooks.co.uk/*
Penguin Books UK	*http://www.penguin.co.uk/*
Pickabook	*http://www.pickabook.co.uk/*
Powell's	*http://powells.com/*
Red House	*http://www.redhouse.co.uk/*
Richard Nicholson of Chester	*http://www.antiquemaps.com/*

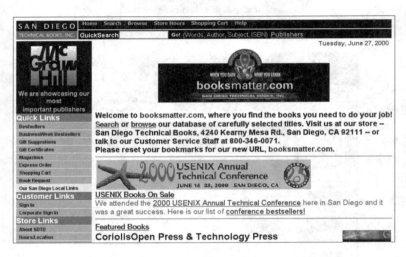

San Diego Technical Books	*http://www.booksmatter.com/*
Saxons	*http://www.saxons.co.uk/*
Scholar's Bookshelf, The	*http://www.scholarsbookshelf.com/*
Sci-Fi	*http://www.sci-fi.co.uk/*
Sportspages	*http://www.sportspages.co.uk/*
Tesco	*http://www.tesco.co.uk/books*

Titanic Incorporated	*http://www.titanic-leisure.com/books.htm*
Varsity Books	*http://www.varsitybooks.com/*
Virgin Books	*http://www.virgin-books.com/*
Waterstones	*http://www.waterstones.co.uk/*
Watkins	*http://www.watkinsbooks.com/*

WH Smith	*http://www.whsmith.co.uk/*

Publishers

Some publishers sell their books on the web, but even those who don't carry full details of their books and outlets where you can purchase them.

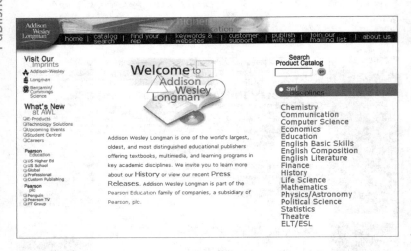

Addison Wesley Longman	*http://www.awl.com/*
Blackwell	*http://www.blackwellpublishers.co.uk/*
Butterworths	*http://www.butterworths.co.uk/*

Cambridge University Press	*http://www.cup.cam.ac.uk/*

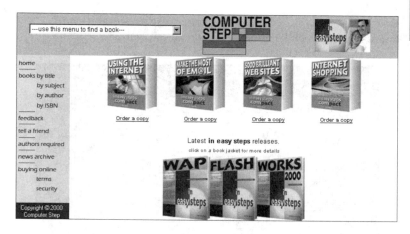

Computer Step (in easy steps)	*http://www.ineasysteps.com/*
DC Thomson	*http://www.dcthomson.co.uk/*
Dorling Kindersley	*http://www.dk.com/*
Ginn	*http://www.ginn.co.uk/*
HMSO	*http://www.hmson.gov.uk/*
Hodder & Stoughton	*http://www.hodder.co.uk/*
Kogan Page	*http://www.kogan-page.co.uk/*
Macmillan	*http://www.macmillan.co.uk/*
McGraw-Hill	*http://www.mcgraw-hill.co.uk/*
Orbit	*http://www.orbit.co.uk/*
Paragon	*http://www.paragon.co.uk/*
Pearson	*http://www.pearson.co.uk/*
Penguin	*http://www.penguin.co.uk/*
Puffin	*http://www.puffin.co.uk/*

Reed   *http://www.reedbusiness.com/*
Sunstone Press Book Publishers   *http://www.sunstonepress.com*

Thompson   *http://www.thompson.com/*

Charities

Although not all of these sites are actually registered charities, they all set out to help those less fortunate.

Health

These charities help fight a particular disease, care for people suffering from it or raise its profile. Or all three.

Action for Blind People	*http://www.vois.org.uk/afbp*
Action for M.E.	*http://www.afme.org.uk/*
Action on Smoking and Health	*http://www.ash.org.uk/*
Age Concern	*http://www.ace.org.uk/*
Alcohol Counselling & Prevention Services	*http://www.vois.org.uk/acaps/*
Alzheimer's Disease	*http://www.vois.org.uk/alzheimers/*
Anthony Nolan Bone Marrow Trust	*http://www.anthonynolan.com/*
Association for International Cancer Research	*http://www.aicr.org.uk/*
Barnardos	*http://www.barnardos.org.uk/*
Bob Champion Cancer Trust	*http://www.helpnet.org.uk/ hlpn06a.html*

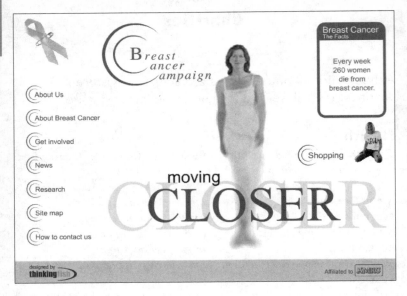

Breast Cancer Campaign	*http://www.bcc-uk.org/*
British Heart Foundation	*http://www.bhf.org.uk/*
British Red Cross Society	*http://www.redcross.org.uk/*
CancerHelp UK	*http://medweb.bham.ac.uk./ cancerhelp/*
Down's Syndrome Assoc., The	*http://www.helpnet.org.uk/hlpn08a .html*
Handicap International	*http://www.globalassistance.org/*
Hearing Concern	*http://web.ukonline.co.uk/ hearing.concern*

Help the Aged   *http://www.vois.org.uk/hta/*
Leukaemia Research Fund   *http://www.leukaemia-research.org.uk/*

order
  your free
cancer
  guide

**information
line**
0845 601 6161

..a voice for life.

IN YOUR AREA   ABOUT US   HELP IS HERE   SUPPORT US   ON LINE SURVEY

Registered charity number 261017

Macmillan   *http://www.macmillan.org.uk/*
Marie Curie   *http://www.mariecurie.org.uk/*
Marie Stopes International   *http://www.mariestopes.org.uk/*
                               index.html
M. E. Association   *http://glaxocentre.merseyside.org/*
                               mea.html
Multiple Sclerosis Society   *http://glaxocentre.merseyside.org/*
                               mss.html
Muscular Dystrophy Campaign   *http://www.muscular-dystrophy.org/*
National AIDS Trust   *http://www.nat.org.uk/*
National Society for the Prevention *http://www.nspcc.org.uk/*
   of Cruelty to Children

Royal National Institute for the
   Blind

http://www.rnib.org.uk/

Royal Society for Mentally
   Handicapped Children and Adults

http://www.mencap.org.uk/

Save the Children Fund

http://www.oneworld.org/scf

Humanitarian

There are a great many organisations which provide international support to
those less well off than ourselves.

Amnesty International	*http://www.oneworld.org/amnesty/*
British Refugee Council	*http://www.gn.apc.org/brcslproject*
Christian Aid	*http://www.oneworld.org/*
	christian_aid/
Creating Hope International	*http://www.creatinghope.org/*
Disaster Training International	*http://www.disastertraining.org/*
East Meets West Foundation	*http://www.eastmeetswest.org/*

Friends of the Earth   *http://www.foe.co.uk/index.html*

HOPE Worldwide	*http://www.hopeww.org/*
IOBG Humanitarian Foundation	*http://www.iobghf.org/*
Oxfam	*http://www.oxfam.org.uk/*
Salvation Army	*http://www.winkcomm.com/saweb*
Samaritans	*http://www.compulink.co.uk/*
	~careware/samaritans/
Sightsavers	*http://www.sightsavers.co.uk/*
Voluntary Service Overseas	*http://www.oneworld.org/vso/*
	index.html
Women's Commission for Refugee	*http://www.intrescom.org/wcrwc.html*
World Care	*http://www.worldcare.org/*

Organisations

Whether it be raising awareness of environmental issues or providing help for underprivileged kids, someone, somewhere is ready to help.

A Way Out	*http://www.awayout.twoffice.com/*
Anne Frank Educational	*http://www.afet.org.uk/*
Association of Blind Piano Tuners	*http://www.uk-piano.org/abpt*
Association of Medical Research Charities	*http://www.amrc.org.uk/*
Breakthrough	*http://www.breakthrough-dhi.org.uk/*
British Youth Council	*http://www.byc.org.uk/*
Charity Net	*http://www.charitynet.org/*
Citizens Advice Bureau	*http://www.poptel.org.uk/cab/*
Donkey Sanctuary, The	*http://www.thedonkeysanctuary*
Duke of Edinburgh's Award	*http://www.sonnet.co.uk/dea/*
Gingerbread	*http://www.gingerbread.org.uk/*

Global Assistance	*http://www.globalassistance.org/*
Greenpeace	*http://www.greenpeace.org/*
Guide Star	*http://www.guidestar.org/*
I Give.com	*http://www.igive.com/*
InterAction	*http://www.interaction.org/*
International Rescue Committee	*http://www.intrescom.org/*
LifeNets	*http://www.lifenets.org/*

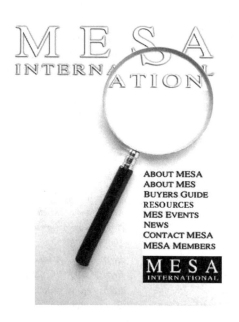

MESA   *http://www.mesa.org/*

National Canine Defence League	*http://www.ncdl.org.uk/*
Netaid	*http://www.netaid.org/*
Operation Mercy	*http://www.mercy.t.se/*
Parrot Line	*http://www.parrotline.org/*
ReliefNet Organizations	*http://www.reliefnet.org/org.html*
Rotary Club	*http://www.rotary.org/*
Round Table	*http://www.interads.co.uk/rtbi/ wokingham/*
Royal Botanic Gardens	*http://www.rbgkew.org.uk/*
Royal British Legion	*http://www.britishlegion.org.uk/*
Royal National Lifeboat Institution	*http://www.rnli.org.uk/*
Scope	*http://www.scope.org.uk/*
St John Ambulance	*http://www.stjohnambulance.org.uk/*

Traidcraft Exchange	*http://www.traidcraft.co.uk/*
Vegetarian Society	*http://www.veg.org/veg/Orgs/ VegSocUK/*
Women's Institute	*http://www.nfwi.org.uk/*
World Foundation for Humanity	*http://worldfoundation.com/*
YMCA	*http://www.ymca.org.uk/*
Youth Hostelling Association	*http://www.yha.org.uk/*

Clothes

Virtually all of the stores here sell clothes directly to the public. Look out for those that offer free carriage as these charges can wipe out the saving made on the actual garment.

Women's Clothes

Why is it that my wife's wardrobe is four times the size of mine (not including the bulging sides) and yet I still get a daily rendition of 'I don't know what to wear'? followed closely by 'I don't have anything to wear'.

57 West Bank	*http://www.57westbank.com/*
Abbie Lynn	*http://www.abbielynn.com/*
Accent Bridal Accessories	*http://www.directproducts.com/accent/*
Access Style	*http://www.accessstyle.com/*
Accetra Apparel Inc	*http://www.accetra.com/*
Advantage Discount Bridal	*http://www.advantagebridal.com/*
After Dark	*http://www.afterdarkevenings.com/*
Agnes.com	*http://www.agnes.com/*
Alese Gregory Sport	*http://www.alesegregorysport.com/*
Alfeo di Linosa	*http://www.studios.it/alfeogep*
Allola Cashmere Fashion Shop	*http://www.allola.net/*
Alluring Nights	*http://www.alluringnights.com/dresses*
Alternative Gowns	*http://www.alt-gowns.com/*

ALOHA AND WELCOME TO ANGELWEAR HAWAII!

Relax....soft focus .... and you're back in the Islands.

Soft plumeria-scented breezes caress your skin and warm ocean waters lap around your ankles bringing you a feeling of peace and total well being.

This is Hawaii, where the tempo of life is just a bit slower and definitely on the casual side. Where opportunities to relax and enjoy life abound, and where friends, family and traditions are valued above all.

These are the Hawaiian Islands, home of AngelWear Hawaii where we believe that if it feels good, it IS good, especially when it comes to loungewear and leisurewear.

Welcome! Please come in and browse.

Aloha! E' komo mai!

Our store has been entered by `023074` visitors!

Click here to <u>enter our store</u> or to learn more <u>about AngelWear</u>

Angelwear	*http://angelwearhawaii.com/*
Ann 'N' Eve Collection	*http://www.annneve.com/*
Any-Wear	*http://www.any-wear.com/*
Art Effect	*http://www.arteffectchicago.com/*
Artigiano	*http://www.artigiano.com/*
Asha Imports	*http://www.asha-imports.com/*
Baa Baa Zuzu	*http://www.baabaazuzu.com/*
Banana Boat of Key West	*http://www.bananaboatkw.com/*

ⓑ. bargainclothing.com   women's store | junior store | plus size store

home | search | your account | customer service | gift services | sign up | log in

Bargain Clothing Corporation   *http://www.bargainclothing.com/*

Batik Center	*http://www.batikcenter.bizland.com/*
Bebe	*http://www.bebe.com/*
Benetton Online	*http://www.benettononline.com/*
Best Bridesmaid	*http://www.bestbridesmaid.com/*
Best Prom Dresses	*http://www.bestpromdresses.com/*
Better Sweater	*http://www.bettersweater.com/*
Black Frock	*http://www.blackfrock.com/*
Blacktiegown	*http://www.blacktiegown.com/*

Blue-Eyed Bear   *http://www.blue-eyedbear.com/*

Bo Bo Boutique	*http://www.boboboutique.com/*
Bodysuit.com	*http://www.bodysuit.com/*
BodyTape Inc	*http://www.bodytape.com/*
Boston Proper	*http://www.bostonproper.com/*
Bras Direct	*http://www.brasdirect.co.uk/*
Bridal Creations	*http://www.bridalcreations.com/*
Bridal Marketplace	*http://www.bridalmarketplace.com/*
Bridesmaids.com	*http://www.bridesmaids.com/*
Brooks Brothers Women's wear	*http://www.brooks-brothers.net/* *womensbrooks.htm*
Buy In America	*http://www.buyinamerica.com/*

Byrd Designs	*http://www.byrddesigns.com/*
Caro Fashion-Design	*http://www.caro-modedesign.de/*
Carter Classics	*http://www.carterclassics.com/*
Carushka	*http://www.carushka.com/*
Chelsea Nites	*http://www.chelseanites.com/*
Chic Ladies Fashions	*http://www.chicfashions.co.uk/*
Ciciriello	*http://www.ciciriello.com/*

Clockwork Orange Clothing   *http://www.clockwork-orange.net/*

Clothes Heaven	*http://www.clothesheaven.com/*
Coat Factory	*http://www.freewayfashions.com/*
Coldwater Creek	*http://www.coldwatercreek.com/*
Cotton Clothing Co	*http://www.cottonclothingco.com/*
Couture	*http://coutureinternational.com/*

Couture Online   *http://www.coutureon-line.com/*

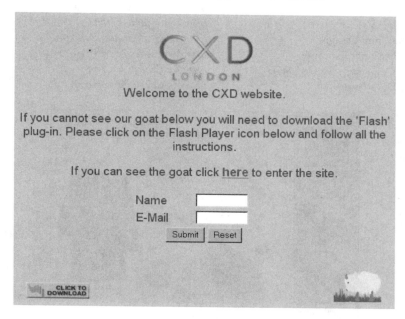

DiFrancia Designer Garters   *http://www.difrancia.com/*
Direct Factory Outlet   *http://emin001.safeshopper.com/*
Dorothy Perkins   *http://www.dorothyperkins.co.uk/*

Draper's and Damon's   *http://www.drapers.com/*
eArmoire   *http://www.earmoire.com/*
Easyshop   *http://www.easyshop.co.uk/*
Egowns.com   *http://www.egowns.com/*
Elevations   *http://www.designelevations.com/*
Elsahaag   *http://www.elsahaag.co.uk/*
Emans Atelier   *http://www.emansatelier.com/*
Enokiworld   *http://www.enokiworld.com/*

Escapeze Fashions	*http://www.escapeze.com/*
Esprit	*http://www.esprit-intl.com/*
Esprit Online Shopping	*http://www.esprit.com/*
Evans	*http://www.evans.ltd.uk/*
Eveningbag.com	*http://www.eveningbag.com/*
Fantasy Apparel	*http://www.fantasyapparel.com/*
Fashion Clothing	*http://www.modaflash.com/*
Fashion Dish	*http://www.fashiondish.com/*
Fashion Junkie	*http://www.fashionjunkie.com/*
Fashion Victim Women's Tees	*http://www.fashionvictim.com/*
Fashionmine	*http://www.fashionmine.com/*

Fassy Fashions	*http://www.fassyfashions.com/*

Fat Face	*http://www.fatface.co.uk/*
Father Nature's Boutique	*http://www.fathernature.com/*
FCUK	*http://www.frenchconnection.com/*
Fezz	*http://www.fezz.net/*
Fine Things	*http://www.fine-things.net/*

FK Company	*http://www.fkcompany.com/*
For Joseph .	*http://www.forjoseph.com/*
Formal Fashions	*http://www.formalfashions.com/*
Fun Fashions Inc.	*http://www.funfashions.com/*
Gad Abouts International	*http://www.gad-abouts.com/*

Ghost	*http://www.ghost.co.uk/*
Goddess Apparel	*http://www.tcfb.com/goddess/*
Good Humans Clothing	*http://www.goodhumans.com/*
Graffiti Online	*http://www.graffitionline.com/*
Gurlwear	*http://www.gurlwear.com/*
Half Price Store	*http://www.1-half-price.com/Womens/*
Harebell	*http://www.harebell.com/*
High On Design	*http://www.highondesign.com/*
Holiday Halters	*http://www.holidayhalters.com/*
Hollywood Boulevard Fashions	*http://hollywoodblvdfashions.bizland.com/*
Hummingbird Activewear	*http://www.hummingbirdwear.com/*
Idojo Fashion House	*http://www.idojo.com/*

In the Mood	*http://www.inthemoodsweetannieltd.com/*
In The Nik Fashions	*http://www.itn.uss.net.au/*
Intermix	*http://www.intermix-ny.com/*
Isabella Bird	*http://www.isabellabird.com/*
Island Threads	*http://www.islandthreads.com/*
Itsybits.com	*http://www.itsybits.com/*
J. Jill	*http://www.jjill.com/*
Jam Packed	*http://www.jampacked.com/dresses*
Jubilees Boutique	*http://www.jubileesboutique.com/*
Judy Parker Hand Knit and Crochet	*http://www.judyknits.com/*

Judy's Clothes

" Now On A Clothesline Near You "

Judy's Clothes	*http://www.judysclothes.com/*

Kakkis Fine Line	*http://www.kakkisfineline.com/*
Kasper ASL	*http://www.kasper.com/*
Kathy Schwartze	*http://www.dressedfortheday.com/*
Katwalk Fashion Showroom	*http://www.thekatwalk.com/*
Kays	*http://www.kaysnet.com/*

Kendall Creek Collections
Trademark Pending

Kendall Creek is a collection of unique, high quality women's fashions and accessories. We invite you to explore our site, and if you find our products appealing, feel free to shop our catalog. You can purchase items "**on-line**" or by contacting us by **e-mail** fax or phone. Gift certificates are also available upon request.

Visit our "**About Us**" page to find out more about Kendall Creek, and don't forget to sign our **guest book**.

Kendall Creek Collections	*http://www.kendallcreek.com/*
Kinghill	*http://www.kingshill.co.uk/*
Knitwear Boutique of Builth Wells	*http://www.midwales.co.uk/knitwear/*
La Posh Designer Boutique	*http://la-posh.com/*
Ladies and Dames	*http://www.ladiesanddames.com/*

Lady Wilderness Apparel	*http://www.lady-wilderness.com/*
LadyBug Originals	*http://www.ladybugoriginals.com/*
LadyBwear.com	*http://www.ladybwear.com/*
L'allure	*http://www.lallure.com/*
Lana Collection	*http://www.lanacollection.com/*
Lapetina	*http://www.lapetina.com/*
Le Galleria	*http://www.dchee.com/*
Leftgear.com	*http://www.leftgear.com/*
Leigh Morgan Fashions Inc	*http://www.leighmorgan.com/*

Leila	*http://www.leilaclothing.com/*

Lilly Pulitzer	*http://www.lillyshop.com/*
Lingerie Online by Bainbridge & Boston	*http://www.bainbridge.co.uk/*
Lipays Women's Wear	*http://www.lipays.com/*
Little Black Dress To Go	*http://www.lbdtogo.com/*
Little House Fashions	*http://www.littlehousefashions.com/*
Livingston Bags	*http://www.beadedbags.com/*
Long Tall Clothing Company	*http://www.tallwomensclothing.com/*
Made in Manchester Ltd.	*http://www.madeinmanchester.net/*
Marcia Ruggeri	*http://www.marciaruggeri.com/*
Marge Rohrer	*http://handwovenstylesbymarge.com/*
Margies Creations	*http://margiescreations.anthill.com/*
Mauriziotoscani	*http://www.mauriziotoscani.com/*

Max Studio	*http://www.maxstudio.com/*

Meena Bazar	*http://www.meenabazar.com/*
Models Gear	*http://www.modelsgear.com/*
Moms At Play	*http://momsatplay.com/*

Montage/Double Take	*http://www.montagedt.com/*
More by Lata	*http://www.morebylata.com/*
Natural Ingredients	*http://www.naturalingredients.com/*

Nellie M. Boutique	*http://www.nelliem.com/*
New Natalies Bridals	*http://www.newnataliesbridals.com/*
Newbury Bond	*http://www.newburybond.com/*
Newport News	*http://www.newport-news.com/*
Ninja Shop-Nunokko Mishima	*http://skybusiness.com/nunokko/*

Now Wear This	*http://www.nowwearthis.com/*
NY Dress Co	*http://www.nydressco.com/*
Nygård International	*http://www.nygard.com/*
Pagan Playground	*http://www.paganplayground.com/*
Peach Berserk	*http://www.peachberserk.com/*
Persefonie	*http://www.persefonie.com/*
Petitediva.com	*http://www.petitediva.com/*
Pick up 'n' Go	*http://www.pickupngo.com/*
PJ Bear	*http://www.pjbear.com/*
Principles	*http://www.principles.co.uk/*
Prom Girl	*http://www.promgirl.com/*
Prom Guide	*http://www.promguide.com/*
Prom-dresses.com	*http://www.prom-dresses.com/*
Promod Shop	*http://www.promodshop.com/*

Promoutlet.com	*http://www.promoutlet.com/*
PunPun	*http://www.punpun.com/*
Purpleskirt.com	*http://www.purpleskirt.com/*
Pzaz.com	*http://www.pzaz.com/*
Quinceanera	*http://www.dressesbylilia.com/*
Quinceanera Dresses	*http://www.quinceaneradresses.com/*
R.S.V. Sport Inc	*http://lifeenergyintelligence.com/*
Raffaela Studio	*http://www.raffaelastudio.com/*
Rampage	*http://www.rampage.com/*
Ready2shop	*http://www.ready2shop.com/*
Reality Boutique	*http://www.realityboutique.com/*

Rivetwear	*http://www.rivetwear.com/*
Roberta Frost	*http://www.robertafrost.com/*
Robyn Boyd	*http://www.robynboyd.com.au/*
S. Robin	*http://www.srobin.com/*

Sara Boutique	*http://www.saraboutique.com/*
Sarah's	*http://www.sarahs-clothes.com/*
Savvy Online	*http://www.savvyonline.com/*
Scarves, Silk and Art	*http://art-and-scarves.com/*

Scott's Sweaters	*http://www.scottssweaters.com/*
Screaming Women	*http://www.pintsize.com/screamingwomen/*
Sec-Ce Designs	*http://sexysuits.com/*
Selective	*http://www.selective.co.uk/*
SewItSeams	*http://www.sewitseams.com/*
SFR Coats and Jackets	*http://www.sfr-creations.com/*
Shewear	*http://www.shewear.com/*
Shop at Anna	*http://www.shopatanna.com/*
Sila	*http://www.sila.com/*

Simply Dresses   *http://www.simplydresses.com/*
Simply Elegant Boutique   *http://www.simplyelegantboutique*
                                  .com/

Skirts and Shirts.com   *http://www.skirtsandshirts.com/*
Sky David Park   http://www.skydavidpark.com/
Smart Images Inc   *http://www.txheat.com/*
SmartArtwear.com   *http://www.smartartwear.com/*
Sophies Circle   *http://www.sophiescircle.com/*
SoYouWanna Dress Better   *http://www.soyouwanna.com/*
Sparkle Plenty Fashions   *http://www.sparkleplenty-fashions*
                                  .com/

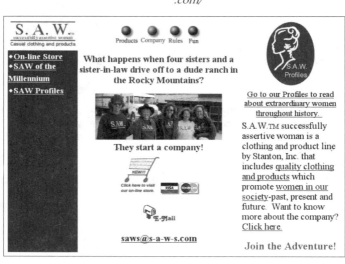

Stanton Inc   *http://s-a-w-s.com/*

STATURE®
EXTRA LENGTH

CONTEMPORARY CLOTHING WITH A Little Extra Length

Stature – clothing for moderately tall women. Stature designs and manufactures clothing for taller women and taller juniors (5' 7" – 6' tall) who simply need "a little extra length" in their contemporary apparel. Stature's comfortable separates fit ladies proportioned with long waists, arms and/or legs. If you are taller than the average woman, but find tall sizes to be too long or oversized, then Stature clothing is just right for you.

Stature manufactures trendy career basics and fashionable casual clothing in womens sizes 4-18. Overstock garments are offered to the public after wholesale orders have been processed. Stature's catalog is available on-line only and displays all clothing currently in inventory. Styles, colors and sizes change on a continual basis so "bookmark" www.StatureClothing.com for future reference.

SusanVale.com	*http://www.susanvale.com/*
Tag Rag	*http://www.tagrag.com/*
Tee-Zone	*http://www.tee-zone.com/*
The Cashmere Company	*http://www.cashmerecompany.com/*
The Dress Suite	*http://www.thedressuite.com/*
The Evening Store	*http://www.theeveningstore.com/*
The Gap	*http://www.gap.com/onlinestore/gap/*
The Leotard Company	*http://www.tlcsport.co.uk*

The Peruvian Connection	*http://www.peruvianconnection.com/*
Theme	*http://www.themesingapore.com/*
Tianello	*http://www.tianello.com/*

Tiaraworld	*http://www.tiaraworld.com/*
Time For Prom	*http://www.timeforprom.com/*
TJ Formal	*http://www.tjformal.com/*
Top Shop	*http://www.tops.co.uk/*
Turnbury Lady Fashions	*http://www.turnburylady.com/*
Unique Wedding	*http://www.uniquewedding.com/*
Unusual Knits	*http://www.maguirecustomknits.com/*
Urban Designs	*http://www.fashionhaven.com/*
Uuma.com	*http://www.uuma.com/*
Veilnet.com	*http://www.veilnet.com/*
VioletPeace	*http://www.violetpeace.com/*
Wicked Kitten	*http://www.wickedkitten.com/*
Wild Women Enterprises	*http://wildwomen-ent.com/*
Winona	*http://www.winona.com/*
Women's Wear	*http://www.ldny.com/*
Womensuits.com	*http://www.womensuits.com/*
World Piece	*http://www.world-piece.com/*
Zona Boutique	*http://www.zonaclothes.com/*
Zoot Fashion	*http://zootfashion.com/*

Men's Clothes

To demonstrate the previous point, there are fewer sites here for men's clothes than for women's clothes. But only just.

2002 Ties.com	*http://www.2002ties.com/*
Absolute Ties	*http://absoluteties.com/*
Alan Flusser Custom Shop	*http://www.bestselections.com/ alanflusser*

Allmensunderwear.com	*http://www.allmensunderwear.com/*
Aloha Hawaiian shirts	*http://alohahawaiianshirts.com/*
Aloha Shirts	*http://www.alohashirts.net/*
Alohaland	*http://www.alohaland.com/*
America's Shirt Catalogue	*http://www.hugestore.com/*
American Male and Company	*http://www.american-male.com/*
Arrowshirt	*http://www.arrowshirt.com/*
As Ties Go By	*http://www.astiesgoby.com/*
AUkdesignershop	*http://www.ukdesignershop.com/*
Barry Manufacturing	*http://www.bettermenswear.com/*
Bavender	*http://www.bavender.com/*
Bespoke Tailors	*http://www.menswear.ie/*
Big Kahuna	*http://www.aloha-bigkahuna.com/*
Blackman Custom Tailor	*http://www.blackmantailor.com/*
BMG Imports	*http://www.bmgimports.com/*
Boston Bow Tie	*http://www.bostonbowtie.com/*
Bow Tie Club	*http://www.bowtieclub.com/*
Boxer Rebellion	*http://www.boxerrebellion.com/*
Bromleys	*http://www.shirts-direct.co.uk/*
Brooks Brothers	*http://www.brooks-brothers.net/*
Burton	*http://www.burtonmenswear.co.uk/*

Butt For You	*http://www.buttforyou.com/*
Buy Ties	*http://www.buyties.com/*

Cafe Coton Menswear	*http://www.cafecoton.co.uk/*
Captains Closet	*http://www.captainscloset.com/*
Caswell's	*http://www.tsfmcaswells.com/*
Chapman & Son	*http://www.chapmanandsons.com/*
Charles Tyrwhitt	*http://www.ctshirts.co.uk/*
Chaud Naturelle International	*http://www.interstart.net/*
Chicagoman.com	*http://chicagoman.com/*
City Boxers	*http://www.cityboxers.com/*
Classic Kit	*http://www.classickit.com/*

Clothing Guy	*http://www.clothingguy.com/*
Corsair Ties	*http://www.corsairties.com/*

Countess Mara	http://www.countessmaraties.com/
Dalton Reade	http://www.daltonreade.com/
D'Angelo Bowties	http://www.dangelobowties.com/
Designer Heaven	http://www.designerheaven.com/
Designer Waistcoats Direct	http://www.waistcoatsdirect.co.uk/
Digities Neckwear	http://www.digities.com/
Discount Designer Menswear	http://www.menswear-discounts.com/
Edward Teach	http://www.edward-teach.com/
Elephant and Castle	http://www.elephantandcastle.com.au/

KENSINGTON TO KILMARNOCK - TENNESSEE TO

<u>Home Page</u> <u>You & Your Order</u> <u>Check Basket</u> <u>Questions?</u> <u>Contact Us</u>

Embleton & King	http://www.embletonking.com/
eSuit.com	http://www.esuit.com/

Ex Officio	*http://www.exofficio.com/*
Execstyle	*http://www.execstyle.com/*
Factory Direct Menswear	*http://www.factorydirectmenswear.com/*
Fiducia Collection	*http://www.fiduciacollection.com/*
Flyz	*http://www.flyz.net/*
Funky Trunks	*http://www.funkytrunks.com/*
Gemelli Uomo	*http://www.nystyle.com/gemelliuomo*
Gentlemen's Corner	*http://www.gentlemenscorneronline.com/*
Gentlemen's Essentials	*http://www.gentlemensessentials.com/*
Gere Internet Ltd	*http://www.gere.org.uk/*
Good Humans Clothing	*http://www.goodhumans.com/*
Harvie & Hudson	*http://www.harvieandhudson.com/*
Hawaiian Shirt	*http://www.hawaiianshirt.net/*
Heralds	*http://www.heraldsmenswear.com/*
Hermosa General Store	*http://www.hermosageneralstore.com/*
Herringbone	*http://www.herringbone.com.au/*
High Seas Trading	*http://www.highseastrading.com/*
Highland Dress Online	*http://www.highland-dress.co.uk/*
Hilditch & Key	*http://www.hilditch.co.uk/*
Hucklecote Country Clothing	*http://www.hucklecote.co.uk/*
Hugestore.com	*http://www.hugestore.com/*
Hunters Tie Partnership	*http://www.luxuryties.com/*
Ike Behar	*http://www.ikebehar.com/*
International Jock	*http://internationaljock.com/*
Invisible Tie Stay	*http://www.tiestaystore.com/*
Island Shirts	*http://islandshirts.com/*

Italy For Men	*http://www.italyformen.com/*
J. David's Custom Clothiers	*http://www.jdavids.com/*
Jeffrey's Collections	*http://www.jeffreyscollections.com/*
Jockey Club Ltd.	*http://www.shortmenssizes.com/*
Kelsey Tailors	*http://www.kelseytailors.co.uk/*
Kiniki	*http://www.kiniki.com/*
Larry Mazer	*http://larrymazer.com/*
Loose Cannon Apparel Ltd	*http://www.loosecannon.net/*
M. Goldberg Clothier	*http://www.mgoldbergclothier.com/*
Mafioso USA	*http://mafiosousa.com/*
Male Manor	*http://www.malemanor.com/*
Maus and Hoffman	*http://mausandhoffman.com/*
Men's Clothing	*http://www.smartcasual.com/*

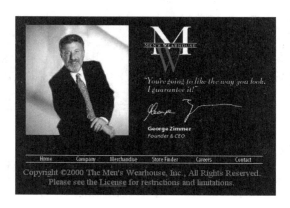

Men's Wearhouse	*http://www.menswearhouse.com/*
Menswear Solutions	*http://www.1menswear.com/menswear*

Milbern Clothing   *http://www.milbern.com/*
Milepost Four   *http://www.milepostfour.com/*

Moonbow Tropics Maui   *http://moonbowtropicsmaui.com/*
Necktie Organizer   *http://www.necktieorganizer.com/*
Novelty Ties by Uniquely Tied   *http://www.noveltyneckties.com/*
Off the Deep End   *http://www.offthedeepend.com/*
Outrageous Comfort   *http://www.outrageouscomfort.com/*
Paolo Capitoni Shirts   *http://www.paolocapitoni.com/*
Papillon Online   *http://www.eshopetc.com/*
Paradise Apparel   *http://www.paradiseapparel.com/*

Paul Fredrick	*http://www.paulfredrick.com/*
Peter Magee	*http://www.pmshirts.com/*
Political Ties	*http://www.politicalties.com/*
Pomeroy's Men's Store	*http://www.missionarysupplies.com/*
Porgy & Bess	*http://www.porgyandbess.com/*

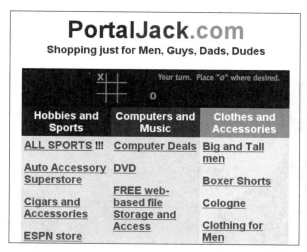

Portal Jack	*http://www.portaljack.com/*
Productopia	*http://productopia.netscape.com/*
Richard David	*http://www.richarddavid.com/*
Rym Stuff	*http://www.rymstuff.com/*
S and K Menswear	*http://www.skmenswear.com/*
Sansabelt Pant World	*http://sansabeltworld.com/*
SaviShopper	*http://www.savishopper.com/*

Sax Design	*http://www.saxdesign.com/*
Seymour Shirts	*http://www.seymour-shirts.co.uk/*
Shirtz	*http://www.shirtz.com.au/*
Shop Fords	*http://shopfords.com/*
Siewert's Tie Shop	*http://webordergifts.com/ties*
Silk Shop London	*http://www.silkshoplondon.com/*
Skivvy	*http://www.skivvy.com/*
Sportique International	*http://www.sportiqueinternational.com/*

Straus Clothing	*http://strausclothing.com/*
Suitable	*http://www.suitable-u.com/*
Suitbank.com	*http://www.suitbank.com/*

SurfRods	*http://www.surfrods.com/*
Tabasco Ties	*http://www.tabascogolfshirts.com/*
Ted the Bear	*http://www.tedthebear.com/*
The Clothes Store	*http://www.the-clothes-store.com/*
The Fashion Man	*http://www.fashionman.com/*
The Neckwear Directory	*http://www.neckweardirectory.com/*
The Shirt Press	*http://www.shirt-press.co.uk/*
The Ties Factory	*http://www.the-ties-factory.com/*
Tie Saver	*http://www.tiesaver.co.uk/*
Tiecrafters	*http://www.tiecrafters.com/*
Tieguys.com	*http://www.tieguys.com/*
Tiemaster	*http://www.tiemaster.com/*
Ties 4 all	*http://www.ties4all.co.uk/*
Tieshop UK	*http://www.tieshop.uk.com/*
TiesTiesNeckties.com	*http://www.tiestiesneckties.com/*
Tom James	*http://www.tomjamesco.com/*
Top Drawers	*http://www.topdrawers.com/*
Top Man	*http://www.topman.co.uk/*
Trillion	*http://www.trillionpalmbeach.com/*
Trois Boutons	*http://www.troisboutons.com/*
Uglies Boxer Shorts	*http://www.uglies.com/*
US Cavalry	*http://www.uscav.com/*
Ventresca	*http://www.ventresca.com/*
WebUndies	*http://www.webundies.com/*
WildTies.com	*http://www.wildties.com/*
Wm Fox	*http://www.wmfox.com/*
World-Ties.com	*http://www.world-ties.com/*

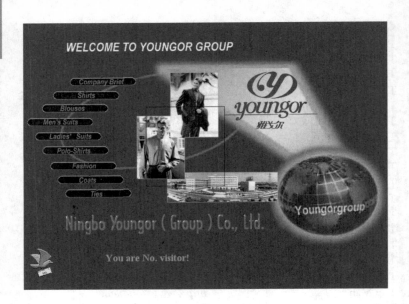

Youngor Group   *http://www.youngorgroup.com/*
Yourunderwear.com   *http://www.yourunderwear.com/*

Children's Clothes

Children grow so fast that they need plenty of clothes but it's often difficult to get the correct size. Many of these clothes stores offer sizing advice.

ABC Global Shopper   *http://www.abcglobalshopper.com/kids*
Alex and Me Solar Protection   *http://www.alexandme.com/*
Alligator Alley Kids   *http://www.alligatoralleykids.com/*

Amber Rose Fleece	*http://www.amberrosefleece.com/*
Annex Shoppe	*http://www.annexshoppe.com/*
Anteater-Togs	*http://www.anteater-togs.com/*
Ara's Pants	*http://www.araspants.com/*

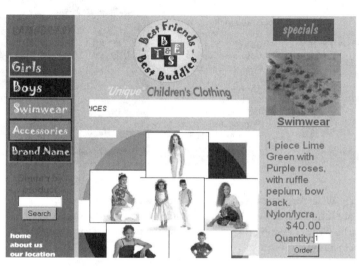

Best Friends Best Buddies	*http://www.bestfriendsbestbuddies.com/*
Bombalulus	*http://www.bombalulus.com/*
Bonfire Babies	*http://www.bonfirebabies.com/*
BoomersKids	*http://www.boomerskids.com/*
Brandoni-USA	*http://www.brandoni-usa.com/*
Breyla Children's Clothing	*http://www.breyla.com/*

Home Feedback Contents Search Links

bubby.com.au

Melbourne's premier indoor play center

Bubby wear

Market Stalls

Gift Shop

Shopping Info

Mums Net

Things to do in Melb

Contact Information

Electronic mail
General Information:
Sales:
Customer Support:
bubbywear@bigpond.com

Telephone
Australia
0403 131 176
International
+61 403 131 176
FAX
+61 3 9824 8220

Bubby Wear Australia	*http://www.bubby.com.au/*
Carol Holm Design	*http://www.holmdesign.com/*
Charlie Crow Dressing up Costumes	*http://www.charliecrow.com/*
Childrens Closet	*http://www.thechildrenscloset.com/*
Chloes Designs	*http://www.chloesdesigns.com/*
Clothes Closet	*http://clothescloset.netfirms.com/*
CO2 Girl	*http://www.co2girl.com/*
Connie's Kids	*http://www.connieskids.com/*
Cookie Crumbs!	*http://www.go.to/cookiecrumbs*
Cotton Moon	*http://www.cottonmoon.co.uk/*
Country Lane Kids	*http://www.countrylanekids.com/*

Crocodile Tears	*http://www.crocodiletears.com.au/*
Crumbsnatchers	*http://www.crumbsnatchers.net/*
Curly Sue	*http://www.curlysue.com/*
DapperLads	*http://www.dapperlads.com/*
Debbie Bliss Knitwear	*http://www.debbiebliss.freeserve.co.uk/*
Designs by Augusta	*http://www.designsbyaugusta.com/*
Dragonfly Children's Clothes	*http://www.dragonflys.co.uk/*
Echo Field Cottons	*http://www.echofield.com/*
Edwards and Co	*http://www.edwardsandco.ndirect*
Emily Kate's	*http://www.emilykates.com/*
Emma T. Clothing	*http://www.emmat.com/*
Emmala Children's Clothing	*http://www.emmala.com/*
Exciting Inc	*http://www.excitinginc.com/*
First Squad	*http://www.militarybratwear.com/*
Fleece Farm	*http://www.fleecefarm.com/*
Flora and Henri	*http://www.florahenri.com/*
French Kids	*http://www.frenchkids.com/*
Frog N' Princess	*http://frogandprincess.anthill.com/*
Gap Kids.com	*http://www.gap.com/onlinestore/ gapkids/*
Gatefish.com	*http://www.gatefish.com/*
Girl Heaven	*http://www.girlheaven.co.uk/*
Go Girl World	*http://www.gogirlworld.com/*
God's Quality Inc.	*http://www.godsquality.com/*
Golden Giraffe	*http://www.goldengiraffe.com/*
Good Humans	*http://www.goodhumans.com/ Shopping/Infants*
Good Lad apparel	*http://www.goodlad.com/*

Guppy Gear	*http://www.guppy-gear.com/*
Hanna Andersson Swedish Quality Clothing	*http://www.hannaandersson.com/*
Heather's World of Children's Clothing	*http://www.heathersclothing.com/*
HipHemp!	*http://www.hiphemp.com/*
Infant Replays	*http://www.infantreplays.com/*
Iriss of Penzance	*http://www.66penzance.fsnet.co.uk/*

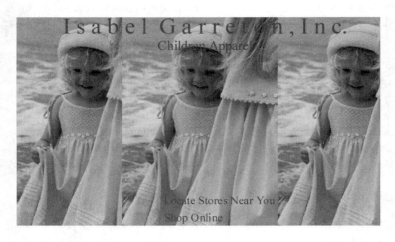

Isabel Garreton Inc.	*http://www.isabelgarreton.com/*
Just 4 Kix	*http://www.just4kix.com/*
Just Kids Clothes	*http://www.justkidsclothes.com/*
Kestrel Designs	*http://www.kestreldesigns.com/*
Kid Canada Clothing	*http://www.kidcanadaclothing.com/*

Kid Knits	*http://www.island.net/~rjbw/kidknits.html*
Kid Style-nyc	*http://www.kidstyle-nyc.com/*
Kids Clothes	*http://www.urchin.co.uk/*
Kids Fashion Center	*http://www.webmall2000.net/fashion/*
Kids Fashion Online	*http://www.sewingmall.com/fashion/kids.htm*
Kids T-shirts	*http://www.kids-t-shirt.com/*
Kids' Clothesline	*http://www.kidscl.com/*
Kidstock	*http://www.kidstockmontana.com/*
Kidswear Directory	*http://www.kidsweardirectory.com/*
Kidz Cargo	*http://www.kidzcargo.com/*
King's Kidz Infant Apparel	*http://www.kingskidz.com/*
Kings and Sages Apparel	*http://www.kingsandsages.com/*
Laugh Out Loud Wear	*http://www.lolwear.com/*
Lauren Alexandra	*http://www.laurenalexandra.com/*
Lil' Cuties Boutique	*http://www.lilcutiesboutique.com/*
Little Boutique	*http://www.littleboutique.com/*
Little Red Coat Co	*http://www.littleredcoat.com/*
Lolly's Tot Shop	*http://www.lollystotshop.com/*
Lucy Jayne Collection	*http://www.lucy-jayne.co.uk/*
Mad River Clothing	*http://www.madriverclothing.com/*
Masque Rays	*http://www.sunproof.com/Children2000.htm*
Material Girl Fashions	*http://www.materialgirlfashions.com/*
Max and Ruby	*http://maxandruby.com/*
Mischiefkids	*http://www.mischiefkids.co.uk/*
MommyDana Sales	*http://www.mommydana.com/*
Momz N' Kids	*http://www.momznkidz.com/*

Nana's Kids Kloset   *http://www.nanaskidskloset.com/*

Sweaters, Books and Gifts
16 Brunswick Walk - Elliot Lake, ON - Canada - P5A 2A8
(705) 461-9322 or FAX (705) 461-9384

Noah's Ark Sweaters   *http://www.noahsarksweaters.com/*
Nowa Li   *http://www.nowali.com/*
Oilily   *http://www.oililyusa.com/*
Okjas Kids   *http://www.k4web.com/kidsclothes*
Originali-tees   *http://www.originali-tees.com/*
OshKosh B'Gosh   *http://www.oshkoshbgosh.com/*

Over The Moon Babywear   *http://www.overthemoon-babywear*
                                     .co.uk/
Pageant Shoppe   *http://www.thepageantshoppe.com/*
Petit Patapon   *http://www.petitpatapon.com/*
Petite Batik   *http://www.petitebatik.com/*
Pippifinn   *http://www.pippifinn.com/*
Pip-Squeeks   *http://www.pip-squeeks.com/*

Precious Child	*http://www.precious-child.com/*
Precious Little Time	*http://www.preciouslittletime.com/*
Pride and Joy	*http://www.pridejoy.org/*
Ptarmigan Kids	*http://www.ptarmigankids.com/*
Punkey Monkey	*http://www.punkeymonkey.com/*
Ragamuffins	*http://www.ragamuffins-children.com/*
RAJ Shop	*http://www.rajinc.com/*
Rich Kids	*http://www.rich-kids.com/*
Robyn Boyd	*http://www.robynboyd.com.au/*
Rooster Jones	*http://www.roosterjones.com.au/*
Sally McCalls	*http://sallymccalls.com/*
Sara's Prints	*http://www.sarasprints.com/*

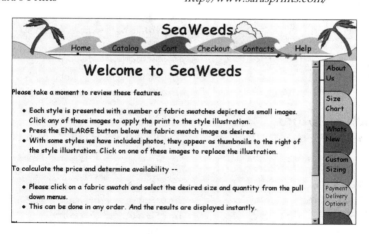

SeaWeeds	*http://www.kvproducts.com/* *SeaWeeds/*

Shoe Zoo	*http://www.shoezoo-mpls.com/*
ShopStars.com	*http://www.shopstars.com/*
Simpleprints	*http://www.simpleprints.com/*
Skadoodles	*http://www.skadoodle.com/*
Spiff Clothing Company	*http://www3.bc.sympatico.ca/spiff*
Splasharoo!	*http://www.zyworld.com/splasharoo*
Splashcity	*http://www.splashcity.com/kids.htm*
Storybook Heirlooms	*http://www.storybookheirlooms.com/*
Tessakids.com	*http://www.tessakids.com/*
That's My Boy	*http://www.thatsmyboy.com/*
TinyBlessings.com	*http://www.tinyblessings.com/*
Tody Bullmoose	*http://www.todybullmoose.com/*
Tot Towels	*http://www.tottowels.com/*
Towel Babys	*http://towelbabys.emerchantpro.com/*
Trotters	*http://www.trotters.co.uk/*
Weebok.com	*http://www.weebok.com/*
When Pigs Fly	*http://www.oinkoink.net/*
Whitney's Wee-Wear	*http://www.wee-wear.com/*

Baby Clothes

Before they get to the 'children' stage, you'll need plenty of baby clothes.

A Anichini	*http://www.anichini.net/*
A Special Day	*http://www.a-special-day.com/*
A Weefurbished Womb	*http://www.weefurbished.com/*
Alexis USA	*http://www.alexisusa.com/*
Anna-Bean Clothing Inc	*http://www.annabean.com/*
ASAP Manufacturing	*http://www.asapmfg.com/*

Babblin' Babies	*http://www.babblinbabies.com/*
Baby Basics Garments	*http://www.babybasicsgarments.com/*
Baby Bee Hat Company	*http://www.babybeehats.com/*
Baby Bib Bottle Holder	*http://www.teidreflow.com/*
Baby Blessing Outfits	*http://whatablessing.bizland.com/*
Baby Blessings	*http://www.babyblessings.com/*
Baby Boxers	*http://www.users.bigpond.com/ BabyBoxers/*
Baby Clothing Online	*http://babyclothingonline.com/*
Baby Fish Blues	*http://babyfishblues.com/*
Baby Gap	*http://www.gap.com/onlinestore/ babygap/*
Baby Hats	*http://babyhats.homestead.com/*
Baby Nouveau	*http://www.babynouveau.com/*
Babyrobes.com	*http://www.babyrobes.com/*
Baby Steps	*http://www.bsteps.com/*
Baby Sunshine	*http://www.babysunshine.co.uk/*
Baby Ultimate	*http://www.babyultimate.com/*
Baby World	*http://www.binary.co.nz/babyw.html*
Baby-101	*http://baby-101.com/*
Babybows	*http://www.babybows.com/*
Babyjay layette	*http://www.babyjay.com/*
Bearskins Baby Wear	*http://www.bearskins.com.au/*
Bella Famiglia	*http://www.bellafamiglia.com/*
Bergstroms Childrens Stores	*http://www.bergstroms.com/*
Big Sky Little Rain	*http://www.bigskylittlerain.com/*
Bobux USA	*http://www.bobuxusa.net/*
Body By Prayer	*http://www.bodybyprayer.com/*

Breyla	*http://www.bcity.com/breyla*
Buy For Kids	*http://www.buyforkids.com/*
Caleb's Corner	*http://www.calebscorner.com/*
Childrenswear.com	*http://www.childrenswear.com/*
Chock Catalog Baby Store	*http://www.chockcatalog.com/*
Christening Boutique	*http://christeningboutique.com/*
ChuckleBumble	*http://www.theimart.com/*
Coccole	*http://www.expoumbria.com/coccole*
Colorado Kids Clothing	*http://www.coloradokidsclothing.com/*
Cookie Baby Inc.	*http://www.cookiebabyinc.com/*
Cute As A Bug	*http://www.cuteasabug.com/*
Dab a Bow	*http://www.dababow.com/*
Dormouse Babywear	*http://www.dormouse.co.uk/index.htm*
Earth Muffinzz Baby Clothes	*http://www.earthmuffinzz.com/*
Earthwear Organic Cotton Originals	*http://www.earth-wear.com/*
Eco baby	*http://www.ecobaby.ie/*
eKid Wear	*http://www.ekidwear.com/*
ekids Playwear	*http://www.ekidsplaywear.com/*
Essential Baby	*http://www.nexusworld.com/ebaby*
Eva Evan	*http://www.evaevan.com/*
Exciting Inc.	*http://excitinginc.com/*
Exclusively Jenny	*http://www.exclusivelyjenny.com/*
EZ-Baby	*http://www.ez-baby.com/*
GahGah.com	*http://www.gahgah.com/*
Good Lad	*http://www.goodlad.com/*
Google Designs	*http://www.googledesigns.com/*
Green Babies	*http://www.greenbabies.com/*
Hi Baby!	*http://www.hibaby.com/*

Hindsight Diapers by Jennifer   *http://www.hindsightdiapers.findhere .com/*

HoneyStuff   *http://www.honeystuffbabies.com/*
James Collier Creations   *http://www.jamescolliercreations.cc/*
Jan's Knits For Kids   *http://www.jansknitsforkids.com/*
Jordan Marie   *http://www.jordanmarie.com/*
Julie's Stuff   *http://www.juliestuff.com/*
Kieraninc.com   *http://www.kieraninc.com/*
Layette Express   *http://www.giftforbaby.net/*
Lilly Patch   *http://www.lillypatch.com/*
Linda Manley   *http://handmade.iocus.com/*
Little Company   *http://www.littles.com/*
Little Lids   *http://www.littlelids.com/*

Little Miracles Christening Clothes	*http://www.christeningbaby.com/*
Little Tapiocas	*http://www.littletapiocas.com/*
Lolly's Tot Shop	*http://www.lollystotshop.com/*
Mackenzie Kay Baby	*http://www.mackenziekay.com/*
Made by Josette	*http://www.eeguide.com/shops/josette/*
Miller-Dexter Silk Christening Gowns	*http://www.miller-dexter.com/*
Mo Charese Heirlooms	*http://www.mochareseheirlooms.bigstep.com/*
Moonjumpers	*http://www.moonjumpers.com/*
Mushroom House Designs	*http://www.mushroomhousedesigns.com/*
Names In Knit	*http://www.namesinknit.com/*
Nap Sack Inc.	*http://napsack-frenchimports.com/*
Only Young Once	*http://www.babyclothers.com/*
Over The Moon Babywear	*http://www.overthemoon-babywear.co.uk/*
Peekaboocanada	*http://www.peekaboocanada.com/*
Petit Patapon	*http://www.petitgift.com/*
Precious	*http://www.preciousbymarymargie.com/*
Preemie Clothes	*http://foraspecialbaby.itool.com/*
Preemie Clothes	*http://www.preemiesleepers.com/*
Preemies Only	*http://www.preemiesonly.com/*
Roaming Wild!	*http://www.roamingwild.com/*
Shannikins	*http://www.shannikins.com/*
Snug As A Bug	*http://www.snugasabug.com/*
Snugglewrap	*http://www.snugglewrap.com/*

Spunky Punk	http://www.spunkypunk.com/
Squash Blossom	http://www.squash-blossom.com/
Stellina Baby Clothes	http://www.stellina.com/
Stik-on-bib	http://www.stik-on-bib.com/
Swim Diapers	http://www.gabbys.net/
Tiny Little Clothes. Inc	http://www.tinylittleclothes.com/
Tiny Treasures Baby Clothes	http://www.baby-clothes-store.com/
Tizzyfits	http://www.tizzyfits.com/
Tody Bullmoose	http://www.todybullmoose.com/
Tootaloo	http://tootaloo.com/
Warm Beginnings by Danielle	http://www.warmbeginnings.com/
Wavin' Baby Designs	http://www.wavinbaby.com/
Wish Upon A Star	http://www.wishkids.com/
Y2wear	http://www.y2wear.com/
Zootjes	http://zootjes.net/

Maternity Wear

Even earlier, is the maternity stage when it's the mum-to-be that needs lots of new clothes.

9 Months Plus	http://www.9monthsplus.com/
A Natural Baby Store	http://www.naturallyforbabies.com/
Abracadabra Maternity	http://www.momshop.com/
Anna Cris Maternity	http://www.annacris.com/
Baby Becoming	http://www.babybecoming.com/
BabyCenter	http://store.babycenter.com/
BabyZone's Maternity Zone	http://www.maternityzone.com/
Basics Direct	http://www.maternity.com/

Be'Be'Maternity	*http://www.bebematernity.com/*
Bellemere	*http://www.bellemere.com/*
Belly Basics	*http://www.nystyle.com/bellyb/*
Belly Belt	*http://www.cyberbaby.com.au/bellybelt*
BellyBand	*http://www.campusdirectory.com/ bellyband/*
Bloom'n Fashion	*http://www.bloom-n.com/*
Blooming Marvellous	*http://www.bloomingmarvellous .co.uk/*
Bumpstart	*http://www.bumpstart.co.uk/*
Carla C. Maternitywear	*http://www.carla-c.com/*
Clark and Lou Inc	*http://www.bellybra.com/*

Designer Maternity Clothing   *http://www.professionalmaternity.com/*

Details Direct	http://www.detailsdirect.com/pregkit.htm
eMommie.com	http://www.emommie.com/
Essential Baby	http://www.essentialbaby.com.au/
Expecting Style	http://www.expectingstyle.com/
Fit For Two	http://www.galeriver.com/
Fit Maternity and Beyond	http://www.fitmaternity.com/
From Here to Maternity	http://www.fromheretomaternity.com/
Generations Maternity	http://www.gmaternity.com/
Gladstone Maternity Outlet	http://www.momstobe.com/
Healthy Legs and Feet Too	http://maternitystockings.com/
Hindy's	http://www.maternityapparel.com/
iMaternity.com	http://www.imaternity.com/
Jaggar	http://www.maternityclothes.com/catalog1.htm
Jake & Me Clothing Company	http://www.jakeandme.com/
Kyra Mommy Wear	http://www.kyrawear.com/
L'Attesa: Stylish	http://www.bestselections.com/lattesa
Labour of Love Maternity	http://www.labouroflovematernity.com/
Ladies in Waiting Maternity Boutique	http://ladiesinwaitingmaternity.com/
Mama Bella	http://www.mamabella.com/
Mama T's Nursing Wear	http://www.mama-ts.com/
Maternal Instinct	http://www.maternal-instinct.com/
Maternity and Beyond	http://www.maternityandbeyond.com/
Maternity and Preemie	http://www.akmaternity.com/
Maternity Blues	http://www.mbbmarketing.com/

Maternity by Veronique — *http://www.veroniqued.com/*
Maternity Closet — *http://www.maternitycloset.com/*
Maternity Clothing with Style — *http://www.stylematernity.com/*
Maternity Company — *http://www.maternityco.com/*
Maternity Directory — *http://www.maternitydirectory.com/*
Maternity For Less — *http://maternity4less.com/*
Maternity Matters — *http://www.maternitymatters.com/*
Maternity Outfitters Inc — *http://www.maternityoutfitters.com/*
Maternity Profile — *http://www.maternityprofile.com/*

Maternity Wear

Nursing Wear

Just for Baby

Send E-Mail

Newsletter/
What's New

New Spring Merchandise has arrived! Check out the latest in <u>Maternity Casual and Dressy wear</u> with a touch of spring!

Maternity Stop — *http://www.maternitystop.com/*
Modern Maternity — *http://www.modernmaternity.com/*
Modern Maternity — *http://www.1webamerica.net/*
Mom & Me Maternity — *http://www.momandmematernity.com/*
Mom and Me — *http://www.mom-and-me.com/*

Mom's Maternity and Childrens' Store	*http://www.momsmaternity.com/*
Mom's to Be	*http://www.momstobefashions.com/prod01.htm*
Mom's Tops	*http://users.ev1.net/~momstops/default.htm*
Mommy and Me	*http://www.featureweb.com/mommyandmebc/*
Moms to be	*http://stores.suncommerce.com/momstobefashion/*
Moms to Be Factory Outlet	*http://www.momstobefashions.com/*
Moms Trends	*http://www.momstrends.com/*
Monterrosa Embroidery	*http://www.monterrosa.com/*
Motherhood is Special	*http://heirloomsbyhollylynn.homestead.com/*
Motherhood Maternity	*http://www.motherhood.com/*
Mothers In Motion Inc.	*http://www.mothers-in-motion.com/*
Mothers' Online Thrift Shop	*http://www.motshop.com/*
Mumsies	*http://www.mumsies.com/*
Naissance	*http://naissancematernity.com/*
Ninemonths-etc.com	*http://www.ninemonths-etc.com/*
One Hot Mama	*http://www.onehotmama.com/*
Pamper Mum	*http://www.pampermum.com.au/*
Pea in the Pod	*http://www.apeainthepod.com/*
Pickles and Ice Cream	*http://www.plusmaternity.com/*
Professional Expectations	*http://www.maternityleasing.com/*
Pumpkin Maternity	*http://www.nystyle.com/pumpkin*
Save-A-Bundle	*http://www.save-a-bundle.com/*

Sax Maternity	*http://www.saxmaternity.com/*
Special Addition	*http://www.eden.com/~spec_add/*
Strawberry Baby Buntings	*http://buntings.com/*
theMaternityShop.com	*http://www.thematernityshop.com/*
Thyme Maternity	*http://www.maternity.ca/*
Two in One Maternity Wear	*http://www.twoinone.com.au/*
Village Belle	*http://www.villagebelle.com/*

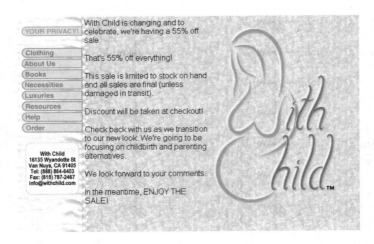

YOUR PRIVACY!

Clothing
About Us
Books
Necessities
Luxuries
Resources
Help
Order

With Child
16135 Wyandotte St
Van Nuys, CA 91405
Tel: (888) 864-5403
Fax: (818) 787-2467
info@withchild.com

With Child is changing and to celebrate, we're having a 55% off sale.

That's 55% off everything!

This sale is limited to stock on hand and all sales are final (unless damaged in transit).

Discount will be taken at checkout!

Check back with us as we transition to our new look. We're going to be focusing on childbirth and parenting alternatives.

We look forward to your comments.

In the meantime, ENJOY THE SALE!

With Child   *http://www.withchild.com/*

Shoes

If you do buy from an online shoe-shop, check the postal charges carefully because shoes are heavy and so delivery can be expensive. Also make sure the online store offers an exchange if the shoes don't fit properly.

123Shoes.com	*http://www.123shoes.com/*
800shoes.com	*http://800shoes.com/*
A Shop 4 Shoes	*http://www.platform-shoes.com/*
A Step Above	*http://www.astepaboveshoes.com/*
A Step Apart	*http://shoes-comfort-fashion.com/*
Alan's Shoes	*http://www.shoes.com/*
All Clogged Up	*http://anywears.sanjoseweb.com/*
Allen Edmonds	*http://www.allenedmonds.com/*
Altama	*http://www.altama.com/tactical.html*
Antshoes	*http://www.antshoes.com.au/*
Aquila Shoes	*http://www.aquila.com.au/*
Arcopedico Shoes	*http://www.arcopedicoshoes.com/*
Atelier Fusaro Shoes	*http://www.fusaro.de/*
Aurora Shoes	*http://www.aurorashoes.com/*
Barrington Outfitters	*http://gbshoes.com/*
Bay Street Shoes	*http://www.baystreetshoes.com/*
Belleville Shoe	*http://www.bellevilleshoe.com/public/*
Best Shoes	*http://www.thebestshoes.com/*
BN Safety Footwear	*http://www.bnsafetyfootwear.com/*
BootBarn.com	*http://www.bootbarn.com/*
Boots Online	*http://www.bootsonline.com.au/*
Botticelli	*http://www.botticellishoes.com/*
Breyer International	*http://www.breyerintl.com/*
Brown Shoes	*http://www.brown-shoes.com/*
Burch's Fine Footwear	*http://www.burchs.com/*
Butcher and Company	*http://www.butcherco.com/*
Capps Shoe Company	*http://www.capps-shoe.com/*
Celtic Sheepskin Company	*http://www.celtic-sheepskin.co.uk/*

Chester Boot Shop   *http://www.chesterboot.com/*

CHETS SHOES ON LINE

Directory

HOME

IRISH SETTER
BOOTS

VASQUE
HIKERS

LACROSSE
SPORT

LACROSSE
SAFETY

WORX

ON LINE
CATALOG

O CHETS SHOES!

Since 1947, Chets has been the name
to trust in footwear and clothing for
men and women. We specialize in
outdoor footwear and work footwear by
IRISH SETTER, RED WING, VASQUE,
WORX, LACROSSE, and cold climate
clothing by CARHARTT.

Chets also can set up and supply
safety footwear and slip and fall
reduction programs for companies,
both locally and nationally.

Chet's Shoes	*http://www.chetsshoes.com/*
Ciabattificio Silvia	*http://www.pistoia-export.it/silvia*
Clobber Leather	*http://www.clobberleather.com.au/*
Clog Shoppe	*http://www.theclogshoppe.com/*
Clog Store	*http://theclogstore.com/*
Clogs-N-More	*http://www.clogsnmore.com/*
ClogsOnline.com	*http://www.clogsonline.com/*
Clogworld	*http://www.clogworld.com/*
Cloudwalkers	*http://www.cloudwalkers.com/*
Correct Shoe Fitters	*http://www.correctshoefitters.com/*

Crary Shoes   *http://www.craryshoes.com/*
Creo Interactive   *http://www.creointeractive.com/*
Crummies   *http://www.handcraftedshoes.com/*
Cudas   *http://www.cudas.com/*

Dale's Shoes   *http://www.dales-shoes.com/*
Dansko Inc   *http://www.dansko.com/*
Davidson Shoes Plus   *http://www.shoestoboot.com/*
Dee Shoes   *http://deeshoes.com/*
Deer Stags Shoes   *http://www.deerstags.com/*
Di Bucci Shoes   *http://www.dbshoes.com/*
Dinoia Shoes   *http://www.italianshoestore.com/*

Dunham Boots	*http://dunhamboots.com/*
Edgewear.com	*http://www.edgewear.com/shoes.html*
Eshoes	*http://www.eshoes.net/*
Espadrilles	*http://espadrillesetc.com/*
Ethical Wares	*http://www.veganvillage.co.uk/ethicalwares/*
Exotic Mall	*http://www.exoticmalls.com/top.boots*
Factory Shoe Outlet	*http://www.factoryshoeoutlet.com/*
Fantastique Shoes	*http://www.npnhost.com/footwear*
Fitted Shoe	*http://www.fittedshoe.com/*
Foot Smart	*http://www.footsmart.com/*
FootStock	*http://www.footstock.com/*
Footwear Directory	*http://www.footweardirectory.com/*
Foster's Shoes	*http://www.fostersshoes.com/*
Frumps	*http://www.frumps.com/*
Gravis Footwear	*http://www.gravisfootwear.com/*
Great Lakes Shoe Company	*http://www.mephistogreatlakes.com/*
Great Plains Moccasin Factory	*http://www.uvisions.com/moccasin*
Grenda Shoe Corporation	*http://www.grendha.com/*
Guat Shoes	*http://www.guatshoes.co.uk/*
Happy Feet	*http://www.happyfeet.com/*
Hard Time Boots	*http://www.hardtimeboots.com/*
Howards Shoes	*http://www.howardsshoes.com/*
Hush Puppies Shoes	*http://hushpuppiesshoes.com/*
Inge's Footwear	*http://www.ingesfootwear.com/*
Ippy Clog and Sandal Company	*http://www.shore.net/~mia/*
J.W. Bray Slippers	*http://www.jwbray.com/*
Jgear	*http://www.jgearusa.com/*

Joewear	*http://www.joewear.com/*
Just Our Shoes	*http://www.justourshoes.com/*
K and L Boots	*http://www.kandlboots.com/*
Kaibab Moccasins	*http://www.kaibabmocs.com/*
Kamps Shoes	*http://www.kampshoes.com/*
Key West Sandal Factory	*http://www.kwsf.com/*
Lavahut	*http://www.lavahut.com/feet.htm*
Leatherlife Sheepskins	*http://www.uggboots.ws/*
Lee's Shopping Mall	*http://www.leesonline.com/index.html*
Les Newmans	*http://www.lesnewmans.com/*
Lonnie's Ballroom	*http://www.lonniesdance.com/*
Louie	*http://www.netlouie.com/*
Marley of London	*http://www.marleylondon.com/*
Meredith Trading Post	*http://www.meredithtradingpost.com/*
Michele Olivieri	*http://moshoes.com/*
Mischief	*http://www.mischiefkids.co.uk/ footwear.html*
MO	*http://www.moorder.com/*
Moccasin Shop	*http://www.mocshop.com/*
MyFavoriteShoe.com	*http://www.myfavoriteshoe.com/*
Nation-Wide Bootworks	*http://www.wolverineworkboots.com/*
New England Shoe Outlet	*http://newenglandshoe.com/*
Nicole Shoes	*http://www.nicoleshoes.com/*
New Balance	*http://www.newbalancestlouis.com/*
Online Shoes	*http://www.onlineshoes.com/*
Overland Sheepskin	*http://www.overland.com/se2/ sheepskin_slippers.htm*
Pappagallo	*http://clothes-line.net/*

Rockport
RESOLE CENTER

Rockport™

Enter the
Catalog

This catalog
courtesy of:
the WALKING
experience
Rockport* Shops
326 N. Santa Cruz
Ave.
Los Gatos, CA 95030
Toll Free
1-888-762-5999
Order_Desk@walking-
shoes.com

Rockport* Shoes

'the WALKING experience' Collection

Your favorite Rockport* shoes for men and women are available here. Rockport* shoes are engineered for comfort and complemented by a fundamental sense of style.

Rockport* shoes make you feel like walking!

Rockport™

Enter the Catalog

Shoe Parlor	*http://www.shoeparlor.com/*
Shoe Superstore	*http://www.shoesuperstore.com/*
Shoe Town	*http://www.sbshoetown.com/*
Shoebuy.com	*http://www.shoebuy.com/*
Shoecomfort.com	*http://www.shoecomfort.com/*
Shoemadness	*http://www.shoemadness.com/*
Shoepad	*http://www.shoepad.com/*
Shoes of The Fisherman	*http://www.shoesofthefisherman.com/*
Shoes On The Net	*http://www.shoesonthenet.com/*
Shoe-Shack.com	*http://www.shoe-shack.com/*

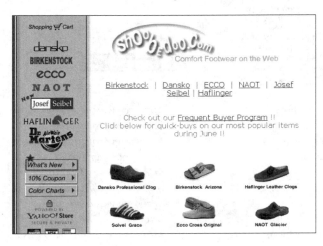

Shoo Be Doo	*http://www.shoobedoo.com/*
Shop Outerwear.com	*http://www.shopouterwear.com/*
Siam Leather Goods	*http://www.siamleathergoods.com/*

Sole Survivor	*http://leathersandals.com/*
Stacy Adams Men's Shoes	*http://www.stacyadams.com/*
Steger Mukluks and Moccasins	*http://www.mukluks.com/*
Stegmann	*http://clogz.com/*
Stravers	*http://www.stravers-adam.demon.nl/*
Studio HD2 Shoes	*http://www.studio-hd2.com/*
Sunrise Shoes	*http://www.sunriseshoes.net/*
Sunsports Sandal	*http://www.sunhemp.com/*
Supreme Comfort Footwear	*http://www.workboots.org/*
Sutor Mantellassi	*http://www.sutormantellassi.com/*
Tanner's Cobbler Shop	*http://www.tanners-cobbler.com/*
Taylor'd Footwear	*http://www.taylor-dfootwear.com/*
Teva Sport Sandals	*http://www.tevasandals.com/*
Timberline Outfitters	*http://www.tlpg.com/*
Tokio Kumagaï	*http://www.tokiok.com/*
Tony Shoes Inc.	*http://www.tonyshoes.com/*
Tony's Shoe Store	*http://www.shoestoreusa.com/*
Tozzok	*http://www.tozzok.com/*
Tradition World	*http://www.traditionworld.com/*
Vegetarian Shoes	*http://www.vegetarian-shoes.co.uk/*
Via Moda	*http://www.viamoda.com/*
Via Veneto Shoes	*http://viavenetoshoes.com/*
Walk Shop	*http://walkshop.com/*
Walking Company	*http://www.walkingco.com/*
Walking on Water	*http://www.walkingonwater.com/*
Wicked Road Warrior	*http://www.wickedroadwarrior.com/*
Worksite Footwear	*http://www.worksitefootwear.com/*
Zappos.com	*http://www.zappos.com/*

Computers

If you've got a computer, the Internet is a great place to make it better by installing more software or adding to the hardware.

Hardware

Not only complete computer systems, but components are available to buy on the web. Most companies also provide technical specifications of their products and many provide free drivers for their hardware.

3Com	*http://www.3com.com/*
Adaptec	*http://www.adaptec.com/*
AMD	*http://www.amd.com/*
APC	*http://www.apcc.com/*
Apple Computer, Inc.	*http://www.apple.com/*
ATI Technologies	*http://www.atitech.ca/*
Cirrus Logic	*http://www.cirrus.com/*
Cisco	*http://www.cisco.com/*
Cyrix	*http://www.cyrix.com/*
Dell Computers	*http://www.dell.com/*
Diamond	*http://www.diamondmm.com/*
eMachines	*http://www.e4me.com/*
Fujitsu	*http://www.fujitsu.com/*
HAL-PC	*http://www.hal-pc.org/*

Hayes Corporation   *http://www.hayes.com/*

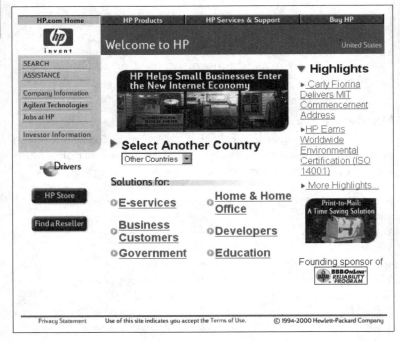

Hewlett-Packard   *http://www.hp.com/*
Hitachi   *http://www.hitachi.com/*
IBM Corporation   *http://www.ibm.com/*
Intel Corp.   *http://www.intel.com/*
Iomega   *http://www.iomega.com/*

Kingston Technology	*http://www.kingston.com/*
Matrox	*http://www.matrox.com/*
Motorola	*http://www.mot.com/*
NEC Online	*http://www.nec.com/*
NVIDIA	*http://www.nvidia.com/*
OPTi	*http://www.opti.com/*

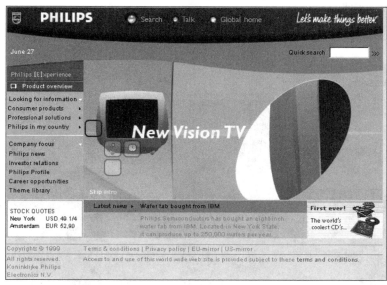

Philips	*http://www.philips.com/*
Quantex	*http://www.quantex.com/*
Quantum	*http://www.quantum.com/*
Rockwell	*http://www.rockwell.com/*

Samsung	*http://www.samsung.com/*
Seagate	*http://www.seagate.com/*
Sony	*http://www.sony.com/*
Sun Microsystems	*http://www.sun.com/*
SyQuest	*http://www.syquest.com/*
Toshiba	*http://www.toshiba.com/*
U.S. Robotics	*http://www.usr.com/*
Unisys	*http://www.unisys.com/*
Western Digital Corporation	*http://www.wdc.com/*

Xircom	*http://www.xircom.com/*
Zilog Inc.	*http://www.zilog.com/*

Computers Software

Software

There are countless Internet sites that offer software which can be downloaded either for free or for a nominal sum.

Download Shop   *http://www.downloadshop.co.uk/*
Download.com   *http://www.download.com/*
Downloads at MSN   *http://msn.co.uk/Page/4-30.asp*

EuroNet - TUCOWS   *http://tucows.euro.net/*
Free Stuff Link Center   *http://centerfree.hypermart.net/*
FreeSoft97 Freeware   *http://www.freesoft97.mcmail.com/*
Grey Olltwit's Freeware   *http://www.adders.org/freeware/*

109

Linux Software Archive	*http://linux.davecentral.com/*
Microsoft Download Center	*http://www.microsoft.com/downloads/* *search.asp*
Netscape	*http://www.netscape.com/*
Rocketdownload.com	*http://www.rocketdownload.com/*
TUCOWS	*http://tucows.ukonline.co.uk/*
UK Games	*http://www1.zdnet.com/cgwuk/*
VNU	*http://www.vnunet.com/download*
WinFiles.com	*http://www.winfiles.com/*
WinZip Download Page	*http://www.winzip.com/download.htm*
ZDNet Software	*http://www.zdnet.co.uk/software/*

Games

The vast majority of downloadable programs are games for PCs. Some of these sites also deal in games for consoles like Sega, Nintendo and Playstation.

24 Hour Games	*http://www.free-gaming.com/*
3D Files	*http://www.3dfiles.com/*
3D Gamers	*http://www.3dgamers.com/*
3D Spotlight	*http://www.3dspotlight.net/*
3D Updates	*http://www.3dupdates.com/*
Access Software	*http://www.accesssoftware.com/ctg/* *golf/*
Acdownload.com	*http://acdownload.com/*
All Games Network	*http://www.allgames.com/*
ASC Games	*http://www.ascgames.com/*
Beam International	*http://www.beam.com.au/*
BiowareNews	*http://www.biowarenews.com/*

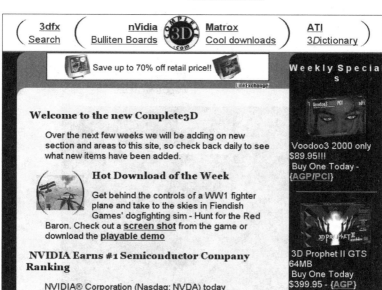

ComputerGameFan	*http://www.compufan.com/*
Cosmo3D	*http://www.cosmo3d.com/*
CrazyGames	*http://www.crazygames.net/*
Cyber Pet Game	*http://www.angelfire.com/hi3/game/*
DaGameBoyz	*http://www.dagameboyz.com/*
Daily Telefrag	*http://www.dailytelefrag.com/*
DemoFleet	*http://demofleet.virtualave.net/*
DOS Games Page	*http://www.dosgames.com/*
Dr. Mushroom's Shareware Depot	*http://www.drmushrm.com/shareware/ games.html*
Dragon Spawn	*http://www.dalhart.com/ DragonSpawn/*

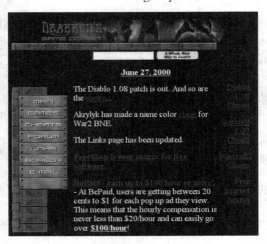

Drakken's Game Domain   *http://www.gamethreat.com/*

Eidos Interactive	*http://www.eidosinteractive.com/*
Emulators Online	*http://www.vghq.com/*
Encompass Gaming	*http://www.encompassgaming.com/*
ESPN Fantasy Games	*http://games.espn.go.com/*
Extacy Games	*http://www.extacygames.com/*
FilePlanet	*http://www.fileplanet.com/*
Free Games Net	*http://www.free-games-net.com/*
Freeality Download Computer Games	*http://www.reverse-lookup.com/ windowst.htm*
FreeGames	*http://freegames.org/*
Funster Multiplayer Word Games	*http://www.funster.com/*
Game Addict	*http://www.gameaddict.net/*
Game Forge	*http://www.game-forge.com/*
Game Nexus	*http://www.gamenexus.com/*
Game Search	*http://www.gamesearch.co.uk/*
Game Stats	*http://www.gamestats.com/*
GameArchives	*http://www.gamearchives.com/*
GameArena	*http://www.gamearena.net/*
Gamer's Portal	*http://www.internet-top.com/*
Gamers Central	*http://www.gamerscentral.net/*
Gamers Depot	*http://www.gamersdepot.com/ main.htm*
Gamers Gazette	*http://www.gamersgazette.com/*
Gamers Homepage	*http://gamershomepage.com/*
Gamers Net	*http://www.thegamers.net/*
Gamers Syndicate	*http://www.gamersyndicate.com/*
Gamers' CyberMall	*http://gcm.hypermart.net/*
Gamersnews	*http://www.gamersnews.com/*

GamerXtreme	*http://www.gamerxtreme.com/*
Games Domain	*http://www.gamesdomain.co.uk/*
Games Express	*http://www.gamesexpress.net/*
GameScan.com	*http://www.GameScan.com/*
GameShadow Networks	*http://www.gameshadow.com/*
GamesHoncho	*http://www.busprod.com/rastus/ gameshoncho/*

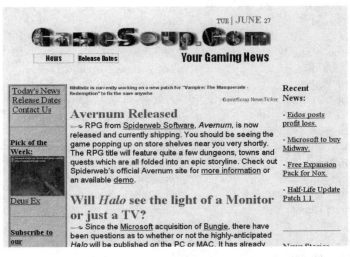

GameSoup.Com	*http://www.gamesoup.com/*
Gamespot	*http://www.gamespot.com/*
Gamesta.com	*http://www.gamesta.com/*
Gamesville Bingo Zone	*http://www.bingozone.com/*
Gamez Unlimited	*http://www.gamezunlimited.com/*

Gamezilla!	*http://www.gamezilla.com/*
GamezNet	*http://www.gameznet.com/3dgames*
GameZone.com	*http://www.gamezone.com/*
Gaming Zone	*http://www.pcpros.net/~cejay/pcgames/*
Gamingfx	*http://gamingfx.com/*
Gem's Games	*http://gemsgames.game-poi nt.net/*
GibWorld	*http://www.gibworld.com/*

Charts — the world's most popular entertainment charts

Global100.com

[Home] [Items Archive] [Requests Archive] [Personal Card] [Login] [Contact]

New brand, new company, new web site (formerly known as World Charts)

Add your site to the charts now!
(Before someone else does...)

[PC Games] [Video Games]
[Albums] [Singles]
[Movies] [TV Shows]
[Web Sites] [Home Pages]
[Females] [Males]

Global100.com provides you with charts of different kinds of products. These charts are compiled from votes submitted by visitors of global100.com. Every few hours we take a new unofficial calculation. Here we show you the last calculations for each of the charts.

Last calculation 27-Jun-00 at 21:33

Top Home Pages

TC	TW	Title	Publisher
1	1	Sabrina	Eric W. Schwartz
2	2	ZZ Studios	James Bruner
3	3	The Foxx Den	Chris Yost

Hottest:

54	90	Forever Knight Romance Love Page	Lauren
62	87	Enya The Angel	Simone M. Kajiki
77	96	Outrageous Talent: A Tribute to Michelle Kwan	Shallah's Universe

Voted by Noel Rosenberg at 22:02

GameSpot

Voted by Noel Rosenberg at 22:02

Pictures

Last calculation 27-Jun-00 at 21:02

23 *June 2000*

Top Web Sites

Global100.com   *http://www.global100.com/*

Happy Puppy's Games & Demos Page	*http://www.happypuppy.com/ compgames/pc/*
IDG Games Network	*http://www.pcgamesmag.com/*
IGN PC	*http://pc.ign.com/*
Jumbo Games	*http://www.jumbo.com/pages/games/*
Kay Bee Toys	*http://www.kbtoys.com/*
Kebie.com	*http://www.kebie.com/*
LadyDragon.Com	*http://www.ladydragon.com/*
LucasArts	*http://www.lucasarts.com/*
Making Games Better	*http://www.voodooextreme.com/ reverend/Main.html*
Maxmedia Interactive Drama	*http://www.achilles.net/~jgreen/ multimed.html*
Media and Games Online	*http://www.mgon.com/*
MobyGames	*http://www.mobygames.com/*
NegativeZero	*http://www.negativezero.com/*
Oldman Murray's Game Reviews	*http://www.oldmanmurray.com/*
OnTracks	*http://www.ontracks.co.uk/*
Patch Central	*http://www.patchcentral.com/*
PBeM News	*http://www.pbem.com/*
PC Game.com	*http://www.pcgame.com/*
PC Game Review	*http://www.pcgr.com/*
PC Game Watch	*http://www.pcgamewatch.com/*
PC Gamers	*http://www.pcgamers.net/*
PC Gameworld	*http://www.pcgameworld.com/ buygames.htm*
PC Patches.com	*http://www.pcpatches.com/*

Plugin Online Fantasy	*http://members.xoom.com/ pluginonline/*
Productive Play Company	*http://www.prodplay.co.uk/*
Profile	*http://www.planetquake.com/profile/*
Review Nexus	*http://www.reviewnexus.com/*
Riddler	*http://www.riddler.com/hub.cgi*
Soleau Software	*http://www.soleau.com/*
Sports Illustrated For Kids Games	*http://www.sikids.com/games/ index2.html*
Stomped	*http://www.stomped.com/*
Strategy Shrine	*http://strategyshrine.gamereactor.net/*
Studio Magique	*http://www.magique.com/*
The Crystallized Network	*http://www.crystallized.com/*
Top Load Games	*http://www.topdownloads.net/*
Top Ten Demo Channel	*http://www.bignetwork.com/tt/*
We Come To Play.com	*http://www.wecometoplay.com/*
Wise Owl Educational Software	*http://www.hometown.aol.com/ wiseowlsw*
ZDNet Games Library	*http://www.zdnet.com/swlib/ games.html*

Internet Search

If you want to find a particular piece of information, or you want to find a site that will provide you with the information you need, you could try a search engine. The trouble is that when you enter your query into a search engine, you invariably get either nothing, or 10,000 websites to wade through. It's for this reason that books like this are so popular.

4anything.com *http://www.4anything.com/*
Alcanseek *http://www.alcanseek.com/*

All 4 One *http://www.all4one.com/*
All-in-One *http://www.albany.net/allinone/*
AltaVista Search UK *http://www.altavista.co.uk/*
AnySearch *http://www.anysearch.com/*
Ask Jeeves (UK) *http://www.ask.co.uk/*
Ask Jeeves (US) *http://www.askjeeves.com/*
Avatar Search *http://www.avatarsearch.com/*
Bigfoot *http://www.bigfoot.com/*
Bigstuff *http://www.bigstuff.com/*

Dogpile	*http://dogpile.com/*
Excite United Kingdom	*http://www.excite.co.uk/*
FAST Search	*http://www.alltheweb.com/*
Google	*http://google.com/*
HotBot	*http://www.hotbot.com/*
Infoseek UK	*http://www.infoseek.com/*
LookSmart	*http://www.looksmart.com/*
Lycos	*http://www.lycos.co.uk/*
Meta Search	*http://metasearch.com/*
MSN Web Search	*http://search.msn.co.uk/*
Netscape Search	*http://home.netscape.com/home/internet-search.html*
Northern Light	*http://www.northernlight.com/*
PeekABoo	*http://peekaboo.net*
SearchUK	*http://www.searchuk.com/*
UK Max	*http://www.ukmax.com/*
UK Plus	*http://www.ukplus.co.uk/*
WebCrawler	*http://www.webcrawler.com/*
Webseek	*http://www.ctr.columbia.edu/webseek/*
Yahoo	*http://www.yahoo.com/*

PC Help

Computer manuals are notoriously difficult to understand. If you get stuck, you could try one of these sites to help you get unstuck.

British Computer Society	*http://www.bcs.org.uk/*
Computer Home Help	*http://www.almac.co.uk/homehelp/*
HelpDesk.com	*http://www.helpdesk.com/*

| MacUser OnLine | *http://www.macuser.co.uk/* |
| Microsoft Windows Update | *http://windowsupdate.microsoft.com/* |

Web Design

Web pages are constructed using a language called HTML (HyperText Markup Language). You can buy programs which will help you create web pages without having to go into HTML, but it is still worth having some knowledge about it.

A Beginner's Guide to HTML

http://burks.bton.ac.uk/burks/internet/ web/html_bg/html_bg.htm

About HTML

http://html.miningco.com/compute/ html/

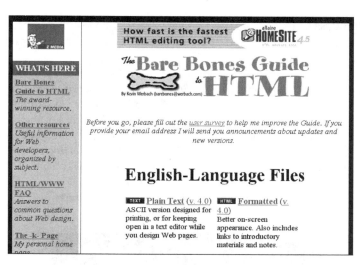

Bare Bones Guide to HTML

http://werbach.com/barebones/ barebone.html

Enhanced HTML 2000

http://www.enhance.co.uk/

HTML Compendium

http://www.htmlcompendium.org/

HTML Home Page

http://www.w3.org/markup/

HTML Quick Reference Guide

http://www.cc.ukans.edu/~acs/docs/ other/html_quick.shtml

| Introduction to HTML | *http://snowwhite.it.brighton.ac.uk/ ~mas/mas/courses/html/html.html* |
| Web Pages for Absolute Beginners | *http://subnet.virtual-pc.com/li542871/ intro.html* |

Animated GIFs

These are the little movies you see on webpages that make the page just a little more interesting.

Animated GIF Collection	*http://www.gifanimations.com/*
GIF Construction Set	*http://www.mindworkshop.com/ alchemy/gifcon.html*
GraphicCorp Animations	*http://www.developer.com/downloads/ Graphiccorp/Indexanimations.html*
Making Animated GIFs	*http://www6.uniovi.es/gifanim/ gifmake.htm*
Stepping Stones Animation	*http://www.ssanimation.com/ gallery.html*

| Web Graphics | *http://www.njet.net/heikki* |
| Webpedia | *http://animations.webpedia.com/* |

Education

Learning is a lifelong activity and there's no shortage of ways to learn on the Internet.

Learning

These sites have superb educational content which, although aimed mainly at kids, adults will find enthralling.

Arthur C Clarke *http://www.acclarke.co.uk/*
BBC Education *http://www.bbc.co.uk/education/home/*
Blackboard *http://www.blackboard.com/*
British Council *http://www.britishcouncil.org/ education/*
CH4 Schools *http://schools.channel4.com/*
Digital Education Network *http://www.edunet.com/*
Education 4 Kids *http://www.edu4kids.com/*
Education Place *http://www.eduplace.com/*
Educational.com/ *http://www.educational.com/*
Enchanted Learning *http://www.enchantedlearning.com/*
Fun Factory *http://www.esw.co.uk/funfactory/*
Funschool.com *http://www.funschool.com/*
GCSE Bytesize *http://db.bbc.co.uk/education-bytesize/ pkg_main.p_home*
Gurlpages.com *http://www.gurlpages.com/*

Kids.com	*http://www.kidscom.com/*
Math.com	*http://www.math.com/*
Maths Games	*http://atschool.eduweb.co.uk/ufa10/games.htm*
Schools Net	*http://www.schoolsnet.com/*
Schools Online	*http://sol.ultralab.anglia.ac.uk/pages/schools_online/*

Sesame Street	*http://www.ctw.org/*
Studyweb	*http://www.studyweb.com/*
Thinkquest.org	*http://www.thinkquest.org/*
Top Marks	*http://www.topmarks.co.uk/*

Yahooligans   *http://www.yahooligans.com/*

Yuckiest Website   *http://www.yucky.com/*

Museums

It's difficult to know quite where to put this, but as they are all educational…

Andy Warhol Museum   *http://www.warhol.org/*
Archaeology at MSU   *http://emuseum.mankato.msus.edu/*
Arthur C Clarke's 'Eye to   *http://www.nmsi.ac.uk/on-line/clarke/*
   the Future'
Beaulieu Car Museum   *http://www.beaulieu.co.uk/*

Black Country Museum — *http://www.woden.com/dudley/ museum.html*

British Museum — *http://www.british-museum.ac.uk/*

Brooklands Museum — *http://www.motor-software.co.uk/ brooklands/*

Butler Institute of American Art — *http://www.butlerart.com/*

Carnegie Museum of Art — *http://www.clpgh.org/cma/*

Cleveland Museum of Art — *http://www.clemusart.com/*

Contemporary Arts Museum of Houston — *http://www.camh.org/*

Crocker Art Museum — *http://www.sacto.org/crocker/*

Fine Arts Museums of San Francisco	*http://www.thinker.org/index.shtml*
Getty Information Institute	*http://www.ahip.getty.edu/*
Getty, J.Paul Museum	*http://www.getty.edu/museum/*
Hammond Museum	*http://www.hammondmuseum.org/*
Imperial War Museum	*http://www.iwm.org.uk/*
Ironbridge Gorge Museum	*http://www.ironbridge.org.uk/*
Jane Austen Museum	*http://www.janeaustenmuseum.org.uk/*
Jewish Museum	*http://www.ort.org/communit/ jewmusm/home.htm*
London Transport Museum	*http://www.ltmuseum.co.uk/*
Millenium Dome Experience	*http://www.new-millenium- experience.co.uk/*

Motorsports Hall of Fame	*http://www.mshf.com/*

Museum of Classical Archaeology	http://www.classics.cam.ac.uk/ark.html
Museum of Contemporary Art	http://www.mca.com.au/
Museum of East Asian Art	http://www.east-asian-art.co.uk/
Museum of the History of Science	http://www.mhs.ox.ac.uk/

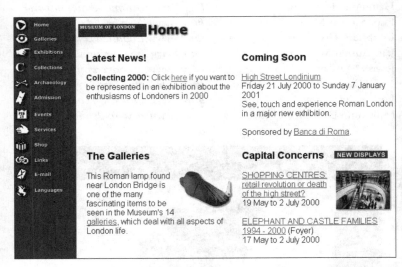

Museum of London	http://www.museum-london.org.uk/
Museum of the Moving Image	http://www.bfi.org.uk/museum/
Museum of Science	http://www.mos.org/
Museum of Science & Industry (UK)	http://www.msim.org.uk/
Museum of Science & Industry (US)	http://www.msichicago.org/

National Gallery of Art	*http://www.nga.gov/*
National Gallery of Australia	*http://www.nga.gov.au/*
National Gallery of Victoria	*http://www.ngv.vic.gov.au/*
National Maritime Museum	*http://www.nmm.ac.uk/*
National Museum of Photography, Film & Television	*http://www.nmpft.org.uk/*
National Museum of Scotland	*http://www.nms.ac.uk/*
National Portrait Gallery	*http://www.npg.si.edu/*
National Railroad Museum	*http://www.nationalrrmuseum.org/*

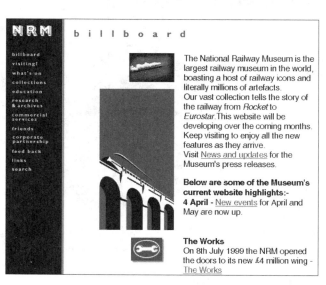

National Railway Museum	*http://www.nmsi.ac.uk/nrm/*

National Tramways Museum	*http://www.tramway.co.uk/about.html*
Natural History Museum	*http://www.nhm.ac.uk/*
Royal Air Force Museum	*http://www.rafmuseum.org.uk/*
Royal Naval Museum	*http://www.compulink.co.uk/*
Science Museum	*http://www.nmsi.ac.uk/*

**VISIT THE SHERLOCK HOLMES MUSEUM
FOR CRIME MYSTERY AND SUSPENSE!**

The Sherlock Holmes Museum
221b Baker Street, London England.

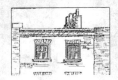

Sherlock Holmes and Doctor Watson lived at 221b Baker Street between 1881-1904, according to the stories written by Sir Arthur

Sherlock Holmes Museum	*http://www.sherlock-holmes.co.uk/*
Sikh Museum	*http://www.sikhmuseum.org/*
Smithsonian Institution	*http://www.si.edu/*
The Tech Museum of Innovation	*http://www.thetech.org/*
Victoria and Albert Museum	*http://www.nal.vam.ac.uk/*

Universities

There is no shortage of colleges and universities across the world at which you can further your studies. These are just some from Australia, New Zealand, UK and the US.

Aberdeen University (UK)   *http://www.abdn.ac.uk/*
Aberystwyth University (UK)   *http://www.aber.ac.uk/*
Arizona State University (US)   *http://www.asu.edu/*
Aston University (UK)   *http://www.aston.ac.uk/*

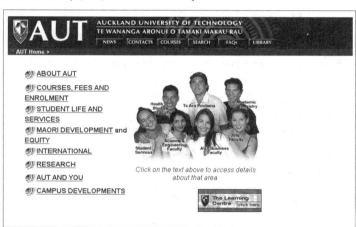

Click on the text above to access details about that area

Auckland University of   *http://www.aut.ac.nz/*
     Technology (NZ)
Australasian College for Emergency   *http://www.acem.org.au/open/*
     Medicine (AU)   *documents/home.htm*

Australian College of Law (AU)	*http://come.to/contract*
Australian International Hotel School (AU)	*http://hotelschool.cornell.edu/aihs/*
Australian National University (AU)	*http://www.anu.edu.au/*
Avondale College (AU)	*http://www.avondale.edu.au/*
Bangor University (UK)	*http://www.bangor.ac.uk/*
Bath University (UK)	*http://www.bath.ac.uk/*
Bible College of Victoria (AU)	*http://www.bcv.aus.net/*
Birmingham University (UK)	*http://www.birmingham.ac.uk/*

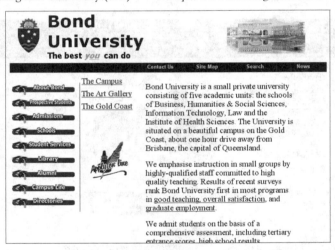

Bond University
The best *you* can do

Contact Us   Site Map   Search   News

About Bond
Prospective Students
Admissions
Schools
Student Services
Library
Alumni
Campus Life
Directories

The Campus
The Art Gallery
The Gold Coast

Bond University is a small private university consisting of five academic units: the schools of Business, Humanities & Social Sciences, Information Technology, Law and the Institute of Health Sciences. The University is situated on a beautiful campus on the Gold Coast, about one hour drive away from Brisbane, the capital of Queensland.

We emphasise instruction in small groups by highly-qualified staff committed to high quality teaching. Results of recent surveys rank Bond University first in most programs in good teaching, overall satisfaction, and graduate employment.

We admit students on the basis of a comprehensive assessment, including tertiary entrance scores, high school results.

Bond University (AU)	*http://www.bond.edu.au/*
Bradford University (UK)	*http://www.bradford.ac.uk/*
Brigham Young University (US)	*http://www.byu.edu/*

Bristol University (UK)	*http://www.bris.ac.uk/*
Brown University (US)	*http://www.brown.edu/*
Brunel University (UK)	*http://www.brunel.ac.uk/*
California State University (US)	*http://www.csuchico.edu/*

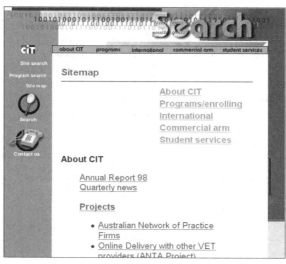

Canberra Institute of Technology (AU)	*http://www.cit.act.edu.au/*
Cardiff University (UK)	*http://www.cf.ac.uk/*
Carnegie Mellon University (US)	*http://www.cmu.edu/*
Central Institute of Technology (NZ)	*http://www.cit.ac.nz/*
Central Metropolitan College (AU)	*http://www.cmctafe.wa.edu.au/*

Central Queensland University (AU)	*http://www.cqu.edu.au/*
Centralian College (AU)	*http://www.ozemail.com.au/~centcoll/*
Charles Sturt University (AU)	*http://www.csu.edu.au/*
Christchurch Polytechnic (NZ)	*http://www.chchp.ac.nz/*
Christian Heritage College (AU)	*http://www.chc.qld.edu.au/*
City University (UK)	*http://www.city.ac.uk/*
City University of New York (US)	*http://www.cuny.edu/*
Colorado State University (US)	*http://www.colostate.edu/*
Curtin University of Technology (AU)	*http://www.curtin.edu.au/*
Cyberuni (NZ)	*http://www.cyberuni.ac.nz/*
Dartmouth College (US)	*http://www.dartmouth.edu/*
Deakin University (AU)	*http://www.deakin.edu.au/*
Duke University (US)	*http://www.duke.edu/*
Dundee University (UK)	*http://www.dundee.ac.uk/*
Durham University (UK)	*http://www.durham.ac.uk/*
Edith Cowan University (AU)	*http://www.cowan.edu.au/*
Emerald Agricultural College (AU)	*http://www1.tpgi.com.au/users/eac/index.html*
Essex University (UK)	*http://www.sx.ac.uk/*
Exeter University (UK)	*http://www.exeter.ac.uk/*
Fairfield College (NZ)	*http://www.faircol.co.nz/*
Flinders University (AU)	*http://www.flinders.edu.au/*
Florida State University (US)	*http://www.fsu.edu/*
Glasgow University (UK)	*http://www.gla.ac.uk/*
Global Virtual University (NZ)	*http://www.gvu.ac.nz/*
Gold Coast Institute of TAFE (AU)	*http://www.gcit.qld.edu.au/*

Griffith University (AU)	*http://www.gu.edu.au/*
Guildhall London (UK)	*http://www.lgu.ac.uk/*
Harvard University (US)	*http://www.harvard.edu/*
Hull University (UK)	*http://www.hull.ac.uk/*
Hutt Valley Polytechnic (NZ)	*http://www.hvp.ac.nz/*
Illinois Institute of Technology (US)	*http://www.iit.edu/*
Imperial College (UK)	*http://www.ic.ac.uk/*
Indiana University (US)	*http://www.indiana.edu/*
International Pacific College (AU)	*http://www.ipca.edu.au/*
International Pacific College (NZ)	*http://www.ipc.ac.nz/*
Iowa State University (US)	*http://www.iastate.edu/*
James Cook University of North Queensland (AU)	*http://www.jcu.edu.au/*
Kansas University (US)	*http://www.ukans.edu/*
Keele University (UK)	*http://www.keele.ac.uk/*
Kingston-upon-Thames (UK)	*http://www.kingston.ac.uk/*
La Trobe University (AU)	*http://www.latrobe.edu.au/*
Lake Tuggeranong College (AU)	*http://www.laketuggeranongs.act.edu.au/*
Leeds University (UK)	*http://www.leeds.ac.uk/*
Leicester University (UK)	*http://www.leicester.ac.uk/*
Lincoln University (NZ)	*http://www.lincoln.ac.nz/*
Liverpool University (UK)	*http://www.liv.ac.uk/*
London Business School (UK)	*http://www.lbs.ac.uk/*
London School of Economics (UK)	*http://www.lse.ac.uk/*
London University (UK)	*http://www.lon.ac.uk/*
Loughborough University (UK)	*http://www.lut.ac.uk/*
Macleay College (AU)	*http://www.macleay.edu.au/*

Macquarie University (AU)   *http://www.mq.edu.au/*
Manchester University (UK)   *http://www.man.ac.uk/*
Manukau Institute of   *http://www.manukau.ac.nz/*
    Technology (NZ)

Massachusetts Institute of   *http://www.mit.edu/*
    Technology (US)
Massey University (NZ)   *http://www.massey.ac.nz/*
Michigan State University (US)   *http://www.msu.edu/*
Minnesota State University (US)   *http://www.msus.edu/*
Mississippi State University (US) *http://www.msstate.edu/*
Monash University (AU)   *http://www.monash.edu.au/*
Murdoch University (AU)   *http://www.murdoch.edu.au/*

Murray Mallee Community College (AU)	*http://www.ruralnet.net.au/~mmcc/index.html*
NC State University (US)	*http://www.ncsu.edu/*
Nelson Polytechnic (NZ)	*http://www.nelpoly.ac.nz/*
New College UNSW (AU)	*http://www.newcollege.unsw.edu.au/*
New York University (US)	*http://www.nyu.edu/*

Newcastle University (UK)	*http://www.ncl.ac.uk/*
North Adelaide School of Art (AU)	*http://www.artelaide.com.au/nasa/*
North Dakota University (US)	*http://www.nodak.edu/*
Northern Territory University (AU)	*http://www.ntu.edu.au/*

Northland Polytechnic (NZ)	*http://www.northland.ac.nz/*
Northwestern University (US)	*http://www.nwu.edu/*
Nottingham University (UK)	*http://www.nott.ac.uk/*
Ohio State University (US)	*http://www.ohio-state.edu/*
Oklahoma State University (US)	*http://www.okstate.edu/*
Open Learning Australia (AU)	*http://www.ola.edu.au/*
Open Polytechnic of New Zealand (NZ)	*http://www.topnz.ac.nz/*
Open University (UK)	*http://www.open.ac.uk/*
Oregon State University (US)	*http://www.orst.edu/*
Otago Polytechnic (NZ)	*http://www.tekotago.ac.nz/*
Oxford University (UK)	*http://www.ox.ac.uk/*
Pennsylvania State University (US)	*http://www.psu.edu/*
Princeton University (US)	*http://www.princeton.edu/*
Purdue University (US)	*http://www.purdue.edu/*
Queens (UK)	*http://www.qub.ac.uk/*
Queen's College (AU)	*http://www.queens.unimelb.edu.au/*
Queensland University of Technology (AU)	*http://www.qut.edu.au/*
Reading University (UK)	*http://www.reading.ac.uk/*
Redlands College (AU)	*http://www.redlands.qld.edu.au/ contact.htm*
Rensselaer Polytechnic Institute (US)	*http://www.rpi.edu/*
Rice University (US)	*http://www.rice.edu/*
Rochester Institute of Technology (US)	*http://www.rit.edu/*
Royal Melbourne Institute of Technology (AU)	*http://www.rmit.edu.au/*

SAE Technology College (AU)	*http://www.saecollege.edu.au/*
San Diego State University (US)	*http://www.sdsu.edu/*
San José State University (US)	*http://www.sjsu.edu/*
Santa Clara University (US)	*http://www.scu.edu/*
Sheffield University (UK)	*http://www.shef.ac.uk/*

Smithsonian Institution (US)	*http://www.si.edu/*
Southampton University (UK)	*http://www.soton.ac.uk/*
Southern Cross University (AU)	*http://www.scu.edu.au/*
Southland Polytechnic (NZ)	*http://www.southpoly.ac.nz/*
Spotswood College (NZ)	*http://tipnet.taranaki.ac.nz/~iscraigp/ spotswood*

St Andrews University (UK)	*http://www.st-and.ac.uk/*
St.Mark's College (AU)	*http://www.adelaide.edu.au/stmarks/index.html*
Stanford University (US)	*http://www.stanford.edu/*
State University of New Jersey (US)	*http://www.rutgers.edu/*

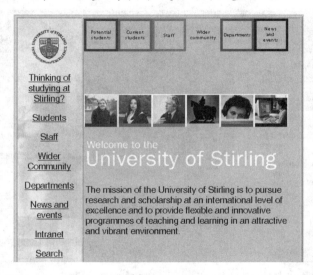

Stirling University (UK)	*http://www.stir.ac.uk/*
Surrey University (UK)	*http://www.surrey.ac.uk/*
Sussex University (UK)	*http://www.sussex.ac.uk/*
Swansea University (UK)	*http://www.swan.ac.uk/*
Swinburne University of Technology (AU)	*http://www.swin.edu.au/*

Tabor College Australia (AU)   *http://www.tabor.edu.au/*

Texas A&M

U N I V E R S I T Y
College Station, Texas 77843
(979) 845-3211

Texas A&M University (US)   *http://www.tamu.edu/*
Trinity College (AU)   *http://www.trinity.unimelb.edu.au/*
UC Berkeley (US)   *http://www.berkeley.edu/*
UCLA (US)   *http://www.ucla.edu/*
UNC-Chapel Hill (US)   *http://www.unc.edu/*
Universal College of Learning (NZ)   *http://www.ucol.ac.nz/*
University at Buffalo (US)   *http://www.buffalo.edu/*
University of Adelaide (AU)   *http://www.adelaide.edu.au/*
University of Alberta (US)   *http://www.ualberta.ca/*

University of Arizona (US)   *http://www.arizona.edu/*
University of Auckland (NZ)   *http://www.auckland.ac.nz/*
University of Ballarat (AU)   *http://www.ballarat.edu.au/*
University of California,   *http://www.uci.edu/*
   Irvine (US)

University of California,   *http://www.ucr.edu/*
   Riverside (US)
University of California,   *http://www.ucsb.edu/*
   Santa Barbara (US)
University of Cambridge (UK)   *http://www.cam.ac.uk/*
University of Canterbury (NZ)   *http://www.canterbury.ac.nz/*
University of Chicago (US)   *http://www.uchicago.edu/*

University of Colorado (US)	*http://www.colorado.edu/*
University of Delaware (US)	*http://www.udel.edu/*
University of Edinburgh (UK)	*http://www.ed.ac.uk/*
University of Georgia (US)	*http://www.uga.edu/*
University of Idaho (US)	*http://www.uidaho.edu/*
University of Illinois (US)	*http://www.uiuc.edu/*
University of Iowa (US)	*http://www.uiowa.edu/*
University of Maryland (US)	*http://www.umd.edu/*
University of Melbourne (AU)	*http://www.unimelb.edu.au/*
University of Melbourne (AU)	*http://www.unimelb.edu.au/*
University of Michigan (US)	*http://www.umich.edu/*
University of Minnesota (US)	*http://www.umn.edu/*
University of Missouri - Columbia (US)	*http://www.missouri.edu/*

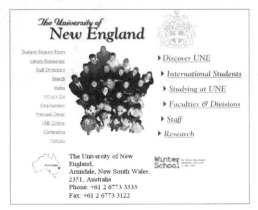

University of New England (AU)   *http://www.une.edu.au/*

University of New South
   Wales (AU)   *http://www.unsw.edu.au/*

University of Newcastle (AU)   *http://www.newcastle.edu.au/*

University of Notre Dame (AU)   *http://www.nd.edu.au/*
University of Notre Dame (US)   *http://www.nd.edu/*
University of Oregon (US)   *http://www.uoregon.edu/*
University of Otago (NZ)   *http://www.otago.ac.nz/*
University of Pennsylvania (US)   *http://www.upenn.edu/*
University of Phoenix (US)   *http://www.uophx.edu/*
University of Queensland (AU)   *http://www.uq.edu.au/*
University of South Australia (AU)   *http://www.unisa.edu.au/*

University of Southern California (US)	*http://www.usc.edu/*
University of Southern Queensland (AU)	*http://www.usq.edu.au/*
University of Sydney (AU)	*http://www.usyd.edu.au/*
University of Tasmania (AU)	*http://info.utas.edu.au/*
University of Technology, Sydney (AU)	*http://www.uts.edu.au/*
University of Texas (US)	*http://www.utexas.edu/*
University of the Sunshine Coast (AU)	*http://www.usc.edu.au/*
University of Utah (US)	*http://www.utah.edu/*
University of Virginia (US)	*http://www.virginia.edu/*

University of Waikato (NZ)	*http://www.waikato.ac.nz/*

University of Washington (US) — *http://www.washington.edu/*
University of Western Australia (AU) — *http://www.uwa.edu.au/*
University Of Western Sydney (AU) — *http://www.uws.edu.au/*
University of Wisconsin-Extension (US) — *http://www.uwex.edu/*
University of Wisconsin-Madison (US) — *http://www.wisc.edu/*
University of Wollongong (AU) — *http://www.uow.edu.au/*
Victoria University of Technology (AU) — *http://www.vu.edu.au/*
Victoria University of Wellington (NZ) — *http://www.vuw.ac.nz/*
Virginia Tech (US) — *http://www.vt.edu/*
Waiariki Polytechnic (NZ) — *http://www.waiariki.ac.nz/*
Waikato Polytechnic (NZ) — *http://www.twp.ac.nz/*
Wairarapa Community Polytechnic (NZ) — *http://wairarapa.ac.nz/*
Wanganui Polytechnic (NZ) — *http://www.whanganui.ac.nz/*
Warwick University (UK) — *http://www.warwick.ac.uk/*
Washington State University (US) — *http://www.wsu.edu/*
Wellington Polytechnic (NZ) — *http://www.wnp.ac.nz/*
Whitireia Community Polytechnic (NZ) — *http://www.whitireia.ac.nz/*
Yale University (US) — *http://www.yale.edu/*
York University (UK) — *http://www.york.ac.uk/*

Entertainment

Apart from the Internet being entertaining, it can also provide you with help when seeking entertainment.

Booking

Buzznet	*http://www.buzznet.com/*
Dinenet Menus Online	*http://www.menusonline.com/*
E! Online	*http://www.eonline.com/*
Electric Minds	*http://www.minds.com/*
Entertainment Drive	*http://www.edrive.com/*
Epicurious	*http://www.epicurious.com/*

Mr. Showbiz   *http://www.mrshowbiz.com/*

Oustide Online	*http://outside.starwave.com/*
Parent Soup	*http://www.parentsoup.com/*
Pathfinder	*http://www.pathfinder.com/*
Playbill Online	*http://piano.symgrp.com/playbill/*
Rocktropolis	*http://www.rocktropolis.com/*

Salon	*http://www.salonmagazine.com/*
Swoon	*http://www.swoon.com/*
T@p online	*http://www.taponline.com/*
The Old Farmer's Almanac	*http://www.almanac.com/*
The Onion	*http://www.theonoion.com/*
Walter Miller's Home Page	*http://pages.prodigy.com/hell/water/*
Word	*http://www.word.com/*
You Don't Know Jack	*http://www.bezerk.com/*
Zoloft	*http://www.spectacle.com/*

Cinema

I'd never been a great cinema goer, until using the Internet to find out what's on, where it's on and what the films are about. You can also book tickets over the Internet on some of these sites.

A Hot Ticket   *http://www.lastminute.com/lmn/*
ABC Cinemas   *http://www.abccinemas.co.uk/*
Apollo Cinemas   *http://www.apollocinemas.co.uk/*
BBC Online – Asian Films   *http://www.bbc.co.uk/networkasia/*
                            film/index.shtml
Bollymania   *http://www.dharms.ndirect.co.uk/*
Bollywood Central   *http://www.tcreng.com/bollywood/*

THE FILES
THE LINKS
THE DATABASE
THE PHOTOGRAPHS
THE POLL
THE GUESTBOOK
THE CHEAT
THE SCHEDULE
THE SONGS
THE SOFTWARE
THE AUTOR
THE REPORTERS
INDEPENDENT MOVIES
CASTING CENTER

www.bollywood.de

The Bollywood Movie Database

THE FILES	**THE LINKS**	**THE DATABASE**	**THE PHOTOGRAPHS**
Filmography, autograph address, biodata, links to dedicated	A search engine for links dedicated to Bollywood and India in general. Be it news,	Take **over 3800 movies**, store them all in a database accessible on the	Photographs, exclusive to us, cause none of those have

Bollywood Movie Database   *http://www.wupper.de/sites/unnet/*

British Cinema A To Z	*http://www.msu.edu/user/wigodski/ beatdown/bcfeat1.htm*
British Film Institute	*http://www.bfi.org.uk/*
British Films Catalogue	*http://www.britfilms.com/*
Centenary of the Cinema	*http://www.rchme.gov.uk/cinema.html*
Cinema Theatre Association	*http://www.cinema-theatre.org.uk/*
Cyber Bollywood	*http://www.cyberbollywood.com/*
Empire	*http://www.empireonline.co.uk/*
Film and Cinema in London	*http://www.thisislondon.co.uk/html/ hottx/film/top_direct.html*
Film Finder	*http://www.yell.co.uk/yell/ff/*
Film Unlimited Preview	*http://www.filmunlimited.co.uk/*
Filmweek	*http://film.reviews.co.uk/*
Freepages – Cinema Guide	*http://cinema.scoot.co.uk/*
Hot Gossip UK – Movies, Film & Cinema	*http://www.camelotintl.com/hotgossip/ film.html*
ICU Cinema	*http://www.su.ic.ac.uk/clubsocs/scab/ cinema/*
Internet Movie Database	*http://uk.imdb.com/*
List of U.K. Cinemas	*http://www.aber.ac.uk/~jwp/cinemas/*
London International Film School	*http://www.lifs.org.uk/*
New York – Quad Cinema	*http://www.quadcinema.com/*
Picture House Cinemas	*http://www.picturehouse-cinemas.co.uk/*
Popcorn.co.uk	*http://www.popcorn.co.uk/*
Scoot – Cinema Guide	*http://cinema.scoot.co.uk/*
Showcase Cinemas	*http://www.showcasecinemas.co.uk/*

UCI Cinemas   *http://www.uci-cinemas.co.uk*
Virgin Net – Cinema Listings   *http://www.virgin.net/cinema/*

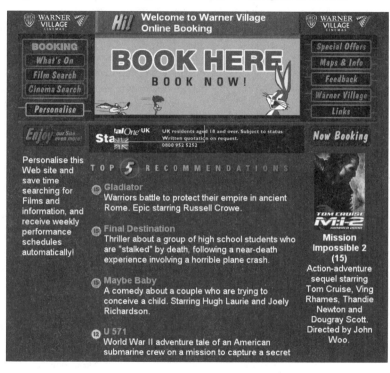

Warner Village   *http://www.warnervillage.co.uk/*

DVD/Video

Home video is gradually being taken over by DVD which provides a far superior picture and is easier to locate a part of the film you want to see. It is also far more durable than video tape.

Black Star Videos   *http://www.blackstar.co.uk/video/*
Blockbuster Video   *http://www.blockbuster.co.uk/*
Choices Direct   *http://www.choicesdirect.co.uk/*
Code Free DVD   *http://www.codefreedvd.com/*
DVD Depot   *http://www.dvddepot.co.uk/*

DVD Express   *http://euro2.dvdexpress.com/*

DVD File.com	*http://www.dvdfile.com/*
DVD Films	*http://www.dvdfilms.co.uk/*
DVD Shopping Den	*http://www.region2.co.uk/*
DVD World	*http://www.dvdworld.co.uk/*
DVDnet	*http://www.dvdnet.co.uk/*

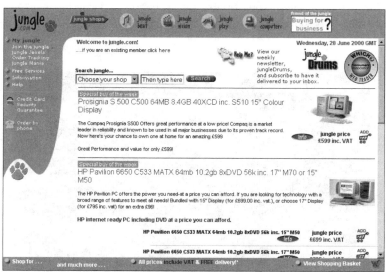

Jungle.com	*http://www.jungle.com/*
MTV UK & Ireland	*http://www.mtv.co.uk/*
Music & Video	*http://www.msn.co.uk/page/14-128.asp*
The Video Shop	*http://www.videoshop.co.uk/*
VideoNet	*http://www.videonet.co.uk/*

VideoParadise   *http://www.videoparadise.com/*
VideoZone   *http://www.videozone.co.uk/*
Yalplay   *http://www.yalplay.com/welcome.htm*

Theatre

There's nothing quite like the theatre, and the Internet can help you find a play or a show and some sites will even allow you to book online.

Aloud.com   *http://www.aloud.com/*

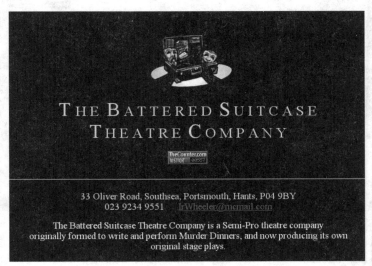

THE BATTERED SUITCASE
THEATRE COMPANY

33 Oliver Road, Southsea, Portsmouth, Hants, P04 9BY
023 9234 9551   IrWheeler@mcmail.com

The Battered Suitcase Theatre Company is a Semi-Pro theatre company
originally formed to write and perform Murder Dinners, and now producing its own
original stage plays.

Battered Suitcase Theatre   *http://www.batteredsuitcase.*
    Company   *mcmail.com/*

Bloomsbury Theatre *http://www.ucl.ac.uk/ BloomsburyTheatre/*

Bristol Old Vic Theatre School *http://oldvic.drama.ac.uk/*

British Theatre *http://britishtheatre.miningco.com/*

Children's Theatre Pages *http://members.aol.com/theatreuk/*

Dress Circle (Musical Theatre) *http://www.dresscircle.co.uk/*

Edinburgh Festival Theatre *http://www.eft.co.uk/*

English Theatre Company *http://www.lissma.se/etc.html*

Highlights in Theatreland *http://www.msn.co.uk/Page/8-59.asp*

Hot Tickets (Theatre) *http://www.thisislondon.co.uk/html/ hottx/theatre/top_direct.html*

Lichfield Youth Theatre	*http://www.mark-smith.ndirect.co.uk/lyt/*
London Theatre Guide	*http://www.londontheatre.co.uk/*
London Theatre Ticket Sales	*http://home.clara.net/rap/half/*
London's West End Theatre Guide	*http://www.demon.co.uk/albemarlelondon2/*
National Theatre	*http://www.nt-online.org/*
New Theatre Publications	*http://www.new-playwrights.demon.co.uk/*

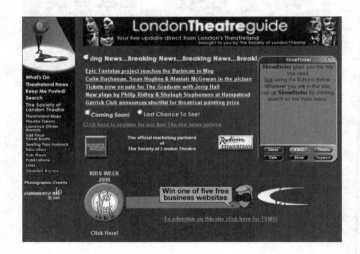

Official London Theatre Guide	*http://www.OfficialLondonTheatre.co.uk/*

Polka Children's Theatre	*http://www.polkatheatre.com/ index2.htm*
Queen's Film Theatre, Belfast	*http://www.qub.ac.uk/qft/*
Royal Lyceum Theatre Company	*http://www.infoser.com/infotheatre/ lyceum/*
Royal Shakespeare Company	*http://www.rsc.org.uk/*

Scene One	*http://www.sceneone.co.uk/s1/theatre*
The Globe	*http://www.rdg.ac.uk/AcaDepts/ln/ Globe/Globe.html*
The Stage	*http://www.thestage.co.uk/*

Theatre Historical Society of America
http://www2.hawaii.edu/~angell/thsa/

Theatre Internet Questionnaire
http://www.dewynters.com/question/InternetQuestionnaire.htm

Theatre Systems Group
http://www.mod.uk/dgics/dcsa_web/tsg.htm

Theatre Web
http://www.uktw.co.uk/offers.html

UK Theatre Web
http://www.uktw.co.uk/

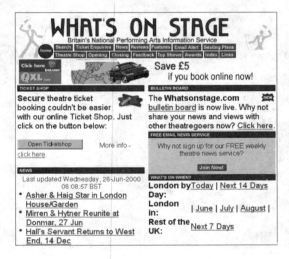

What's On Stage
http://www.whatsonstage.com/

Workshop Theatre
http://www.leeds.ac.uk/theatre/foyer.htm

Youth Action Theatre
http://www.shadlox.demon.co.uk/yat/

TV

Use these sites to find out what's on and what will be on, and also what was on.

ABC-TV	*http://www.abc-tv.net/*
Anglia Television	*http://www.anglia.tv.co.uk/*
Anglia Television Online	*http://www.angliatv.co.uk/*
BBC Online – Schedules	*http://www.bbc.co.uk/television/*
Cable Guide	*http://www.cableguide.co.uk/bread*
Challenge TV	*http://www.challengetv.co.uk/*
Channel 5 Television	*http://www.channel5.co.uk/*
Channel Four	*http://www.channel4.com/*
Classic Kids TV	*http://www.geocities.com/ TelevisionCity/1011/*

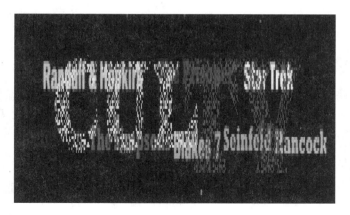

Cult TV   *http://www.metronet.co.uk/cultv/*

Cult TV Memorabilia *http://www.tv-memorabilia.demon
.co.uk/links.htm*

Discovery Channel Online *http://www.discovery.com/*
EuroTV *http://www.eurotv.com/*
Film and TV Craft and Technology *http://www.fatcat.co.uk/*
Guardian Unlimited – TV Listings *http://www.guardianunlimited.co.uk/
TV/*

Internet TV 0171 *http://www.0171.com/index3.html*

ITV	*http://www.itv.co.uk/*
Kaysnet	*http://www.kaysnet.com/*
Mark-It!	*http://www.horizonimages.com/*
Meridian Broadcasting	*http://www.meridian.tv.co.uk/*
Radio Times Guide	*http://www.rtguide.beeb.com/*
Rapture TV	*http://www.rapture.co.uk/*
Satellite TV	*http://members.aol.com/wotsat/*
Satellite TV Europe	*http://www.satellite-tv.co.uk/*
Sky	*http://www.skynow.co.uk/*

Sky Digital	*http://www.sky.com/digital/*

Techno TV Systems	*http://www.techno.cpd.co.uk/*
Teletext TV Plus	*http://www1.teletext.co.uk/tvplus/*
Television Ark	*http://www.tv-ark.co.uk/*
Thames TV	*http://www.geocities.com/Hollywood/5144/*
Time TV	*http://www.timetv.co.uk/*
TV	*http://www.tvchannel.co.uk/*
TV Travel Shop	*http://www.tvtravelshop.co.uk/snm/*
TV Zone	*http://www.visimag.com/tvzone/*
UK Terrestrial Cult TV	*http://members.tripod.com/~ukculttv/*
United Kingdom Cable TV Stations	*http://www.ultimatetv.com/tv/uk/cable.html*
What's On?	*http://msn.co.uk/page/8-60.asp*

Web-Radio

You don't need a radio to receive radio. You can get a huge range of radio broadcast via the Internet.

100 Years of Radio Web	*http://www.alpcom.it/hamradio*
A Net Station	*http://www.advice-net.com/*
Boom Booom Net Radio	*http://www.bmbient.demon.co.uk/blazznet/*
Broadcast.com	*http://www.broadcast.com/*
BRS Web Radio	*http://www.web-radio.com*
Classic Free-Net from Classic FM	*http://www.timetobreathe.net/classicfm/*
DigiBand Radio	*http://www.digiband.com*
First Music	*http://www.firstmusic.com/radio/*

Galaxy FM	*http://www.galaxyfm.co.uk/*
Internet Top 40 Countdown	*http://www.top40countdown.com/*
Live Online	*http://www.live-online.com/*
Live Radio on the Internet	*http://www.frodo.u-net.com/radio.htm*
MIT List of Radio Stations	*http://wmbr.mit.edu/stations/list.html*
MSN Web Events: Radio	*http://webevents.msn.com/radio.asp*
Net Radio Links	*http://www.bodo.com/radio.htm*
NetRadio ISDN Zone	*http://www.netradio.net/isdn*
NetRadio.com	*http://www.netradio.net/*

On Now	*http://www.onnow.com/*
Radio Free New Orleans	*http://www.neworleansonline.com/*
	rfno.htm

Radio Free Underground	*http://www.stitch.com/studio/*
Radio Net	*http://www.radionet.com/*
Radio Online	*http://www.radio-online.com/*
Radio Sonic Net	*http://radio.sonicnet.com/*
Radio Tower	*http://www.radiotower.com*
Rode Boef Real Web Radio	*http://www.gironet.nl/home/rodeboef/*
Sound Market	*http://www.soundmarket.net/ webradio/*
Spinner.com	*http://www.spinner.com*
The Wizard Free	*http://www.imagescape.com/wzrd*
Ultimate Radio Station List	*http://www.ubl.com/radio/*
Virgin Net Radio	*http://www.virgin.net/radio*
WFMU Radio 91.1 FM	*http://www.wfmu.org*
Whatsnew.com	*http://www.whatsnew.com/*
Word On the Net	*http://www.wordnet.couk.com/*
X-radio	*http://www.x-radio.com*
Zero9 – Radio	*http://www.bionicsite.com/zero9/*

Web-TV

You can also receive TV programmes via the Internet.

Microsoft Interactive TV: Overview	*http://www.microsoft.com/DTV*
Philips Magnavox Internet TV	*http://www.philipstraining.com/webtv/ intv62.html*
Web TV	*http://www.webtv.net*
WebTV FAQ	*http://www.owenmeany.com/faq.html*
WebTV Networks	*http://webtv.net/*
WebTV Usability Review	*http://www.useit.com/alertbox/ 9702a.html*

Finance

Whatever aspect of financial dealings you need to find out about, you'll find it here.

Information

Most financial dealings, including banking, is a complete mystery to most of us. But the Internet can provide advice on virtually every aspect of finance including share dealing and investment.

Bank Rate Monitor	*http://www.bankrate.com/*
Credit Report	*http://www.consumerinfo.com/*
Day Trader News	*http://www.daytradernews.net/*
FinAid	*http://www.finaid.org/*

Financial Times	*http://www.ft.com/*

FT Your Money   *http://www.ftyourmoney.com/*
Infopages   *http://www.infopages.net/*

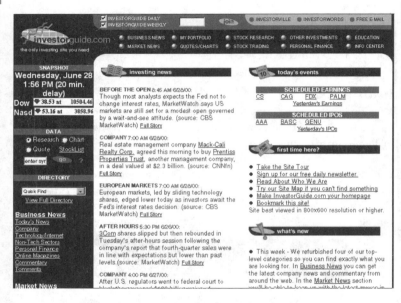

InvestorGuide   *http://www.investorguide.com/*
Marketguide   *http://www.marketguide.com/*
SmartMoney   *http://www.smartmoney.com/*
The Economist   *http://www.economist.com/*
The Street.com   *http://www.thestreet.com/*
Wall Street Journal   *http://www.wsj.com/*
Yahoo Finance   *http://biz.yahoo.com/*

Banking

Money makes the world go around, says the song. The trouble with conventional banking is that you can only make the revolve at certain times. More and more banks are offering 24-hour online banking giving you the opportunity to make transactions and view your account at any time. The only thing you have to visit the bank for is to withdraw hard cash.

Abbey National Group *http://www.abbeynational.co.uk/*
Adams National Bank *http://www.adamsbank.com/*
Advest *http://www.advest.com/*

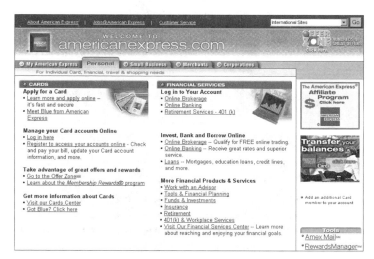

American Express *http://www.americanexpress.com/*

American National Bank	*http://www.accessanb.com/*
American Savings Bank	*http://www.asbhawaii.com/*
AmSouth Bank	*http://www.amsouth.com/*
Associated Bank	*http://www.assocbank.com/*

Banca Intesa	*http://www.bancaintesa.it/*
Banco Central Do Brasil	*http://www.bcb.gov.br/*
BancWest Corporation	*http://www.bancwestcorp.com/*
Bank America	*http://www.bankamerica.com/*
Bank of America	*http://www.bankofamerica.com/*
Bank of Cleveland	*http://www.bankofcleveland.com/*
Bank of Commerce	*http://www.bankofcommerce.net/*

Bank of Estonia   *http://www.ee/epbe/en/*
Bank of Finland   *http://www.bof.fi/*
Bank of Hawaii   *http://www.boh.com/*

Bank of Ireland   *http://www.bank-of-ireland.co.uk/*
Bank of Israel   *http://www.bankisrael.gov.il/*
Bank of Japan   *http://www.boj.or.jp/*
Bank of Latvia   *http://www.bank.lv/*
Bank of Lebanon   *http://www.bdl.gov.lb/*
Bank of Lenawee   *http://www.bankoflenawee.com/*
Bank of Lithuania   *http://www.lbank.lt/*
Bank of Mexico   *http://www.banxico.org.mx/*

Bank of Montreal	*http://www.bmo.com/*
Bank of Mozambique	*http://www.bancomoc.mz/*
Bank of New York	*http://www.bankofny.com/*
Bank of Newport	*http://www.bankofnewport.com/*
Bank of Papa New Guinea	*http://www.datec.com.pg/*
Bank of Portugal	*http://www.bportugal.pt/*

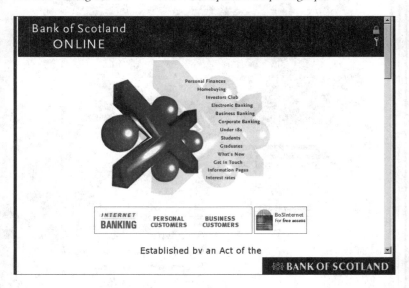

Bank of Scotland	*http://www.bankofscotland.co.uk/*
Bank of Slovenia	*http://www.bsi.si/*
Bank of Thailand	*http://www.bot.or.th/*
Bank of the Southwest	*http://www.bankofthesouthwest.com/*

Bank of Wales	*http://www.bankofwales.co.uk/*
Bank of Zambia	*http://www.boz.zm/*
Bank One	*http://www.bankone.com*

Bank United	*http://www.bankunited.com/*
BankLink	*http://www.banklink.com/*
Banque de France	*http://www.banque-france.fr/*
Barclays Bank	*http://www.barclays.co.uk/*
Bay-Vanguard Federal Savings Bank	*http://www.bayvanguard.com/*
Bermuda Monetary Authority	*http://www.bma.bm/*
Bulgarian National Bank	*http://www.bnb.bg/*
Capital Bank	*http://www.capitalbank.co.uk/*

Capital Federal Savings   *http://www.capfed.com/*
Capital One Financial   *http://www.capitalone.com/*
Central Bank of Armenia   *http://www.cba.am/*
Central Bank of Barbados   *http://www.centralbank.org.bb/*
Central Bank of Bosnia   *http://www.cbbh.gov.ba/*
Central Bank of Chile   *http://www.bcentral.cl/*
Central Bank of China   *http://www.cbc.gov.tw/*
Central Bank of Cyprus   *http://www.centralbank.gov.cy/*
Central Bank of Iceland   *http://www.sedlabanki.is/*
Central Bank of Jordan   *http://www.cbj.gov.jo/*

Central Bank of Malta

➡ ENTER

Central Bank of Malta   *http://www.centralbankmalta.com/*
Central Bank of Swaziland   *http://www.centralbank.sz/*

Central Bank of the Netherlands Antilles	*http://centralbank.an/*
Central Bank of the Republic of Turkey	*http://www.tcmb.gov.tr/*
Central Bank of Trinidad and Tobago	*http://www.central-bank.org.tt/*
Central Bank of Uruguay	*http://www.bcu.gub.uy/*
Central Carolina Bank	*http://www.ccbonline.com/*
Central Reserve Bank of El Salvador	*http://www.bcr.gob.sv/*
Centura	*http://www.centura.com/*
Charter One Financial	*http://www.charterone.com/*

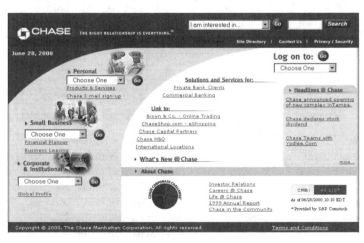

Chase Manhattan Bank	*http://www.chase.com/*
Chevy Chase Bank	*http://www.chevychasebank.com/*

Citibank (UK)	*http://www.citibank.com/uk/*
Citibank US	*http://www.citibank.com/us/*
Citigroup	*http://www.citigroup.com/*

Citizens Bank	*http://www.citizensbank.com/*
Colonial Bank	*http://www.colonialbank.com/*
Columbia Bank	*http://www.columbiabank.com/*
Commerce Bank	*http://www.commerceonline.com/*
Commercial Federal Bank	*http://www.comfedbank.com/*
Commercial National Bank	*http://www.cnbthebank.com/*
Community First	*http://www.cfbx.com/*
Compass Bank	*http://www.compassweb.com/*
Co-operative Bank	*http://www.co-operativebank.co.uk/*

Croatian National Bank	*http://www.hnb.hr/sadr.htm*
Cross Country Bank	*http://www.crosscountrybank.com/*
Czech National Bank	*http://www.cnb.cz/en/*
De Nederlandsche Bank	*http://www.dnb.nl/*
Deutsche Genossenschaftsbank	*http://www.dgbank.de/*
Dime Savings Bank	*http://www.dime.com/*
Dresdner Kleinwort Benson	*http://www.dresdnerkb.com/*
Eastern Bank	*http://www.easternbank.com/*
Eastern Caribbean Central Bank	*http://www.eccb-centralbank.org/*
Egg	*http://www.egg.com/*

Federal Reserve Bank	*http://www.kc.frb.org/*
Fidelity Federal Savings Bank	*http://www.fidfed.com/*

First American Bank.	*http://www.firstambank.com/*
First Citizens Bank	*http://www.firstcitizens.com/*
First Federal Of Michigan	*http://www.charterone.com/*
First National Bank of Maryland	*http://www.cba.am/*
First National Bank of Missouri	*http://www.firstnatlbank.com/*
First National Bank of Mount Dora	*http://www.fnbmd.com/*
First National Bank of Omaha	*http://www.fnbomaha.com/*
First National Bank of Texas	*http://www.fnbtexas.com/*
First of America Bank	*http://www.foa.com/natcity/*
First Republic Bank	*http://www.firstrepublic.com/*
First Union	*http://www.firstunion.com/*

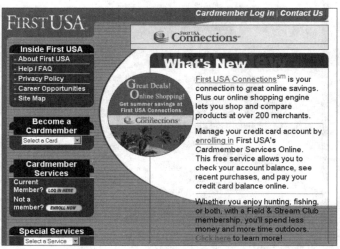

First USA   *http://www.firstusa.com/*

| Firstar Bank | *http://www.firstar.com/* |
| Firstrust Bank | *http://www.firstrustbank.com/* |

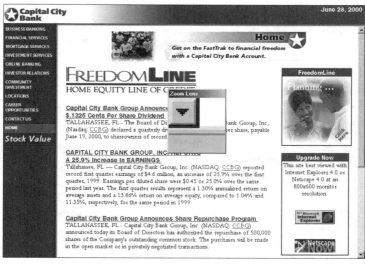

FL - Capital City Bank	*http://www.ccbg.com/*
Flagstar Bank	*http://www.flagstar.com/*
Fleet Bank	*http://www.fleet.com/*
Franklin National Bank	*http://www.fnb.net/*
GA - SunTrust Banks	*http://www.suntrust.com/*
Gateway National Bank	*http://www.gatewaybank.com/*
GreenPoint Bank	*http://www.greenpoint.com/*
Grindlays Private Banking	*http://www.pb.grindlays.com/*
Guaranty Federal Bank	*http://www.gfbank.com/*

Gulf Coast Bank & Trust Company	*http://www.gulfbank.com/*
Halifax Bank	*http://www.halifax.co.uk/*
Houston Savings Bank	*http://www.houstonsavings.com/*

HSBC	*http://www.banking.hsbc.co.uk/*
Istituto di Credito Sammarinese	*http://www.ics.sm/*
JP Morgan & Co. Incorporated	*http://www.jpmorgan.com/*
Kaufman Brothers	*http://www.kbro.com/*
Key Bank in Maine	*http://www.key.com/*
KeyCorp	*http://www.keybank.com/*
Keystone Financial	*http://www.keyfin.com/*
KY - Star Bank	*http://www.starbank.com/*
LaSalle Banks	*http://www.lasallebanks.com/*

Legal & General	*http://www.landg.com/*
Lloyds TSB	*http://www.lloydstsb.co.uk/*
M&I Bank	*http://www.mibank.com/*
MA - Central Bank	*http://www.centralbk.com/*

MBNA	*http://www.mbnainternational.com/*
Mellon	*http://www.mellon.com/*
Mellon Personal Loans	*http://www.mellon.com/*
Mercantile Bankshares Corporation	*http://www.mercantile.net/*
Monetary and Foreign Exchange Authority of Macau	*http://amcm.macau.gov.mo/*
Monetary Authority of Singapore	*http://www.mas.gov.sg/*

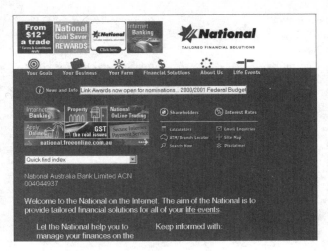

National Australia Bank	*http://www.national.com.au/*
National Bank of Commerce	*http://www.nbcbank.com/*
National Bank of Moldova	*http://www.bnm.org/*
National Bank of the Republic of Macedonia	*http://www.nbrm.gov.mk/*
National City	*http://www.foa.com/*
National City	*http://www.national-city.com/*
National Savings	*http://www.nationalsavings.co.uk/*
National Westminster Bank	*http://www.natwest.co.uk/*
NationsBank	*http://www.nationsbank.com/*
Nationwide	*http://www.nationwide.co.uk/*
Norinchukin Bank	*http://www.nochubank.or.jp/*
North Korean Financial Institutions	*http://www.kimsoft.com/korea/*

Northern Rock	*http://www.northernrock.co.uk/*
Oesterreichische Nationalbank	*http://www.oenb.co.at/*
PhoenixVille Federal Savings	*http://www.phoenixfed.com/*
PNC Bank Corp.	*http://www.pncbank.com/*
Providian Financial	*http://www.providian.com/*
Rayne State Bank & Trust Co.	*http://www.bankonnet.com/*
Republic Bancorp	*http://www.rbmi.com/*
Reserve Bank of Australia	*http://www.rba.gov.au/*

Reserve Bank of NZ	*http://www.rbnz.govt.nz/*
Riggs Bank	*http://www.riggsbank.com/*
Royal Bank of Scotland	*http://www.rbs.co.uk/*
San Diego Commercial Finance	*http://www.sdcf.com/*

Sanwa Bank California	*http://www.sanwa-bank-ca.com/*
Scripps Bank	*http://www.scrippsbank.com/*
Smile	*http://www.smile.co.uk/*
Standard Bank	*http://www.sboff.com/*
State Street Corporation	*http://www.statestreet.com/*
Summit Bank	*http://www.summitbank.com/*

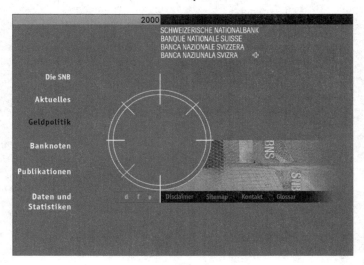

Swiss National Bank	*http://www.snb.ch/*
The Co operative Bank	*http://www.co-operativebank.co.uk/*
TN - SouthTrust Bank	*http://www.southtrust.com/*
UniCredito Italiano	*http://www.credit.it/*
Union Planters Bank	*http://www.unionplanters.com/*

University National Bank of Chicago	*http://www.uninatbk.com/*
US Trust	*http://www.ustrust.com/*
US Trust Boston	*http://www.ustrustboston.com/*
Virgin Direct	*http://www.virgin-direct.co.uk/*
Wachovia Corp	*http://www.wachovia.com/*
Washington Mutual	*http://www.washingtonmutual.com/*
Webster Bank	*http://www.websterbank.com/*
Wells Fargo	*http://www.wellsfargo.com/*
WesBanco	*http://www.wesbanco.com/*

Woolwich	*http://www.woolwich.co.uk/*
Zions Bank	*http://www.zionsbank.com/*

Investments

Making your money work for you seems to be more important than ever to ensure a reasonable degree of comfort in later years. But beware – prices can fall as well as rise.

Check Free Investment Services	*http://www.secapl.com/*
CNBC	*http://www.cnbc.com/*
CNN Financial Network	*http://www.cnnfn.com/*
Cyber Cash	*http://www.cybercash.com/*
Datek	*http://www.datek.com/*
Dow Jones	*http://www.dowjones.com/*
Fidelity Investments	*http://www.fidelity.com/*

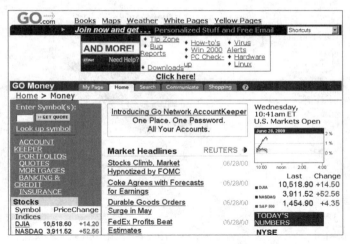

Go   *http://money.go.com/*

Individual Investor	*http://www.individualinvestor.com/*
IMoney Manager	*http://www.moneymanager.com.au/*
Money Online	*http://www.money.com/*
Nasdaq	*http://www.nasdaq.com/*
Personal Wealth	*http://www.personalwealth.com/*
Prudential	*http://www.prudential.com/*
Quicken.com	*http://www.quicken.com/*
Quote.com	*http://www.quote.com/*
The Motley Fool	*http://www.fool.com/*
Waterhouse Securities Inc.	*http://www.waterhouse.com/*

Loans

There never seems to be any shortage of people who are prepared to offer to lend you money. If you do need to borrow, it makes sense to shop around for the best deal.

AccuBanc Mortgage Corporation	*http://www.accubanc.com/*
Anchor Mortgage	*http://www.anchormortgage.com/*
APT Funding	*http://www.aptfunding.com/*
Besthomeloan.com	*http://www.besthomeloan.com/*
Capstead Mortgage Corporation	*http://www.capstead.com/*
Carloan.com	*http://www.carloan.com/*
Century Oak	*http://www.centuryoak.com/*
CMI Mortgage info	*http://www.cmi-mortgageinfo.com/*
Dominion Corporation	*http://www.dominfin.com/*
E-Loan	*http://www.eloan.com/*
E-Mortage1	*http://www.e-mortgage1.com/*
GetSmart	*http://www.getsmart.com/*

Microsurf Internet Services	*http://www.microsurf.com/*
Mid-Atlantic Financial Group	*http://www.ihomeloans.com/*
Money Hunter	*http://www.moneyhunter.com/*
Mortgage Direct	*http://www.mortgagedirect.com/*
Mortgage Edge	*http://www.mortgageedge.com/*
Mortgage Market Information Services	*http://www.interest.com/*
Mortgage Resource	*http://www.mortgage-resource.com/*
Mortgage Select	*http://www.mortgageselect.com/*
Mortgage101.com	*http://www.mortgage101.com/*
Mortgage-Net	*http://www.mortgage-net.com/*
Norwest Corporation Personal Loans	*http://www.ntrs.com/is/*
Norwest Online	*http://www.norwest.com/*
RMCVanguard	*http://www.rmcv.com/*
The Mortgage Network	*http://www.themortgagenetwork.com/*
The Mortgage Outlet	*http://www.themortgageoutlet.com/*
Worldloan.com	*http://www.worldloan.com/*

Share Trading

Some people make their living buying and selling shares. The Internet has made the task considerably easier by providing up-to-the minute prices.

American Stock Exchange	*http://www.amex.com/*
Buy and Hold	*http://www.buyandhold.com/*
Charting UK Shares	*http://www.metronet.co.uk/bigwood/shares/*
Check Your Shares	*http://www.msn.co.uk/page/12-88.asp*

Citywire	*http://www.citywire.co.uk/*
CMC Group	*http://www.forex-cmc.co.uk/*
CMC Group	*http://www.cmcplc.com/*
Copenhagen Stock Exchange	*http://www.xcse.dk/uk/*
E*Trade	*http://www.etrade.com/*
E*Trade (UK)	*http://www.etrade.co.uk/*
Ellis & Partners Ltd	*http://www.ellisandpartners.co.uk/*
Interactive Investor International	*http://www.iii.co.uk/*
Internet Stock Report	*http://www.internetnews.com/stocks/*
London Stock Exchange	*http://www.londonstockex.co.uk/*
Malcolm Hills	*http://www.powerup.com.au/~mhills/ mal1.htm*
Motley Fool UK	*http://www.fool.co.uk/*
Nasdaq UK	*http://www.nasdaq-uk.com/*
New York Stock Exchange	*http://www.nyse.com/*
NO Global Markets	*http://www.ino.com/*
Stockmarket	*http://www.moneyworld.co.uk/stocks/*
StockMaster	*http://www.stockmaster.com/*
StockSelector.com	*http://www.stockselector.com/*
Stocktrade	*http://www.stocktrade.co.uk/*
Teleshare	*http://www.teleshare.co.uk/*
The Share Centre	*http://www.share.co.uk/*
The Share Centre	*http://www.share.com/*
UK-iNvest.com	*http://www.uk-invest.com/*
Union CAL	*http://www.unioncal.com/*
Virtual Stock Exchange	*http://www.virtualstockexchange.com/*
Wall Street City	*http://www.wallstreetcity.com/*
Xest	*http://www.xest.com/*

Food & Drink

I'm always amazed that people want to make such a meal out of having a meal. Even to the extent of spending half a day preparing it and then inviting friends around in the evening to consume it. Food is simply fuel for our bodies. It's a good thing that we don't hold a party every time the car needs petrol.

Drinks

These sites all have one thing in common: sampling their contents can leave you in no fit state to operate a computer.

About Scotch Whisky	*http://www.scotchwhisky.com/*
Absolut Vodka	*http://www.absolutvodka.com/*
ACATS Internet Bar Pages	*http://www.epact.se/acats/*
Alcohol	*http://www.mindbodysoul.gov.uk/ alcohol/alcmenu.htm*
Allied Domecq	*http://www.allieddomecqplc.com/*
Bacardi	*http://www.bacardi.com/*
Baileys PleasureDome	*http://www.baileys.com/*
Beer & Pubs UK	*http://www.blra.co.uk/*
Beerstalker	*http://www.beerstalker.co.uk/*
Breweriana - Pub paraphernalia	*http://www.eagle.co.uk/breweriana*
Canadian Mist	*http://www.canadianmist.com/*

Captain Morgan Rum   *http://www.rum.com/*
Chivas Regal   *http://www.chivas.com/*

Courvoisier   *http://www.courvoisier.com/*
Diageo   *http://www.diageo.co.uk/*
Drink Store   *http://www.drinkstore.com*
DrinkBoy   *http://www.drinkboy.com/*
Drinks   *http://uk.daawat.com/drinks.htm*
Drinks.com   *http://www.drinks.com/*
Epicurious Drinking   *http://food.epicurious.com/d_drinking/*
           d00_home/drinking.html

Food and Drink - Wine Course   *http://www.bbc.co.uk/foodanddrink/*
           winecourse/index.shtml

Grand Marnier	*http://www.grand-marnier.com/*
Hop Back Brewery	*http://www.hopback.co.uk/*
IDrink	*http://www.idrink.com/*
Jack Daniels	*http://www.jackdaniels.com/*
Jamaica Standard Products	*http://www.caribplace.com/foods/*
	jspcl.htm

Jim Beam	*http://www.jimbeam.com/*
Last Call	*http://www.lstcall.com*
Millennium - Drinking Game	*http://www.ecis.com/~weasel/*
	millennium.txt
Now 365	*http://www.now365.com/*
Pub World	*http://www.pubworld.co.uk/*

Red Dwarf - Drinking Game	*http://www2.hunterlink.net.au/ ~dejmb/rd_drink.htm*
Scotch Doc	*http://www.scotchdoc.com/*
Stoli Central	*http://www.stoli.com/*
Sunday Times Wine Club	*http://www.sundaytimeswineclub .co.uk/*

Tetley's Bitter	*http://www.smoothlydoesit.co.uk/*
The World of Spirits	*http://www.spirits.ch/welcome.htm*
Think About Drink	*http://www.wrecked.co.uk/*
Victoria Wine	*http://www.victoriawine.co.uk/*

Mixing Drinks

Should it be shaken or stirred? Mixing cocktails is quite an art, I understand. Apparently not the actual pouring of assortments of brightly coloured liquids into a pot, it's the bottle juggling that really makes a good cocktail waiter.

Bar Drinks   *http://www.bardrinks.com/*
Cecilia's Book of Martinis   *http://www.brecknet.com/cecilias/*
                                    martini.html

Mojito

The balmy, mambo-dancing, cocktail-sipping halcyon days of Cuba are long gone. We never find today's Hemingways on Havana's terraces. But that sweet bygone era of Mafia-supported elegance has bequeathed us the Mojito, a cooling, effervescent libation.

The Mojito was born in Cuba during this century's teen years. Simple enough and old enough to be claimed as the creation of more than a few bartenders, this classic is most closely tied to Cuba's famous La Bodeguita del Medio bar. This establishment's bartenders worked hard to popularize the drink during the '30s and '40s often resorting to name-dropping, most notably that of Ernest Hemingway. Their efforts paid off. Soon popular with Havana's hipsters, the Mojito lifted fresh mint out of its bit part as a mere cocktail garnish. An easy blend of sugar, mint leaves, lime juice, rum, ice, and soda water (strictly in that order), a Mojito (pronounced "moe-HEE-toe") is served in a tall glass sparkling with bubbles and greenery, garnished with a sprig of mint on top.

Cocktail   *http://www.hotwired.com/cocktail*
Cocktail Culture   *http://www.geocities.com/Paris/5289/*
                                    cocktail.html
Cocktail.com   *http://www.cocktail.com/ski/*
Cocktails   *http://cocktails.miningco.com/*
Cupid's Cocktail Recipes   *http://einstein.et.tudelft.nl/~janroel/*
                                    cup_love/cup_cocx.html

Swank-O-Rama
"DEDICATED TO BETTER LIVING THROUGH COCKTAIL CULTURE"

Welcome to the Jet-Age at Swank-O-Rama where you can live the international jet-set cocktail lifestyle on the Internet. Whether you are a secret agent, a playboy, a "La Dolce Vita" jet-setter , a super-model or just someone looking for an lifetime of fabulous fun you are all welcome. Join us in the cocktail lounges of the world as we dance the night away to the suave sound of Sergio Mendes and Brazil '66. Cast off your flannel shirts and pour out your pitchers of beer and join us in your suits and cocktail dresses as we sip martinis and toast the high life. We'll mambo through the night with the fire of a volcano and then toast the dawn with champagne as cigarettes smolder forgotten in ashtrays and Frank Sinatra sings. Above all we will be fabulous!

Soft Drinks

It's best to keep off the hard stuff – it's not good for you. It's much better to stick to drinks which are packed out with sugar and ingredients that are identified with an 'e' number.

The Beverage Network   *http://www.thebevnet.com*
Coca-Cola   *http://www.cocacola.com/*

Dr Pepper   *http://www.drpepper.com/*
Mello Yello   *http://www.melloyello.com*
Mr Pibb!   *http://bluWeb.com/us/chouser/info/*
                                     pibb/

National Soft Drink Association   *http://www.nsda.org*

| OK Soda | *http://spleen.mit.edu/ok.html* |
| SodaFountain.com | *http://www.sodafountain.com/* |

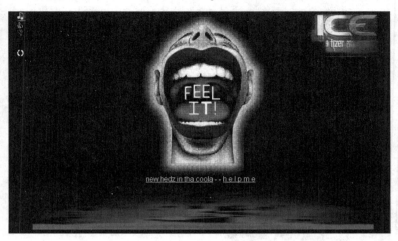

| Tizer | *http://www.tizer.co.uk/* |
| Wet Planet Beverages | *http://www.joltcola.com/* |

Home Cooking

I specialise in things that come out of tins. If you want to develop beyond that stage, visit some of these sites which offer lots of help for the beginner or the expert and some excellent recipes.

A la Carte TV	*http://www.alacartetv.com/*
Albertsons	*http://www.albertsons.com/*
AllRecipes.com	*http://www.allrecipes.com/*

American Foods	*http://www.americanfoods.com/*
Better Baking	*http://www.betterbaking.com/*

Betty Crocker	*http://www.bettycrocker.com/*
CD Kitchen	*http://www.cdkitchen.com/*
Chefs Catalog	*http://www.chefscatalog.com/*
Chefs-store	*http://www.chefs-store.com/*
Cheftalk	*http://www.cheftalk.com/*
Chetday	*http://www.chetday.com/*
Chicken Recipe	*http://www.chickenrecipe.com/*
Cookbooks	*http://www.cookbooks.com/*
Cookie Recipe	*http://www.cookierecipe.com/*
Cooking Compass	*http://www.cookingcompass.com/*
Cooking Light	*http://www.cookinglight.com/*

Cooking With Kids   *http://www.cookingwithkids.com/*

Cooking.com   *http://www.cooking.com/*
Cooks Illustrated   *http://www.cooksillustrated.com/*
Cuisinenet   *http://www.cuisinenet.com/*
Culinary Café   *http://www.culinarycafe.com/*
Culinary Pleasures   *http://www.culinarypleasures.com/*
Culinary.com   *http://www.culinary.com/*
Culinary.net   *http://www.culinary.net/*
CulinaryChef.Com   *http://www.culinarychef.com/*
Cutlery   *http://www.cutlery.com/*

Cyberdiet   *http://www.cyberdiet.com/*

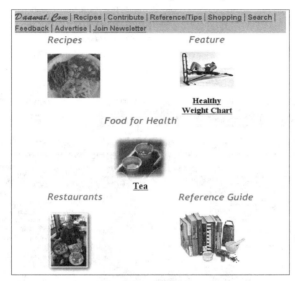

Daawat.Com   *http://www.daawat.com/*
Dean de Luca   *http://www.deandeluca.com/*
Delicious Decisions   *http://www.deliciousdecisions.org/*
Delicious India   *http://www.deliciousindia.com/*
Diabetic Gourmet   *http://www.diabeticgourmet.com/*
Eat.com   *http://www.eat.com/*
e-Cuisines.com   *http://www.e-cuisines.com/*
eHow.com   *http://www.ehow.com/*
Epicurean   *http://www.epicurean.com/*

Epicurious	*http://www.epicurious.com/*
Epicurus.com	*http://www.epicurus.com/*
Fatfree.com	*http://www.fatfree.com/*
Food	*http://www.food.com/*
Food Consultants	*http://www.foodconsultants.com/*
Food Institute.com	*http://www.foodinstitute.com/*

Food Safety	*http://www.foodsafety.gov/*
Food TV	*http://www.foodtv.com/*
Foodvision	*http://www.foodvision.com/*
French Culinary	*http://www.frenchculinary.com/*
Gist	*http://www.gist.com/*
Global Gourmet	*http://www.globalgourmet.com/*

Good Cooking	*http://www.goodcooking.com/*
Gourmet Connection	*http://www.gourmetconnection.com/*
Gourmet Market	*http://www.gourmetmarket.com/*
Great Food	*http://www.greatfood.com/*
Happy Cookers	*http://www.happycookers.com/*

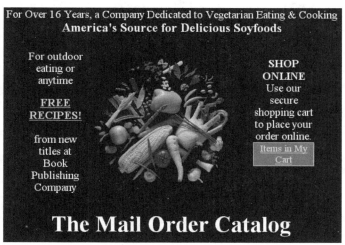
Healthy Eating	*http://www.healthy-eating.com/*
HGTV	*http://www.hgtv.com/*
Homearts.com	*http://www.homearts.com/*
Homechef	*http://www.homechef.com/*
iChef.com	*http://www.ichef.com/*
India Tastes	*http://www.indiatastes.com/*
Kitchen Emporium	*http://www.kitchenemporium.com/*

Kitchenlink — *http://www.kitchenlink.com/*
Lets eat oc.com — *http://www.letseatoc.com/*
Living Foods — *http://www.living-foods.com/*

Martha Stewart — *http://www.marthastewart.com/*
Merry Christmas.com — *http://merry-christmas.com/recipes.htm*

Minute Meals — *http://www.minutemeals.com/*
Mollie Katzen — *http://www.molliekatzen.com/*
Mosiman Academy — *http://www.mosiman.com/*
My Meals — *http://www.my-meals.com/*
My-Recipe.com — *http://www.my-recipe.com/*
Outlaw Cook — *http://www.outlawcook.com/*

Soup Recipe	*http://www.souprecipe.com/*
Star Chefs	*http://www.starchefs.com/*

Starbucks	*http://www.starbucks.com/*
Tavolo	*http://www.tavolo.com/*
Texas Cooking	*http://www.texascooking.com/*
The Food Web	*http://www.thefoodweb.com/*
Top Secret Recipes	*http://www.topsecretrecipes.com/*
Ucook.com	*http://www.ucook.com*
Vegetable Patch, The	*http://www.vegetablepatch.net/*
Vegetarian Society	*http://www.vegsoc.org/*
Veggies Unite	*http://www.vegweb.com/food/*

Vegkitchen.com	*http://www.vegkitchen.com/*
Vegweb	*http://www.vegweb.com/*
Webvan	*http://www.webvan.com*
Your Kitchen	*http://www.your-kitchen.com/*

Yum Yum	*http://www.yumyum.com/*

Ingredients

You can't make anything without the ingredients. These sites have lots of them and lots of tips about what to do with them.

Alaska Seafood Marketing Institute	*http://www.alaskaseafood.org/ recipes.htm*
Crate and Barrel	*http://www.crateandbarrel.com/*

Eat Chicken	*http://www.eatchicken.com/*
Foodline	*http://www.foodline.com/*
Home Grocer	*http://www.homegrocer.com/*

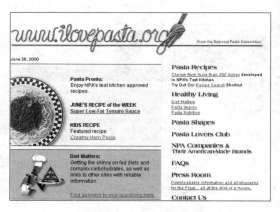

I love pasta	*http://www.ilovepasta.org/*
Ingredients	*http://www.ingredients.com/*
Mushrooms.com	*http://www.gmushrooms.com/*
Net Grocer	*http://www.netgrocer.com/*
Our Daily Bread	*http://www.our-daily-bread.com/*
Schwans	*http://www.schwans.com/*
Send.com	*http://www.send.com/*
Shoprite	*http://www.shoprite.com/*
Sweet Lobster	*http://www.sweetlobster.com/*
Tuna	*http://www.tunaking.com/*
Why Milk?	*http://www.whymilk.com/*
Zagats.com	*http://www.zagats.com/*

Supermarkets

More and more supermarkets are offering online ordering for the weekly groceries. You have to plan in advance to ensure there is a 'delivery slot' at a time that someone can be at home to receive it.

ABCO Foods   *http://www.abcofoods.com/*
Acme Markets   *http://www.acmemarkets.com/*
Asda   *http://www.asda.co.uk/*
Food City   *http://www.foodcity.com/*
Food Ferry   *http://www.foodferry.co.uk/*
FoodFare   *http://www.foodfare.com/*
Glasgow's Online Shop   *http://www.groceries.org.uk/*

Harrods Online   *http://www.harrods.com/*

HomeGrocer.com	*http://www.homegrocer.com/*
Online British Foodstore	*http://www.3ex.com/*
Pathmark Stores	*http://www.pathmark.com/*
Pavilions	*http://www.pavilions.com/*
PC Foods	*http://www.pcfoods.com/*

Price Chopper Supermarkets	*http://www.pricechopper.com/*
Safeway	*http://www.safeway.com/*
Sainsbury's	*http://www.sainsburystoyou.co.uk/*
Shaw's Supermarkets	*http://www.shaws.com/*
Somerfield	*http://www.somerfield.co.uk/*
Tesco	*http://www.tesco.co.uk/software/*
ValuPage	*http://www.supermarkets.com/*
Waitrose Supermarkets	*http://www.waitrose.co.uk/*
Woolworths	*http://www.woolworths.co.uk/*

Government & Politics

There are lots of sites relating to the powers that be from all countries. Many of these sites have links to other sites within the same government-run organisation.

Government

It's comforting to know that the the people charged with making decisions about our lives are so accessible.

Australian Commonwealth Government	*http://www.fed.gov.au/*
British Governments & Elections	*http://www.psr.keele.ac.uk/area/uk/ uktable.htm*
Cabinet Office	*http://www.cabinet-office.gov.uk/*

Canadian Government	*http://canada.gc.ca/*

CCTA Government Information Service	*http://www.open.gov.uk/*
Criminal Justice System	*http://www.criminal-justice-system.gov.uk/*
Falkland Islands Government	*http://www.falklands.gov.fk/*
GCHQ Government Communications HQ	*http://www.fas.org/irp/world/uk/gchq/*
Government Agencies	*http://www.ngfl.gov.uk/ngfl/govern/gov_agency_list.html*

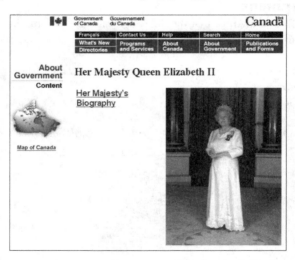

| Her Majesty Queen Elizabeth II | *http://canada.gc.ca/howgoc/queen/quind_e.html* |
| Indian Government | *http://www.indiagov.org* |

Information from the Irish State	*http://www.irlgov.ie/*
Isle of Man Government	*http://www.gov.im/*
New Zealand Government	*http://www.govt.nz/*
Scottish Local Government Index	*http://www.oultwood.com/localgov/scotland.htm*

Good Afternoon

Welcome to the White House

President Clinton's First Internet Address to the Nation
June 24, 2000

Clinton-Gore Administration's Budget Framework

The White House	*http://www.whitehouse.gov/*
UK Government Communications HQ	*http://www.gchq.gov.uk/*
UK Local Government Index	*http://www.oultwood.com/localgov/england.htm*
UK Local Government Sites	*http://sun1.bham.ac.uk/turnersj/local.html*

| UK Public Services and Local Government | http://www.hants.gov.uk/services.html |

UK Royal Family	http://www.royal.gov.uk/
UK Taxation Directory	http://www.uktax.demon.co.uk/home.htm
US Government	http://www.government.com/
US Government and Regulatory Bodies	http://www.pharmweb.net/pwmirror/pwk/pharmwebk.html
Welsh Local Government Index	http://www.oultwood.com/localgov/wales.htm

Politics

Politicians are a very special breed of people: they all seem to have the ability to answer a question without actually answering it.

All Politics	*http://www.allpolitics.com/*
All Things Political	*http://www.federal.com/Political.html*
Australian Labour Party	*http://www.alp.org.au/*
Australian Parliament	*http://www.aph.gov.au/*
Australian Politics	*http://ccadfa.cc.adfa.oz.au/~adm/ politics/politics.html*
Australian Republican Movement	*http://www.republic.org.au/*
British Party Websites	*http://www.psr.keele.ac.uk/area/uk/ localweb.htm*

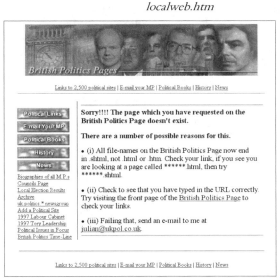

British Politics Pages

Links to 2,500 political sites | E-mail your MP | Political Books | History | News

Political Links
E-mail Your MP
Political Books
History
News

Biographies of all M.P.s
Councils Page
Local Election Results
Archive
uk.politics.* newsgroup
Add a Political Site
1997 Labour Cabinet
1997 Tory Leadership
Political Issues in Focus
British Politics Time-Line

Sorry!!!! The page which you have requested on the British Politics Page doesn't exist.

There are a number of possible reasons for this.

• (i) All file-names on the British Politics Page now end in .shtml, not .html or .htm. Check your link, if you see you are looking at a page called ******.html, then try ******.shtml.

• (ii) Check to see that you have typed in the URL correctly. Try visiting the front page of the British Politics Page to check your links.

• (iii) Failing that, send an e-mail to me at julian@ukpol.co.uk.

Links to 2,500 political sites | E-mail your MP | Political Books | History | News

British Politics	*http://www.ukpol.co.uk/indexa.htm*
British Politics	*http://www.geocities.com/CapitolHill/ Lobby/5436/*

Christian Democratic Party	*http://www.cda.nl/*
Communist Party USA	*http://www.hartford-hwp.com/cp-usa/*
Conservative Party (UK)	*http://www.conservative-party.org.uk/*
Democratic National Committee	*http://www.democrats.org/*
Green Parties Worldwide	*http://www.greens.org/*
Institute of World Politics	*http://www.iwp.edu/*
Labour Party (UK)	*http://www.labour.org.uk/*
Liberal Party (UK)	*http://www.libparty.demon.co.uk/*
New Communist Party	*http://www.geocities.com/CapitolHill/2853/*
Political Parties	*http://www.4politicalparties.com/*
Politics.com	*http://www.politics.com/*
Reform Party	*http://www.reformparty.org/*
Republican National Committee	*http://www.rnc.org/*
Republican Party	*http://www.fiannafail.ie/*
Sinn Fein	*http://sinnfein.ie/*
The Australian Democrats	*http://www.democrats.org.au/*
The Commons	*http://www.the-commons.com/*
The Conservative Party	*http://www.conservative-party.org.uk/*
UK Economics & Politics	*http://dspace.dial.pipex.com/geoff.riley/*
UK Online Politics	*http://www.ukonline.co.uk/ukonline/frame_pols.html*
Ulster Democratic Party	*http://www.udp.org/main.html*
World Politics	*http://www.press.jhu.edu/press/journals/wp/wp.html*

Health

Personally, I'm not sure whether it is a good idea to provide medical material to laymen – it could lead to hyperchondria. These websites are packed with information about staying healthy and how to heal yourself. It should be stressed that if you are unwell, your GP should be consulted, not your favourite website.

Alternative Medicine

Some people swear by it, others dismiss it as hokus-pokus. Perhaps the safest stance is to place it somewhere between those two extremes. Indeed alternative medicine is frequently referred to as complimentary medicine meaning that it can be used alongside, but should not replace conventional medicine.

Acupuncture.com	*http://www.acupuncture.com/*
Acupuncture References	*http://www.americanwholehealth.com/ library/acupuncture*
Acupuntura	*http://www.acupuntura.org/*
All Herb	*http://www.allherb.com/*
American Apitherapy Society	*http://www.apitherapy.org/*
American Back Society	*http://www.americanbacksoc.org/*
Aroma Direct	*http://www.aromagift.com/*
Bhakti Yoga	*http://www.webcom.com/~ara/*

British School of Homoeopathy *http://www.homoeopathy.co.uk/*
Buteyko Asthma Education *http://www.buteyko-usa.com/*

ASTHMA: Buteyko's <u>Cure</u>.

Welcome to the Buteyko home page, created by a number of former asthmatics who have all experienced the immediate and dramatic beneficial effects of Professor Buteyko's therapy for asthma.

All site queries to <u>Peter Kolb</u>, Biomedical Engineer

<u>Introduction</u>

Explanations for doctors and medical scientists

- <u>Summary for doctors:</u> Peter Kolb
- <u>Biochemical basis for KP Buteyko's theory on the diseases of deep respiration:</u> Kazarinov
- <u>Carbon Dioxide:</u> Yandell Henderson
- <u>Genes, Carbon Dioxide and Adaptation:</u> Ray Peat PhD
- <u>Energy, Structure and Carbon Dioxide: A realistic view of the organism:</u> Ray Peat PhD

Clinical Trials

- <u>Russian Clinical Trial</u>
- <u>MJA:Clinical Trial in Brisbane</u>

Buteyko Breath Reconditioning Technique *http://www.wt.com.au/~pkolb/ buteyko.htm*
Buteyko Health Centre *http://www.buteyko.com/*
Buteyko Institute of Breathing & Health *http://www.buteyko.com.au/*
Buteyko Method *http://www.buteykovideo.com/*
Buteyko Online *http://www.buteyko.co.nz/*
Canadian Chiropractic Association *http://www.ccachiro.org/*
Canadian Neuro-Optic Research Institute *http://www.cnri.edu/*

Causal Kinesiology	*http://www.kineko.com/*
Chiropractors' Association of Australia Limited	*http://www.caa.com.au/*

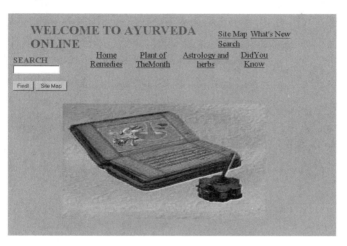

Common Ayurvedic Herbs	*http://ayurveda.virtualave.net/*
Dan Tao, The Way of Transformation	*http://www.erols.com/dantao/*
Foundation for Traditional Chinese Medicine	*http://www.ftcm.freeserve.co.uk/*
Guide to Aromatherapy	*http://www.fragrant.demon.co.uk/*
Guide to Transcendental Meditation	*http://www.tm.org/*
Health Kinesiology UK	*http://www.healthk.co.uk/*
Herb and Juice Stop	*http://www.mindspring.com/~morfil/ shop.htm*

Homeo Doctor — *http://www.tiruchicity.com/homeo*

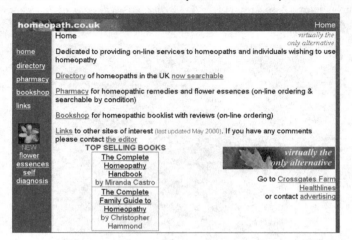

Homeopath — *http://www.homeopath.co.uk/*

Homeopathic Drugs — *http://community.net/~neils/faqhom.html*

Institute for Classical Homeopathy — *http://www.classicalhomoeopathy.org/*

International Chiropractic Pediatric Association — *http://www.4icpa.org/*

International Chiropractors Association — *http://www.chiropractic.org/*

International College of Applied Kinesiology — *http://www.icak.com/*

International Federation of Aromatherapists — *http://www.ifa.org.au/*

International Trepanation Advocacy Group *http://www.trepan.com/*

Introduction to Aromatherapy *http://www.eclipse.co.uk/iys/*

Yoga

Karma Yoga: Path of Selfless Action

Namaste - derived from the Sanskrit word, *Namaskaar*, meaning 'I honor the divine in you'.

I honor the place in you in which the entire universe dwells. I honor the place in you which is of love, of truth, of light, and of peace. When you are in that place in you

Action performed for the purpose of satisfying a desire has the effect of generating new desires that require additional actions. Addiction to pleasure (in any form) is a good example of this. Once the desire is satisfied it generates more desire which n eeds to be satisfied ad infinitum. In Karma Yoga one seeks to end this cycle by not being attached to the outcome of any thing he does. Actions are performed based on what seems appropriate in a given situation. The person performing the action has no con cern about whether the end result is "good" or "bad." Since the actions are not performed for self-gratification the person is free of them. As a result of not being attached to the outcome a person can become completely involved in what ever he is doing. A surprising result is that life becomes more interesting and engaging because your focus is totally in the present. In this way yogis seek to end the eternal cycle of death and rebirth.

[Return to Yoga Paths list]

Karma Yoga: Path of Selfless Action *http://www.talamasca.org/avatar/yoga3.html*

Lanes Health *http://www.laneshealth.com/*

National Institute of Ayurvedic Medicine *http://www.niam.com/*

Oasis By Design *http://www.angelfire.com/hi/oasisbydesign/*

Raja Yoga Meditation and Poetry Page *http://www.quicklink.com/~joneve/*

Trepanation Trust *http://www.trepanation.com/*

General Health

All of us should look after our bodies and with care, they'll last a lifetime. From your head to your toes, and all parts between, there is no shortage of advice on the Internet.

American Heart	*http://www.americanheart.org/*
Body, The	*http://www.thebody.com/*
BUPA	*http://www.bupa.co.uk/*
Delicious Decisions	*http://www.deliciousdecisions.org/*
First Aid	*http://firstaid.ie.eu.org/*
Fitness Online	*http://www.fitnessonline.com/*
Harley Street Dental Practice	*http://www.harley-street-dental.com/*

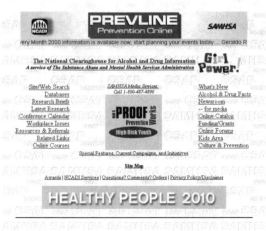

Health	*http://www.health.org/*

Health Central	*http://www.healthcentral.com/*
Healthatoz	*http://www.healthatoz.com/*
Healthfinder	*http://www.healthfinder.gov/*

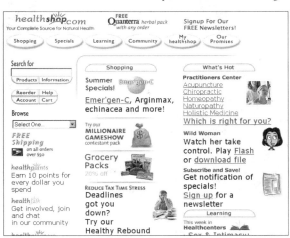

Healthshop	*http://www.healthshop.com/*
Intelihealth	*http://www.intelihealth.com/*
Managing Stress	*http://www.managingstress.com/*
Medicare	*http://www.medicare.gov/*
Mediconsult	*http://www.mediconsult.com/*
Medscape	*http://www.medscape.com/*
Nutravida	*http://www.nutravida.com/*
Self Care	*http://www.selfcare.com/*
Vegetarian Society	*http://www.vegsoc.org/*
Vitamins	*http://www.vitamins.com/*

Web MD   *http://www.webmd.com/*

Your Health   *http://www.yourhealth.com/*

Medicine

You can buy your medicines over the Internet as well as get advice on their use.

Drug Library   *http://www.druglibrary.org/*
Drugstore   *http://www.drugstore.com/*
Pharmaceutical Information   *http://www.pharminfo.com/*
Pharmacy2U   *http://www.pharmacy2u.co.uk/*

Parenting

The problem we found when bringing up children is that seemingly every other parent in the world thinks they are the experts. The way they did it was right for their child and will, therefore, be right for every other child and if you do it a different way, you're wrong. Some websites fall into that category but there are many more which will offer sound unbiased advice based on tried and trusted methods.

AAP	*http://www.aap.org/*
Baby World	*http://www.babyworld.co.uk/*
BBC Education – Pregnancy	*http://www.bbc.co.uk/education/ health/parenting/pregnant.shtml*

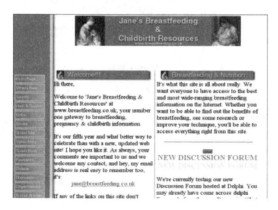

Breastfeeding & Childbirth	*http://www.breastfeeding.co.uk/*
British Pregnancy Advisory Service	*http://www.bpas.demon.co.uk/*

Childcare Now!	*http://www.childcare-now.co.uk/*
Dads.com	*http://www.dads.com/*
Having it All - Kids & a Career	*http://www.bbc.co.uk/education/having/index.shtml*

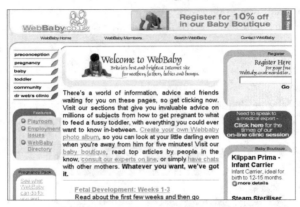

Web Baby	*http://www.webbaby.co.uk/*

Men's Health

The issues surrounding men's health are slightly different from those of women and so here are a few sites which look at men's very special needs.

Black Health Net	*http://www.blackhealthnet.com/*
Black Men's Health	*http://www.blackmenshealth.org/*
Dr. Koop's Community: Men's Health	*http://www.drkoop.com/resource/mens*

Gay Men's Health Crisis   *http://www.gmhc.org/*
Gay Men's Health Summit   *http://www.temenos.net/summit/*

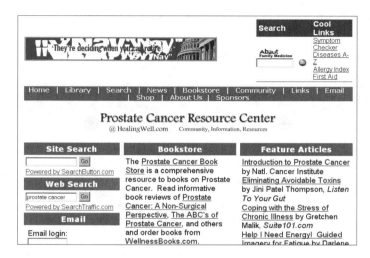

Healing Well   *http://www.healingwell.com/*
                                  prostatecancer/
Health Central   *http://www.healthcentral.com/*
Health Concerns Among Gay Men   *http://www.thebody.com/sowadsky/*
                                  gaymen.html
Health Library   *http://www.healthlibrary.com/*
Health Net   *http://www.health-net.com/*
Health Touch   *http://www.healthtouch.com/*

Impotence World Association	*http://www.impotenceworld.org/*
InteliHealth	*http://www.intelihealth.com/*
Male Health Center	*http://www.malehealthcenter.com/*
Men's Health	*http://www.menshealth.com/*
Men's Health - Clinique	*http://www.clinique.com/ mhealth.html*

Men's Health - Keen.com	*http://www.keen.com/*
Men's Health - ThirdAge.com	*http://www.thirdage.com/health/mens/*
Men's Health Book Store	*http://www.wellnessbooks.com/men/*
Men's Health Consulting	*http://www.menshealth.org/*
Men's Health Network	*http://www.menshealthnetwork.org/*

Men's Health Online	*http://www.mhealth.ru/*
Men's Health Topics - Testicular Cancer	*http://www.uro.com/tcancer.htm*
MSN Men's Health	*http://content.health.msn.com/*
National Prostate Cancer Coalition	*http://www.4npcc.org/*
Prostate Health	*http://www.prostatehealth.com/*
Reuters Health Information	*http://www.reutershealth.com/*
Urology Opinion	*http://www.a-urology.com/*
Virtual Library – Men's Health Issues	*http://www.vix.com/men/health/health.html*

Women's Health

The issues surrounding women's health are slightly different from those of men and so here are a few sites which look at women's very special needs.

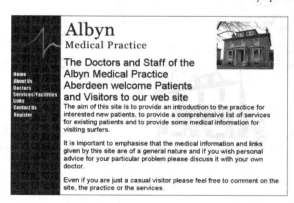

Albyn Medical Practice   *http://www.albyn-medical.co.uk/*

All Cures	*http://www.allhealth-info.com/*
All Health	*http://www.allhealth.com/womens/*
BBC - Women's Health	*http://www.bbc.co.uk/education/ health/womens/*
BBC - Women's Health - STDs	*http://www.bbc.co.uk/education/ health/womens/sexual.shtml*

BUPA - Women's Health	*http://www.bupa.co.uk/*
Canadian Women's Health Network	*http://www.cwhn.ca/indexfr.html*
Cancer and Women's Health Links	*http://www2.cybernex.net/~sune/ blinks.html*
Cestria Health Centre	*http://members.aol.com/ChesterDoc/*
Feeding Question	*http://www.bbc.co.uk/education/ health/parenting/prfeed.shtml*
Fertility & Pregnancy Specialists	*http://www.fertilitytest.co.uk/*

Fibroids - Women's Health	*http://www.womens-health.co.uk/ fibroids.htm*
Fitness During Pregnancy	*http://www.childcare-now.co.uk/ fitpreg.html*
Health Square	*http://www.healthsquare.com/*

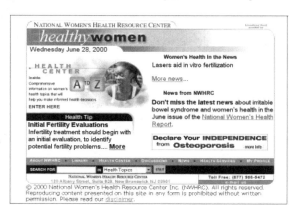

Healthy Women	*http://www.healthywomen.org/*
Jacobs Institute of Women's Health	*http://www.jiwh.org/*
Karen Lee's Virtual Clinic	*http://www.womencare.com/*
Medical Women's Federation	*http://www.m-w-f.demon.co.uk/*
MSN Women Central Health Resources	*http://womencentral.msn.com/health/ default.asp*
National Asian Women's Health Organisation	*http://www.nawho.org/*
National Association of Professionals in Women's Health	*http://www.napwh.org/*

National Women's Health Information Center	*http://www.4woman.org/*
National Women's Health Organisation	*http://www.gynpages.com/nwho*
Natural & Alternative Approaches	*http://www.healthy.net/womenshealth/*
Pregnancy & Women's Health Information	*http://www.womens-health.co.uk/*
Society for Women's Health Research	*http://www.womens-health.org/*
The Mining Company: Women's Health	*http://womenshealth.miningco.com/*
Thrive Online	*http://www.thriveonline.com/health/ womensdoc/womensdoc.today.html*
Vegetarian Pregnancy	*http://www.vegsoc.org/Info/preg.html*
WebMD: Women's Health	*http://women.webmd.com/*
Women's Health	*http://www.womens-health.co.uk/*
Women's Health	*http://www.feminist.com/health.htm*
Women's Health	*http://www.womenshealth.com/*
Women's Health Information Center	*http://www.ama-assn.org/special/ womh/womh.htm*
Women's Health Interactive	*http://www.womens-health.com/*
Women's Health Net International	*http://www.womenshealthnet.com/*
Women's Health Resource Center	*http://www.mayohealth.org/mayo/ common/htm/womenpg.htm*
Work & Pregnancy	*http://www.babyworld.co.uk/ information/working/ work_pregnancy.htm*

Hobbies

Kids of all ages, right up to 70 years and beyond, get a great deal of satisfaction from toys of all types. The Internet has websites from both the manufacturers and the enthusiasts.

Board Games

Many a winter's evening has been spent around a board game of some sort. Some of the most popular and enduring are...

Cluedo   *http://www.cluedo.co.uk/*

Freefungames Board Games	*http://www.freefungames.com/applets/card.htm*
Go	*http://www.britgo.org/gopcres/gopcres1.html*
Monopoly	*http://www.monopoly.com/*
Risk	*http://home.t-online.de/home/losmers/attila.htm*
Scrabble	*http://www.scrabble.com/*
Sorry!	*http://www.hasbro-interactive.com/*

| Trivial Pursuit | *http://www.trivialpursuit.com/* |

Backgammon

This up-market ludo game has some very famous followers including Omar Sharif, I'm told.

Acey Ducey Backgammon
http://www.wingames.com/ adback.html

Backgammon Deluxe
http://www.blackgames.net/ bgammon.htm

FIBSJF
http://www.algonet.se/~svempa

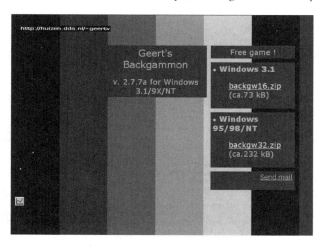

Geert's Backgammon
http://huizen.dds.nl/~geertv

GNU Backgammon
http://www.gnu.org/software/gnubg/ gnubg.html

JellyFish
http://effect.webbie.net/jelly.htm

MVP Backgammon	*http://www.mvpsoft.com/soft-board.html*
Netgammon	*http://www.netgammon.com/*
Pro Backgammon	*http://www.wingames.com/proback.html*
Snowie 3	*http://www.snowie3.com*
Snowie Professional	*http://www.oasya.com/*
The FIBS Bot Page	*http://www.revolver.demon.co.uk/bg/bot/*

Chess

You need a particular way of thinking to master this game, and age doesn't seem to have much to do with it. There have been champions who are only just in their teens.

British Chess Federation

The Watch Oak
Chain Lane
Battle
East Sussex
TN33 0YD

Tel 01424 775222
Fax 01424 775904
Email office@bcf.org.uk

Menu
What's New
National News
Regional News
ChessMoves
Articles
Calendar
Directory
Publicity
Reference
Archive
Grading
Products

The **British Chess Federation (BCF)**, founded in 1904, is the organisation that controls, directs and promotes the playing of chess in England. It is recognised as such by the UK government as well as the World Chess Federation (FIDE). Scotland, Wales, Ireland and the Channel Islands have their own federations.

Grandmaster John Emms is Editor of this web site; Syringa Turvey is Assistant Editor, and will be primarily involved in collecting and reporting county and club news. We look forward to receiving your feedback and contributions.

NEW - ChessMoves for June 2000 - a fully online edition of the BCF's newsletter with news, results, articles, games, photos and a downloadable database of more than 1,800 games - is now available from this site. Go to the

British Chess Federation   *http://www.bcf.ndirect.co.uk/*

British Chess Magazine	*http://www.bcmchess.co.uk/*
Chess Base	*http://www.chessbase.com/*
Chess World	*http://chess.8m.com/*
Garry Kasparov	*http://www.clubkasparov.ru/*
GNU Chess Web Interface	*http://www.net-chess.com/gnu/*
Interchess Email Chess	*http://www.interchess.co.uk/*
International Chess Federation	*http://www.fide.com/*
Internet Chess Club	*http://www.chessclub.com/*
London Chess Centre	*http://www.chess.co.uk/*
Mindscape	*http://www.mindscape.com/*
Rebel Decade	*http://www.rebel.nl/index3.htm*

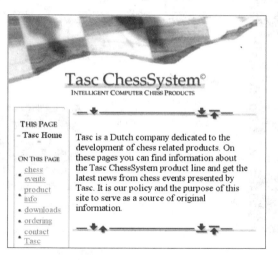

Tasc Chess System	*http://www.tasc.nl/*

Draughts

Using the same board as Chess, Draughts (or Checkers as it is often referred to) is a great deal more straight forward to play.

Actual Checkers   *http://www.atlantsoft.com*

Alquerque Family of Games   *http://web.ukonline.co.uk/*
                                      james.masters/traditionalgames/
                                      draughts.htm

American Checker Federation   *http://www.primenet.com/~krow/*

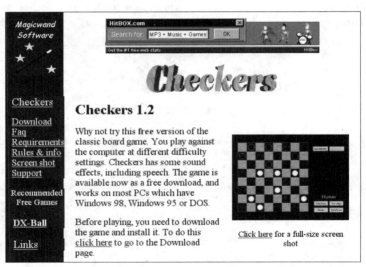

Checkers   *http://www.magicwandsoft.com/*
                                      games/index.html

Checkers & Draughts   *http://members.tripod.com/sgcheckers*
Checkers Information   *http://boardgamecentral.com/checkers/*
Checkers Net Links   *http://boardgames.about.com/*
                                 msub10.htm
Free Fun Games   *http://www.freefungames.com/applets/*
                                 checker/
Grooves Speed Team   *http://www.angelfire.com/games/gst/*
Online Checkers   *http://www.pogo.com*
Pond Checkers   *http://www.pondcheckers.com*
Willow Creek Online   *http://www.wcreekonline.com*

Card Games

I'm amazed at the number of games that can be played with a single pack of cards.

Blackjack   *http://www.freefungames.com/scripts/*
                                 blackjack.htm
Blackjack Depot   *http://www.edepot.com/blackjack.html*
Card Games Playable Over   *http://nxn.netgate.net/*
   The Web   *games2_XcardX.html*
Euchre   *http://www.bright.net/~double/*
                                 euchre.htm
Five by Five Poker   *http://5x5poker.com/*
House of Cards   *http://thehouseofcards.com/*
                                 online_games.html
Poker Races   *http://PokerRaces.com/*

Bridge

I was introduced to this game about 3 years ago and the interesting part about the game of Bridge is that the more you learn the more you realise you've got to learn.

ACBL Board of Governors   *http://www.oz.net/~mamula/bog.html*
Bridge - a fascinating card game!   *http://www.math.auc.dk/~nwp/bridge*

 The Bridge World

INTRODUCTION TO BRIDGE

FOREWORD: Thoughts on Bridge The rewards, beauty, satisfactions and frustrations of the world's most popular card game, described by fans from many walks of life who compete at different levels.

ARTICLE: The Therapeutic Value of Bridge An unusual collection of attributes enables bridge to provide health benefits.

LESSON 1: The Mechanics of Bridge by Alvin Roth and Jeff Rubens

LESSON 2: Bridge Scoring by Alvin Roth and Jeff Rubens

LESSON 3: Introduction to Declarer's Play by Edwin B. Kantar

LESSON 4: Introduction to Defender's Play by Edwin B. Kantar

LESSON 5: Introduction to Bidding by Alvin Roth and Jeff Rubens

Bridge Lessons For Beginners   *http://www.bridgeworld.com/ begin.html*
Bridge Today   *http://www.bridgetoday.com/bt/*
Bridge World   *http://www.bridgeworld.com/*
Contract Bridge   *http://netcafe.hypermart.net/ bridge.html*

Contract Bridge	*http://www.afn.org/~alplatt/bridge.html*
Contract Bridge	*http://www.uq.net.au/~zzjhardy/brmain.html*
Contract Bridge Organisations	*http://bridge.theriver.com/join.html*
Easy Bridge	*http://www.thegrid.net/shan/EasyBridge.htm*
Learn To Play Bridge	*http://www.acbl.org/notices/ltpb.stm*
MSN Gaming Zone - Bridge	*http://www.zone.com/asp/script/default.asp?Game=brdg*
PlayBridge	*http://playbridge.com/*
Tutorial Bridge	*http://learnbridge.com/*
Virtual Bridge Club	*http://www.bridgenfrance.com/*
World Bridge Federation	*http://www.bridge.gr/*

Patience (Solitaire)

If you're really bored, you can even play cards on your own.

Ace Solitaire	*http://acegames.com/solitaire*
Dumb Games Solitaire	*http://www.dumb-games.com/solitaire.asp*
Epsylon Games: Solitaires	*http://www.games.taxxi.com/solit.html*
Free 2 Play	*http://www.homestead.com/free2play/solitaire.html*
Free Fun Games Solitaire	*http://www.freefungames.com/applets/solitaire/*
Gallery Solitaire	*http://www.dplanet.ch/users/adrian.herzog/gallery*
Grump Ventures.com	*http://www.grumpventures.com*

The Solitaire Server

Downloads
Links
Game Descriptions
Email
News
4/04 Redirected old site
to new domain
4/02 Links page added

Welcome to Idiot's Delight, the source for online solitaire. This site features applets for fourteen solitaire variations that can be played in any browser supporting Java. The games allow unlimited undo and have several levels of difficulty to provide a challenging (but winnable) game for all levels of players. The source code and a class archive enabling offline play is available. Click on the name of the desired game to begin play. The applet's help button will display its instructions.

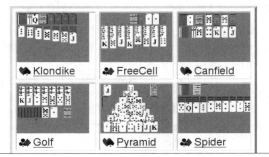

♠ Klondike   ♣ FreeCell   ♠ Canfield

♣ Golf   ♥ Pyramid   ♣ Spider

Idiot's Delight   *http://www.idiotsdelight.net/*
LifeSavers Candystand   *http://www.candystand.com/Solitaire/*
                           default.htm
NetCell   *http://coolios.com/way/cool/cell/*
                           intro.html

PokerSquares.com	*http://www.pokersquares.com*
PokSol	*http://games.yadda.net/poksol*
Solitaire Central	*http://www.solitairecentral.com/ sol_web.html*
Tournament Games	*http://www.tournamentgames.com*

Collections
Beanie Babies

Beanie Babies	*http://www.a2zbeaniebabies.co.uk/*
Beanie Babies Official Club	*http://www.beaniebabyofficialclub .com/*
Beanie Baby Bears	*http://www.beaniebabiebears.co.uk/*
Beanie Box UK	*http://www.beanieboxuk.force9.co.uk/*
Beanie Exchange	*http://www.beanieexchange.net/*
Beanie Stalk UK	*http://www.beaniestalkuk.com/*

Beermats

Beer Collections	*http://www.beercollections.com/*
Beermat index	*http://www.homestead.com/dunny2*

Beermats	*http://www.stormloader.com/olut/*

Beermats	*http://www.pearce7.freeserve.co.uk/* *beermats.htm*
Beermats and Coasters	*http://communities.msn.co.uk/* *BeermatsCoasters/home.htm*
Re: beermats	*http://www.wasquare.com/forums/*
Scanned beer-mats collection	*http://www.home.ch/~spaw1525/* *Welcome.html*

China & Crystal

Collecting Wedgwood	*http://www.suite101.com/article.cfm/* *collecting_china/10729*
Potteries, The	*http://www.thepotteries.org/*
Royal Doulton Collectables Discussion Forum	*http://www.broadband.co.uk/doulton/* *messages/189.html*

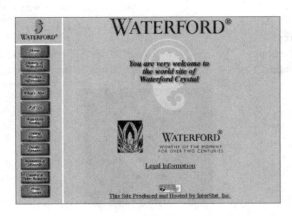

Waterford Crystal	*http://www.waterford-usa.com/*

Cigarette Cards

Card Collectables	*http://www.cardcollectables.co.uk/*
Cigarette and Tea cards	*http://www.microscopy-uk.org.uk/ mag/artaug98/mdcard.html*
Cigarette Cards	*http://www.cardking.bizhosting.com/*
Cigarette Cards Central	*http://www.cigcards.com/*
English Cigarette Card Albums	*http://www.the-forum.com/ephemera/ engcc.htm*

Framed Memories	*http://www.cigarettecards.co.uk/*
Franklyn Cards	*http://ourworld.compuserve.com/ homepages/Franklyn_Roberts/ collect.htm*

243

Pomeranian Cigarette cards	*http://hometown.aol.com/soutra/ pom1.htm*
Tobacco Cards	*http://www.tias.com/stores/arsh/ tobacco-cards-1.html*
Wills cigarette cards	*http://www.collectors.demon.co.uk/ fccwills.html*

Coins

| Coin Dealers Directory | *http://www.numis.co.uk/* |

Coin Link Numismatic Directory	*http://www.coinlink.com/*
Coin News	*http://www.coin-news.com/*
Coin Site	*http://www.coinsite.com/*

Coins of the UK	*http://www.tclayton.demon.co.uk/coins.html*
Collectors.com	*http://www.coin-universe.com/*
Cybercoins	*http://www.nauticom.net/www/coins*
Global Collector	*http://www.globalcollector.ndirect.co.uk/*
Interactive Collector	*http://www.icollector.com/*
Numismatica	*http://www.limunltd.com/numismatica*

| Rare Coins | *http://www.rare-coins.net/* |

S & B Coins	*http://www.users.globalnet.co.uk/ ~brcoin/*
UK Coin Heritage	*http://www.erols.com/annet/clients/ ukch/ukch-index.html*
Worldwide Coins	*http://members.tripod.co.uk/ worldwidecoins/*

Matchboxes

| Matchbox Collecting | *http://www.ntnu.no/~dagfinnr/ matchbox/matchbox.htm* |
| Matchbox Label Collector | *http://members.tripod.com/ ~hans_everink/titel.htm* |

| Matchbox Labels | *http://www.henry.demon.co.uk/mbox/ mboxlabsindex.html* |
| Virtual Matchbox Labels Collection | *http://mkc.onego.ru/~stasdm/* |

Memorabilia

Abundant Horse Racing
  Memorabilia

http://www.derbystuff.com/

BeatleZone
Classic Motorcycle Memorabilia

Collectors Online
Cricket Memorabilia Society

Cult TV Memorabilia

http://www.beatlezone.com/
http://www.dropbears.com/c/
classicmemories/
http://www.csmonline.com/coinworld
http://www-uk.cricket.org/
link_to_database/societies/eng/cms/
http://www.tv-memorabilia.
demon.co.uk/links.htm

Grand Prix Memorabilia	*http://www.gpm.cheltweb.co.uk/*
Holly Buddy - Memorabilia	*http://www.geocities.com/SunsetStrip/ Towers/5236/*
Racing Memorabilia Pages	*http://www.wsnet.com/~sysclp/ postcard.html*
Recollections	*http://www.recollections.co.uk/*

Phone Cards

Culture Phone cards	*http://www.mcs.net/~ifeoma/*
Delphi Phone Card Forum	*http://www0.delphi.com/phonecards/*
Global Collector	*http://www.globalcollector.ndirect .co.uk/*
International Phone Card Exchange	*http://www.ipce.com/*

Phone Card Corner	*http://www.angelfire.com/wy/ cardcorner/*

Swappers Phone Cards	*http://www.geocities.com/Tokyo/Towers/1863/*
World of Phone Cards	*http://www.geocities.com/TheTropics/8370/*

Stamps

American Philatelic Society	*http://www.west.net/~stamps1/aps.html*
Beginner's Guide to Stamp Collecting	*http://alfin.computerworks.net/guide.htm*
Beginning Stamp Collecting	*http://www0.delphi.com/stamps/begin1.html Delphi*
Crown Agents Stamp Bureau	*http://www.casb.co.uk/*

e-Stamp	*http://www.e-stamp.com/*

Global Collector	*http://www.globalcollector.ndirect.co.uk/*
Philatelic.com	*http://www.philatelic.com/*
Philatelists Online	*http://www.philatelists.com/*
Philately	*http://www.philately.com/*
Post Office	*http://www.ukpo.com/*
Stamp Collecting for Kids	*http://www.karoo.net/wilcom/*
Stamp Link	*http://www.stamplink.com/*
Stamp Shows	*http://www.stampshows.co.uk/*
Stamps Mall	*http://www.webcom.com/~tuazon/stamps.html*
Stamps Online	*http://www.stampsonline.com/*
Stamps UK	*http://www.stampsuk.com/*
Wessex Philatelic Auctions	*http://www.wessexphilatelic.com/*

Trading Cards

Beckett Online	*http://www.beckett.com/*
Card Emporium	*http://www.cardemporium.com/*
Card Mall	*http://www.cardmall.com/*
Card Zine	*http://ourworld.compuserve.com/homepages/Read_Fmly*
First Base Trading Cards	*http://www.narrows.com/firstbase/window.html-ssi*
Fleer / Skybox Trading Cards	*http://www.fleercorp.com/*
Pokemon Trading Card Game	*http://www.wizards.com/pokemon/*
Pokemon World	*http://www.pokemon.com/*
SpaceMark Trading Cards	*http://www.spacemark.com/*
The Shakespeare Trading Company	*http://www.bundle.freeserve.co.uk/tradindx.htm*

The World of Cards	*http://www.cardcreations.ndirect.co.uk/*
Trading Cards	*http://www.wwcd.com/priceg/tcpg.html*
Upper Deck Trading Cards	*http://www.upperdeck.com/*

Toys

These are sort of toys for grown-ups that don't get played with.

Aristo Craft Trains *http://www.aristocraft.com/aristo/*

Famous works of art in jigsaw
puzzle form

Toys and Games

Fun Factory | Teddy Bears & Beanie Babies | Collectors Corner | Boys Toys
Childhood Memories | Girls Just Wanna Have Fun | Puzzles, Books & Games

Teddy Bears and Beanie Babies

Gifts Direct - Plush teddy bears with Möet champagne and watches. N W

Chambers Candy Company - Oscar & Bertie are Edwardian Bears, they adorn
delightful sweetie tins.

Gift Delivery Company - cute teddy bears and finger puppets.

| Classic Toys | *http://www.classicengland.co.uk/toysryou.htm* |
| Cyberspace World Railroad | *http://www.mcs.com/dsdawdy/cyberoad.html* |

Matchnbox	*http://www.matchboxtoys.com/*
Modellers Loft Toy Collectables	*http://www.modellersloft.co.uk/* *Vehicles.htm*
TGV - Spotter's Guide	*http://mercurio.iet.unipi.it/tgv/* *spotter.html*
Warhammer	*http://www.games-workshop.co.uk/*
Webville and Hypertext Railroad Company	*http://www.spikesys.com/* *webville.html*

Toy Manufacturers

Most of the major toy manufacturers have a website that gives details of their range of toys and, in some cases, gives you the opportunity to buy directly via the Internet.

Barbie	*http://www.barbie.com/*
Beanie Babies (UK)	*http://www.eurobeenie.co.uk/*
Beanie Babies (US)	*http://www.ty.com/*
Brio	*http://www.brio.co.uk/*
Corgi	*http://www.corgi.co.uk/*
Crayola	*http://www.crayola.com/*
Fisher Price	*http://www.fisher-price.com/*
Furbys	*http://www.furbys.co.uk/*
Goldsea Toys	*http://www.goldseatoy-gift.com/*
Hasbro Toys	*http://www.hasbrotoys.com/* *home.html*
Hornby	*http://www.hornbey.co.uk/*
Kebrico	*http://www.kebrico.ltd.uk/*

K'NEX Central	*http://www.knex.com/*
Knex	*http://www.knex.co.uk/*
Koala Express	*http://www.koalaexpress.com.au/*
Learning Curve International	*http://www.learningcurve.com/*
Lego	*http://www.lego.com/*
Matchbox - Mattel	*http://www.matchboxtoys.com/*
Matchbox Toys	*http://www.matchbox.com/*
Mattel	*http://www.mattel.com/*
Meccano	*http://www.meccano.fr/*

Micro Machines	*http://www.micromachines.co.uk/*
Middle-earth Toys	*http://www.middleearthtoys.com/*
Moose Toys	*http://www.moosetoys.com/*
Nintendo	*http://www.nintendo.com/*
Nintendo Gameboy	*http://www.gameboy.com/*
Playmobil	*http://www.playmobile.de/*

Pokemon	*http://www.pokemon.com/*
Quadro Toys	*http://www.quadro-toys.co.uk/*
Scalextric	*http://www.scalextric.co.uk/*
Schylling Toys	*http://www.schylling.com/*
Sega	*http://www.sega.com/*
Sega Dreamcast	*http://www.dreamcast.com/*
Sony	*http://www.sony.com/*
Sony Playstation	*http://www.playstation.com/*
Tomy	*http://www.tomy.co.uk/*

Toy Suppliers

The sites are like toy shops in your living room (or wherever you happen to have your computer).

Ace Toy Company	*http://www.toy.co.uk/*
Active Toy Company	*http://www.activetoy.co.uk/*
Arcade Toy Shop	*http://www.scoot.co.uk/ arcade_toy_shops/*
Bannisters Matchbox & Toy Cars	*http://www3.mistral.co.uk/trevorb/*
Big Boys Toys	*http://www.bigboystoyz.co.uk/*
British Assoc. of Toy Retailers	*http://www.batr.co.uk/*
British Toy & Hobby Association	*http://www.btha.co.uk/*
Early Learning Centre	*http://www.elc.co.uk/*
eToys	*http://www.etoys.co.uk*
Funstore	*http://www.funstore.co.uk/acatalog/*
Quadro Toys	*http://www.quadro-toys.co.uk/*
Toys 'R' Us	*http://www.toysrus.co.uk/*
Toyzone	*http://www.toyzone.co.uk/*

Home

However humble, there's no place like home. Home is where most of us spend most of our lives and so it follows that homes will reflect the interests and maybe even the characteristics of the owner.

New Homes

Having lived in both new and old houses, there are advantages and disadvantages with both. You can't beat the character of older homes with unusual shaped rooms, interesting windows and high ceilings. Character, I suppose, is the word. But along with that character come draughts, high heating bills due to poor insulation and generally higher maintenance costs. New homes are thermally much more efficient and so heating is significantly reduced and with modern materials like uPVC, they are virtually maintenance free. But when describing the room, phrases about 'rabbit hutches' and 'swinging cats' frequently come to mind.

Antler Homes	*http://www.antlethomes.co.uk/*
Anville Homes	*http://www.anvilleconstruction.co.uk/*
Ashwood Homes	*http://www.ashwoodhomes.co.uk/*
Banner Homes	*http://www.banner-homes.co.uk/*
Barratt Homes	*http://www.ukpg.co.uk/barratt*
Bryant Homes	*http://www.bryant.co.uk/*
David Wilson Homes	*http://www.dwh.co.uk/*

Goldcrest Homes	*http://www.goldcrest.plc.uk*
Laing	*http://www.laing.co.uk/*
McAlpine	*http://www.alfred-mcalpine.co.uk/*

Taylor Woodrow	*http://www.taywood.co.uk/*
Ward Homes	*http://www.ward-homes.co.uk/*
Wimpey Homes	*http://www.wimpey.co.uk/*

Property

I well remember trudging around scores of estate agents getting details of houses for sale. I also remember the postman bringing letters stuffed with property details. The Internet can reduce much of this because more and more estage agents are advertising on the Internet.

Brian & Linda Aaronson	*http://www.realestatehelpline.com/*
Bruce Hardie	*http://hardie.debut.net/*

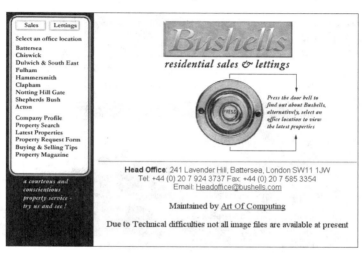

Bushells	*http://www.bushells.com/*
Chancellors	*http://www.chancellors.co.uk/*
CityLet	*http://www.citylet.com/*
Cluttons	*http://www.cluttons.com/*
Dave Wade	*http://www.davewade.net*
Drivers Jonas	*http://www.djonas.co.uk/*
Easier	*http://www.easier.co.uk/*
Egerton	*http://www.egertonproperty.co.uk/*
Euro Properties	*http://www.europropertynet.com/*
Fraser Beach	*http://www.select-e.com/*

Friend & Falcke	*http://www.friendandfalcke.co.uk/*
General Accident	*http://www.gaproperty.co.uk/*
Hamptons	*http://www.hamptons.co.uk/*
Janice Leverington	*http://www.noplacelikehome.com/*
Jeannette Hutchison	*http://www.conejohomes.com/*
Jim Hanrahan	*http://www.sarasota-properties.com/*
John D Wood	*http://www.johndwood.co.uk/*
Judi Wolfson	*http://www.realestatepa.net/*

Judy McCutchin	*http://www.dallashomes.com/*
King Sturge	*http://www.kingsturge.co.uk/*
Knight Frank	*http://www.knightfrank.co.uk/*
Linda Soesbe	*http://www.coloradohomesource.com/*
Lisa DeNardo	*http://www.yourhomeplace.com/*

London Home Net	*http://www.londonhomenet.com/*
Mary Calvert	*http://www.marycalvert.com/*
Nell Shukes	*http://www.nellshukes.com/*
Nigel Wain	*http://www.uniquerealestate.com/*
Nora Ling-Lane	*http://www.noralane.com/*
Property 4 U	*http://www.aproperty4u.com/*
Property Broker	*http://www.propertybroker.co.uk/*
Property Finder	*http://www.propertyfinder.co.uk/*

Property Shop	*http://www.e-propertyshop.com/*
Realtor	*http://www.realtor.com/*
Right Move	*http://www.rightmove.co.uk/*
Ron Resnick	*http://www.teamloudoun.com/*
Russ Harrist	*http://www.realtyshop.net/*

Strettons	*http://www.strettons.co.uk/*
Strutt & Parker	*http://www.struttandparker.co.uk/*
Terry Yapp	*http://www.terryyapp.com*
Thomas & Sally Cook	*http://www.torontorealestate.ca/*
UK Property Shop	*http://www.ukpropertyshop.co.uk/*
Under One Roof	*http://www.underoneroof.co.uk/*
Winkworth	*http://www.winkworth.co.uk/*

Wynne Achatz	*http://www.wynnea.com/*

Removals

Moving home ranks alongside bereavement and divorce in the Top 10 list of stress-inducing activities. At least get a good company to move the contents from your old home to your new home.

Abbey Self Storage	*http://www.abbey-self-storage.co.uk/*
Interpak	*http://www.interpak.co.uk/*
Moves	*http://www.moves.co.uk/*

Pickfords	*http://www.pickfords.co.uk/*

DIY

Doing the job yourself can save a great deal of money. On the other hand it can cost you a great deal if you don't do it properly. Be sure you know what you're doing before embarking on major renovations to your home.

B&Q	*http://www.diy.com/*
Black & Decker	*http://www.blackanddecker.com/*
Bostik	*http://www.bostik.com/*

261

Cookson's Tools   *http://www.cooksons.com/*
Draper Tools   *http://www.draper.co.uk/*

Dulux Paints   *http://www.dulux.com/*
Homebase   *http://www.homebase.co.uk/*
Jewson   *http://www.jewson.co.uk/*
Quickgrip   *http://www.quickgrip.com/*
Screwfix   *http://www.screwfix.com/*
Stanley Tools   *http://www.stanleyworks.com/*
Wickes   *http://www.wickes.com/*

Electrical Goods

The modern home is a highly mechanised environment which takes away much of the drudgery and consequently gives us more time to spend with each other.

Adabra	*http://www.adabra.com/*
Best Stuff	*http://www.beststuff.co.uk/*
Comet	*http://www.comet.co.uk/*
Crazy Electric	*http://www.crazyelectric.com/*
Dixons	*http://www.dixons.co.uk/*
Firebox	*http://www.firebox.com/*

Helpful Home Shopping Co	*http://www.helpful.co.uk/*
iQVC	*http://www.iqvc.com/*
Powerhouse	*http://www.powerhouse-online.co.uk/*
QVC UK	*http://www.qvcuk.com/*
Remote controls	*http://www.remotecontrols.co.uk/*
Tempo	*http://www.tempo.co.uk/*
Unbeatable	*http://www.unbeatable.co.uk/*
Value Direct	*http://www.value-direct.co.uk/*
Web Electricals	*http://www.webelectricals.co.uk/*

Furniture

You need something to sit on, to eat from and something to sleep in. You'll also need other sundry items like cabinets to store or display all the silver and crystal you've accumulated over the years or received as wedding gifts.

Aeromail	*http://www.aero-furniture.com/*
Almara	*http://www.almahome.co.uk/*
Blue Deco	*http://www.craftdesign-london.com/*
Country Desks	*http://www.countrydesks.co.uk/*
Found	*http://www.foundat.co.uk/*

Furniture online	*http://www.furniture-on-line.co.uk/*
Futon Direct	*http://www.futondirect.co.uk/*
Iron Bed Company	*http://www.ironbed.co.uk/*
McCord	*http://www.mccord.uk.com/*

Metal Maniacs	*http://www.wrought-iron-furniture.com/*
Oakridge	*http://www.oakridgedirect.co.uk/*
Sofa Beds	*http://www.sofabeds.co.uk/*
Sofas Direct	*http://www.classicchoice.co.uk/*
Stompa	*http://www.stompa.co.uk/*
Thistle Joinery	*http://www.thistlejoinery.co.uk/*
Vermont Fitness	*http://www.vermontfitness.com/*

Garden

I do like a well-maintained garden. Unfortunately I don't like doing the maintenance. If you do, visit some of these sites.

| British Gardening Online | *http://www.oxalis.co.uk/* |

Crocus	*http://www.crocus.co.uk/*
eSeeds.com	*http://www.eseeds.com/*
Exhibition Seeds	*http://www.exhibition-seeds.co.uk/*
Garden.com	*http://www.garden.com/*

Garden Shop	*http://www.thegardenshop.co.uk/*
Garden World	*http://www.gardenworld.co.uk/*
International Bulb Society	*http://www.bulbsociety.com/*
Nicky's Nursery	*http://www.nickys-nursery.co.uk/seeds*
Pelco	*http://www.pelcogarden.com/*
Seed Potatoes	*http://www.seed-potatoes-international.co.uk/*
Shrubs Direct	*http://www.shrubsdirect.com/*
Woolmans	*http://www.woolmans.co.uk/*

Insurance

We hope we'll never need it, but if the unthinkable should happen, you should be covered. Never insure for less than the full cost of rebuilding plus the new price of all contents.

A1 Insurance	*http://www.a1insurance.co.uk/*
ABBA Home Insurance Direct	*http://members.aol.com/mattcalton/index2.htm*
Arcadian Insurance	*http://www2.jcp.co.uk/arcadian/*
Birmingham Midshires Financial Services	*http://www.birmingham-midshires.co.uk/*
CGU	*http://www.cgudirect.co.uk/*

Welcome to the
Churchill Insurance
Website

"We would be delighted to handle your insurance needs..."

"We already have over 1 million policy holders so we're doing something right..."

Please do have a browse - simply wait or click above

Churchill Insurance	*http://www.churchill.co.uk/*

Clover Insurance Home Insurance	*http://www.clover-insurance.demon.co.uk/household.htm*
Cornhill	*http://www.cornhill.co.uk/*
Direct Line	*http://www.directline.co.uk/*
Eagle Star Direct	*http://www.eaglestardirect.co.uk/*
Edinburgh Solicitors Property	*http://www.espc.co.uk/*
Express Insurance Group	*http://www.expressinsurancegroup.co.uk/*
Fernet Insurance Brokers Ltd	*http://www.fernet.com/uk/*
Guardian Insurance	*http://www.gre.co.uk/home.htm*

| Home Insurance | *http://www.landg.com/homeins/homeins1.html* |
| HomeLine Direct | *http://www.insurance-line.co.uk/homeline.html* |

Home-Net UK	*http://www.midway.co.uk/insurance/home*
HomeQuote Insurance UK	*http://home.quote.co.uk/*
Legal & General UK	*http://www.legal-and-general.co.uk/*
Merlin Insurance Consultants	*http://www.merlins.demon.co.uk/insurance/*
MoneyNet	*http://www.moneynet.ltd.uk/*
Nationwide Finance	*http://www.nwide.freeserve.co.uk/*

NET INSURANCE SERVICES

NIS

Welcome to the leading Independent Insurance site

We belong to the Which? Webtrader Code of Practice

OUR AIM IS TO GIVE INSTANT QUOTES WHENEVER POSSIBLE - SAVING YOU TIME!

Net Insurance Services	*http://www.nis.ndirect.co.uk/*

Rapid Care Insurance   *http://www.domgen.com/*
Reallymoving.com   *http://www.reallymoving.com/*
Royal & Sun Alliance Insurance   *http://www.royal-and-sunalliance.com/*

Car Insurance
If you have had a claim in the last 3 years - which insurers will offer you a quote?
Or if you use your car for business which insurance sites should you visit? Find out with SoreEyes, then click for a quote.

Travel Insurance
Whether you travel on business or for pleasure, for a winter skiing holiday or for a restful beach holiday we can help you to quickly arrange the travel insurance cover that you will require.

Home Insurance
If your house has more than 4 bedrooms or is situated in a flood plain, which insurance sites can offer you cover? Whatever your situation we can help you to quickly find the appropriate insurers.

Bike Insurance
So far, motorbike insurance is not well catered for online, but what there is you can find here.

SoreEyes - Insurance Quotes   *http://www.soreeyes.co.uk/*
                                   body_index.html
Woolwich Insurance Services   *https://secure.woolwich.co.uk/hc/*

Interior Design

To make your house the envy of your friends, you'll need to think about the design of the interior. But interior design will also help you get the most from the available space.

Abiaz   *http://www.abiaz.com/*

Cavendish Interiors	*http://www.cavendishinteriors.co.uk/*
Click Deco	*http://www.clickdeco.com/*
Cross Interiors	*http://www.crossinteriors.com/*

residential design

commercial design

credentials

designed interiors, inc.

Designed Interiors, Inc. focuses on creating human environments to meet your needs for productivity, for beauty, for efficiency, for comfort, and most importantly, for safety. We make an evironmental difference by creating design solutions and selecting products sensitive to the ecosphere.

Good design has its rewards. Think of Designed Interiors as an extension of your self and your image. Designed Interiors helps you create and define your identity through your living, working, and playing environments.

Designed Interiors	*http://www.designedinteriors.com/*
Eclectic Interiors	*http://www.eclecticinteriors.com/*
French Interiors	*http://www.frenchinteriors.com/*
Home Interiors	*http://www.homeinteriors.co.uk/*
Home Portfolio	*http://www.homeportfolio.com/*
Ikea	*http://www.ikea.com/*
Integrated Interiors	*http://www.integratedinteriors.com/*
Interior Design & Decoration	*http://www.iddv.com/*
Interior Internet	*http://www.interiorinternet.com/*
Interiors	*http://www.interiors.com/*

Interiors for a Song	*http://www.interiorsforasong.com/*
Matchroom	*http://www.matchroom.demon.co.uk/*
My Interior Decorator	*http://www.myinteriordecorator.com/*
Old House Interiors	*http://www.oldhouseinteriors.com/*
Style Craft Interiors	*http://www.stylecraftinteriors.com/*
Terence Conran	*http://www.conran.co.uk/*

Village Interiors	*http://www.villageinteriors.com/*

Nik-Naks

It's the little nik-naks that really give the home the character of the occupant. These websites, by and large, sell lots of things you'd like, but not a lot you actually need.

Appeal	*http://www.appeal-blinds.co.uk/*

Argos Online	*http://www.argos.co.uk/*
Battle Orders	*http://www.battleorders.co.uk/*
Bottle Rack, The	*http://www.thebottlerack.com/*
Carpet Right	*http://www.carpetright.co.uk/*
Chadder & Co	*http://www.chadder.com/*

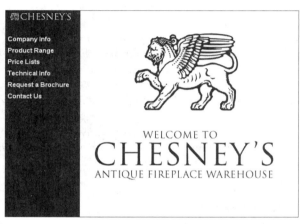

Chesney's	*http://www.antiquefireplace.co.uk/*
CP Hart	*http://www.cphart.co.uk/*
Dyson	*http://www.dyson.com/*
eShop	*http://www.eshop.co.nz/*
Flames	*http://flames.estreet.co.uk/*
Habitat	*http://www.habitat.co.uk/*
Hillarys	*http://www.hillarys.co.uk/*
Holding Company, The	*http://www.theholdingcompany.co.uk/*
Home Zone	*http://www.shoppersuniverse.com/*

House Mail Order	*http://www.housemailorder.co.uk/*
Index Online	*http://www.indexshop.com/*
Innovations	*http://www.innovations.co.uk/*
Liberty	*http://www.liberty-of-london.com/*
Maelstrom	*http://www.maelstrom.co.uk/*
Marks & Spencer	*http://www.marks-and-spencer.co.uk/*
Mathmos	*http://www.mathmos.co.uk/*
Mr Resistor	*http://www.mr-resistor.co.uk/*
Nauticalia	*http://www.nauticalia.co.uk/*
Plümo	*http://www.plumo.com/*
Rabid Home	*http://www.rabidhome.com/*
South Downs Trading Company	*http://www.southdowns.co.uk/*
Sträad Direct	*http://www.straad.co.uk/*
Tie Rack	*http://www.tierack.com/*
West of England Reproduction Furniture	*http://www.reproductionfurniture .com/*

Kitchen Accessories

The kitchen is often described as the centre of a house. There are lots of gadgets you need and even more you'd like available from websites the world over.

All-Clad Online	*http://www.metrokitchen.com/*
Appliance Online	*http://www.applianceonline.co.uk/*
Be-Direct	*http://www.be-direct.co.uk/*
Brabantia	*http://www.brabantia.com/*
Chef's Store	*http://www.chefs-store.com/*

Cook Craft	*http://www.cookcraft.com/*
Cooks Kitchen	*http://www.kitchenware.co.uk/*
Cucina Direct	*http://www.cucinadirect.co.uk/*
Discounts online	*http:/www.discounts.co.nz/*
Divertimenti	*http://www.divertimenti.co.uk/*
Empire Direct	*http://www.empiredirect.co.uk/*
Home Creations	*http://www.myinternet.co.uk/home*
Home Electrical Direct	*http://www.hed.co.uk/*

Internet Cookshop	*http://www.scottsargeant.com/*
Kitchenware	*http://www.kitchenware.co.uk/*
Le Creuset	*http://www.lecreuset.com/*
Magnet	*http://www.magnet.co.uk/*

Pots and Pans   *http://www.pots-and-pans.co.uk/*
Russell Hobbs   *http://www.russell-hobbs.com/*
Small Island Trader   *http://www.smallislandtrader.com/*
Tefal   *http://www.tefal.co.uk/*
Watershed   *http://www.watershedonline.com/*

Whitewear

Whitewear, as it is usually known is generally found in the kitchen or laundry room. The manufacturers are quick to advertise their products on the Internet.

AEG   *http://www.aeg-direct.com/*
Aga & Rayburn   *http://www.aga-rayburn.co.uk/*
Belling   *http://www.belling.co.uk/*
Bosch   *http://www.bosch-direct.com/*
Creda   *http://www.creda.co.uk/*
Electrolux   *http://www.electrolux.co.uk/*
GEC   *http://www.gec.co.uk/*
Hoover   *http://www.hoover.co.uk/*
Hotpoint   *http://www.hotpoint.co.uk/*
Miele   *http://www.miele.co.uk/*
Neff   *http://www.neff.co.uk/*
Panasonic   *http://www.panasonic.co.uk/*
Philips   *http://www.philips.co.uk/*
Servis   *http://www.servis.co.uk/*
Smeg   *http://www.smeguk.com/*
Stoves   *http://www.stoves.co.uk/*
Whirlpool   *http://www.whirlpool.co.uk/*
Zanussi   *http://www.zanussi.com/*

Lifestyle

The term 'lifestyle' seems to cover a multitude of sins.
Perhaps 'miscellaneous' might be more appropriate.

Astrology

Can it really be that one-twelfth of the world's population have the same future
that I have? If you want to know what fortune has in hand for your one-twelfth,
check out some of these sites.

Aquarian Age	*http://www.aquarianage.org/*
Asian Astrology	*http://www.jadegate.com/astro*
Astro Atlas	*http://www.astro.ch/atlas*
Astrola's Metpahysical Den	*http://www.astrola.com/*
Astrological Association of Great Britain	*http://www.astrologer.com/*
Astrological Horoscopes & Forecasts	*http://www.astro-horoscopes.com/*
Astrology	*http://www.canoe.ca/Fun/home.html*
Astrology A to Z	*http://www.astrologer.com/websites/astrol.html*
Astrology Et Al	*http://www.astrologyetal.com/*
Astrology Matrix	*http://www.thenewage.com/*
Astrology Online	*http://www.astrology-online.com/*
Astrology World	*http://www.astrology-world.com/*
Astrology Zone	*http://astrologyzone.go.com/*

Astrology, Runes & Tarot	*http://www.cybershaman.co.uk/*
Barbarann Lang	*http://www.b-lang.freeserve.co.uk/*
Daily Humorscope	*http://www.humorscope.com/*
Esther & Son	*http://www.estherandson.com/*
Hermes Astrology Centre	*http://members.aol.com/aaanum/astro.htm*

JustUs & Associates Publishing
Traditional Astrology Texts, Courses, Software,

Table of Contents

- Our On-Line Shopping Mall
- Carol A. Wiggers Home Page
- Who we are, What we are trying to do
- Pictures of Lilly's Cottage taken by Sue Ward
- Traditional Astrology Glossary
- Frequently Asked Questions (fAQ)
- Still have Questions? Ask Sue Ward!
- JANUS2 Software-U.S. Distributor
- Horary Practitioner

Traditional Horary, Electional & Natal Astrology

JustUs & Associates
Carol A. Wiggers, DMSAstrol., QHP
1420 NW Gilman Blvd., Suite #2164
Issaquah, WA 98027-7001 USA
Phone (425)391-8371 Fax (425)392-1919

Enter Here to Shop Online!

We accept Visa, Master card, Discover card and American Express, Checks, Money Orders and Certified Checks in U.S. Funds

Certified
Safe Shopping Site

Horary Astrology	*http://www.horary.com/*
Horoscopes from Russell Grant	*http://www.russellgrant.com/*
Indolink Astrology	*http://www.genius.net/indolink/Astro/ojSimps1.html*
Jon Sandifer	*http://www.jonsandifer.com/*
Jonathan Cainer	*http://stars.metawire.com/*

Kozmik Horoscopes	*http://www.demon.co.uk/kdm/hscope1.html*
Love Astrology	*http://love.astrology.net/*
Matrix Astrology Software	*http://www.astral.demon.co.uk/*
Metalog Astrology	*http://www.astrologer.com/*
MSN Web Communities: Astrology	*http://communities.msn.com/astrology*
Netstrology: Daily Horoscopes	*http://www.techweb.com/horoscope*
Rob Brezsny's Real Astrology	*http://www.realastrology.com/*
Starlight Astrology	*http://www.starlightastrology.com/*
Sunrise Magazine	*http://www.sunrisemag.com/*
The Astrology Zone	*http://www.pathfinder.com/twep/astrology*
What's in Your Stars	*http://www.msn.co.uk/page/8-150.asp*
Women.Astrology.net	*http://women.astrology.net/*
Your Daily Horoscope	*http://www.4yourhoroscope.com/*
Your Daily Horoscope	*http://www.astrocom.com/horo/daily.htm*
Your Personal Horoscope	*http://www.realitycom.com/webstars/order/personal.html*

Dating

Computer dating is not new, but Internet computer dating is. You enter your details, pay the fee and with luck you'll be matched to your perfect partner.

1-2-1 Internet Dating Agency	*http://www.aquiesce.co.uk/1-2-1/index2.htm*
ABC UK Dating & Personals	*http://www.abcdating.co.uk/*
Absolute Match	*http://www.absolutematch.com/*

American Singles	*http://www.americansingles.com/*
Classical Partners	*http://www.classicalpartners.co.uk/*
Computer Dating	*http://www.computer-dating.com/*

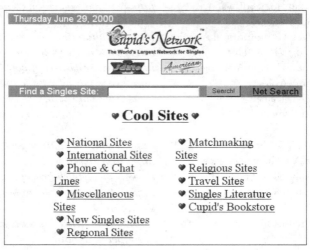

Cupid's Network	*http://www.cupidnet.com/*
Date.com	*http://www.date.com/*
Dateable	*http://www.dateable.com/*
Dating Club	*http://www.datingclub.com/*
Dating Direct	*http://www.datingdirect.co.uk/*
Dating Direct	*http://www.datingdirect.com/*
Dating.com	*http://www.dating.com/*
For Singles	*http://www.forsingles.com/*

Free Dating Agency	*http://www.geocities.com/SouthBeach/Strand/2142*
Free UK Dating Agency	*http://www.lovefinder.co.uk/*
Friendfinder	*http://www.friendfinder.com/*
Gay Dating UK	*http://www.gay-dating.co.uk/dating/indexJ.html*
Justmates	*http://www.justmates.com/*
Kiss.com	*http://www.kiss.com/*
London Dating	*http://www.londondating.co.uk/*
Love Agency	*http://www.loveagency.com/*
Love City	*http://www.lovecity.com/*
Love Happens	*http://www.lovehappens.com/*
Loving You	*http://www.lovingyou.com/*
Match.com	*http://www.match.com/*
Matchmaker.com	*http://www.matchmaker.com/*
On Match	*http://www.onmatch.com/*
One & Only	*http://www.one-and-only.com/*
Online Encounters	*http://www.online-encounters.com/*
Other Singles	*http://www.othersingles.com/*
Pairs	*http://www.pairs.com/*
People 2 People	*http://www.people2people.com/*
Romancero.com	*http://www.romancero.com/*
RSVP	*http://www.rsvp.com.au/*
Search Partner	*http://www.searchpartner.com/*
Singles.com	*http://www.singles.com/*
Six Degrees	*http://www.sixdegrees.com/*
Soulmates	*http://www.soulmates.com.au/*
Swoon	*http://www.swoon.com/*

The Kiss   *http://www.thekiss.com/*
Two's Company Dating Service   *http://www.twoscompany.co.uk/*
Utopia Introduction Agency   *http://www.utopia-dating.freeserve*
                                    .co.uk/
Venus Dating UK   *http://www.venusdating.co.uk/*

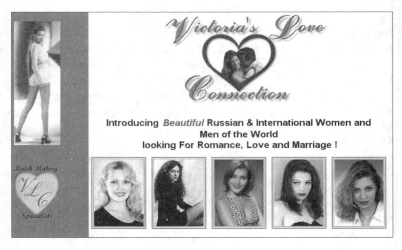

Victoria's Agency   *http://www.victoriasagency.com/*

Internet Chat

If you're feeling lonely, you can have a chat with someone else, or several others, across the Internet. You will probably find that the person you're speaking to is from another part of the world. Some of the chatlines have specific themes so if you use them, you should stick to the designated topics.

Catholicity	*http://www.catholicity.com/*
Chat Box	*http://www.chatbox.com/*
Chat City	*http://www.chatcity.com.au/*
Chat Freak	*http://www.chatfreak.com/*

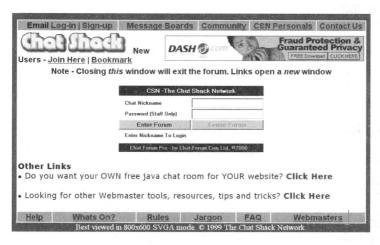

Chat Shack	*http://www.chatshack.net/*
Chat Town	*http://www.chattown.com/*
Chat Web	*http://www.chatweb.net/*
Christian Cafe	*http://www.christiancafe.com/*
Hearme.com	*http://www.hearme.com/*
Hyperchat	*http://www.hyperchat.com/*
ICQ	*http://www.icq.net/*
Internet Relay Chat	*http://www.irchelp.org/*
Keep Talking	*http://www.keeptalking.com/*

L'Hotel Chat	*http://www.hotelchat.com/*
OmniChat!	*http://www.4-lane.com/*
Parachat	*http://www.parachat.com/*
PeopleLink	*http://www.peoplelink.com/*
Quickchat	*http://www.quickchat.org/*
Sneaker Chat	*http://www.sneakerchat.com/*
Teenchat	*http://www.teenchat.co.uk/*
The Palace	*http://www.thepalace.com/*
UKchat	*http://www.ukchat.com/*
Womenchat	*http://www.womenchat.com/*
Yahoo! Chat	*http://chat.yahoo.com/*

Religion

Information about all of the world's religions can be found on the Internet. These are but a few.

About Islam and Muslims	*http://www.unn.ac.uk/societies/islamic/*
Alternative Religions	*http://altreligion.about.com/*
Basics Of Sikhi	*http://www.sikhi.demon.co.uk/*
Belief Net	*http://www.beliefnet.com/*
Biblealive	*http://www.internet-uk.com/bible-a*
British Humanist Association	*http://www.humanism.org.uk/*
British Religion and Philosophy	*http://www.stg.brown.edu/projects/ hypertext/landow/victorian/religion/ philtl.html*
Calendar of Religious Festivals	*http://www.namss.org.uk/fests.htm*
Catholic Encyclopedia	*http://www.knight.org/advent/cathen/ cathen.htm*

Catholic Online On The Web   *http://www.catholic.org/*
Christian Faith Groups   *http://www.religioustolerance.org/*
                               var_rel.htm

Finding God in Cyberspace   *http://www.fontbonne.edu/libserv/fgic/*
                               intro.htm

Welcome to the HOUSE OF GOD

House Of God runs parties fortnighly on Saturdays at **The Factory**, which can be found at the rear of **The Sanctuary** on Digbeth High Street in Birmingham, England. The main room plays Techno & Deep House and the back room plays Hip Hop, Breaks & Drum 'n' Bass.

Times: 10pm - 4am. Cost: £5 members / £6 sinners (before 11pm); £6 members / £7 sinners (after 11pm)

There will also be occasional one-offs at other local venues.

House of God   *http://sun1.bham.ac.uk/taylomsj/hog/*
Introduction to Religion *http://www.uwyo.edu/a&s/relstds/*
                          reli1000.htm
Investigating Islam   *http://www.islamic.org.uk/*
Islamic City   *http://www.islam.org/*
Islamic Gateway   *http://www.ummah.org.uk/*

Islamic Research Academy	*http://www.stir.ac.uk/relstd/afa/ jerusalem/welcome.htm*
Jewish Communities in the U.K.	*http://www.virtual.co.il/communities/ wjcbook/uk/*
Jewish Museum, London	*http://www.ort.org/communit/ jewmusm/home.htm*
Muslim Directory	*http://www.muslimdirectory.co.uk/ newpages/autext.html*
Muslim Prayer Times	*http://salam.muslimsonline.com/*
Mysticism in World Religions	*http://www.digiserve.com/mystic/*
New Religious Movements	*http://cti.itc.virginia.edu/~jkh8x/ soc257/profiles.html*
Quakers	*http://www.quaker.org.uk/*
Religion	*http://www.hbuk.co.uk/ap/journals/rl/*
Religion For The Fun Of It	*http://members.esslink.com/~frenchy/ religion.htm*
Religion in Everyday Life	*http://news.mpr.org/features/199804/ 06_newsroom_religion/*
Religion Links	*http://www.gty.org/~phil/ bookmark.htm*
Religion on the Web	*http://users.ox.ac.uk/~worc0337/ serious/religion.html*
Religions and Religious Studies	*http://www.clas.ufl.edu/users/gthursby/ rel/*
Religious Education Exchange	*http://re-xs.ucsm.ac.uk/*
Sikh Museum	*http://www.sikhmuseum.org/*
Studies in World Christianity	*http://www.div.ed.ac.uk/journals/ studies.htm*

Totally Jewish   *http://www.totallyjewish.com/*
UK Islamic Education   *http://www.ukiew.org/*
Virtual Religion Index   *http://religion.rutgers.edu/vri/*
Voodoo Information Pages   *http://www.arcana.com/shannon/*
                                   voodoo/voodoo.html
Religious Studies - Africa   *http://www.sas.upenn.edu/*
                                   African_Studies/About_African/
                                   ww_relig.html
Watchman Index of Cults and   *http://www.watchman.org/*
   Religions   *indxmenu.htm*
Western Religions   *http://www.mrdowling.com/*
                                   605westr.html

Men

These sites will be of particular interest to men, although there is a great deal
here for everyone.

A Man's Life   *http://www.manslife.com/*
Atlanta Reproductive Health   *http://www.ivf.com/*
   Centre
Bi.org   *http://bi.org/*
Clinique - For Men Only   *http://www.clinique.com/*
FitnessOnline   *http://www.fitnessonline.com/*
GMHC: HIV and AIDS   *http://www.gmhc.org/*
   Information
GMHC: Treatment Issues Index   *http://www.gmhc.org/aidslib/ti/ti.html*
Health Magazines - Healthy Living *http://bewell.healthgate.com/healthy/*
                                   living/

Sex: A Man's Guide   *http://www.sexamansguide.com/b/*
Smack 'em Yack 'em   *http://www.smackem.com/*
Total Man   *http://www.klinks.com/totalman/*
Welcome to the Vita-Men!   *http://www.vita-men.com/*
YMCA   *http://www.ymca.net/*

Women

It has finally been recognised that this is the largest untapped market on the Internet. These sites are aimed specifically at women.

Beme.com   *http://www.beme.com/*
British Women Pilots' Association   *http://www.bwpa.demon.co.uk/*
British Women Racing Drivers Club   *http://www.autolinkuk.co.uk/bwrdc/*

Charlotte Street   *http://www.charlottestreet.com/*

289

Feminist Archive	*http://www.femarch.mcmail.com/*
Freedom UK	*http://www.freedom.co.uk/*
GaytoZ	*http://www.gaytoz.com/*
Handbag.com	*http://www.handbag.com/*
Int'l Council of Jewish Women	*http://www.icjw.org.uk/*
Internet UK Gay Guides	*http://www.gayguide.co.uk/*
Lesbian Archive & Info Centre	*http://www.womens-library.org.uk/*
Life UK	*http://www.lifeuk.org/*
Ministers for Women	*http://www.open.gov.uk/womens-unit/*
National Federation of Women's Institutes	*http://www.nfwi.org.uk/*
National Women's Council of Ireland	*http://www.nwci.ie/*
National Women's Register	*http://www.nwr.org/*
Network of East-West Women	*http://www.neww.org./*
Planet Girl	*http://www.planetgrrl.com/*
Scottish Women's History Network	*http://swhn.gcal.ac.uk/*
Successful Women	*http://www.networkwomenuk.org/*
WNAS	*http://www.wnas.org.uk/*
Women in Publishing	*http://www.cyberiacafe.net/wip/*
Women.com	*http://www.women.com/*
Women's History Review	*http://www.triangle.co.uk/whr/*
Women's National Commission	*http://www.thewnc.org.uk/*
Women's Press	*http://www.the-womens-press.com/*
Women's Resource Centre	*http://www.wrc.uninet.co.uk/*
Women's Royal Voluntary Service	*http://members.tripod.com/~wrvs/*
Women's Unit	*http://www.womens-unit.gov.uk/*

Motoring

I'm sure some people must have been born with petrol in their veins. Motor cars and bikes are the love of some people's lives. For others, they are merely a means of getting from a to b.

Auto Manufacturers

All of the major motor manufacturers have a website which in most cases is their catalogue in a slightly different form. There are, however, some surprises in store on some of the sites.

AC	*http://www.accars.com/*
Alfa Romeo	*http://www.alfaromeo.com/*
Aston Martin	*http://www.astonmartin.com/*
Audi	*http://www.audi.com/*
Bentley	*http://www.rolls-royceandbentley.co.uk/*
BMW	*http://www.bmw.com/*
Bristol	*http://www.bristolcars.co.uk/*
Cadillac	*http://www.cadillac.com/*
Caterham	*http://www.caterham.co.uk/*
Chevrolet	*http://www.chevrolet.com/*
Chrysler	*http://www.chryslerjeep.co.uk/*
Citroen	*http://www.citroen.com/*

Daewoo	*http://www.dm.co.kr/*
Ferrari	*http://www.ferrari.it/*
Fiat	*http://www.fiat.com/*
Ford	*http://www.ford.com/*
Holden	*http://www.hsv.com.au/*
Honda	*http://www.honda.com/*

Hyundai	*http://www.hyundai-car.co.uk/*
Isuzu	*http://www.isuzu.com/*
Jaguar	*http://www.jaguar.com/*
Jeep	*http://www.chryslerjeep.co.uk/*
Kia	*http://www.kia.com/*
Land Rover	*http://www.landrover.com/*
Lexus	*http://www.lexus.com/*
Lotus	*http://www.lotuscars.co.uk/*

Marcos	*http://www.marcos.co.uk/*
Maserati	*http://www.maserati.it/*
Mazda	*http://www.mazda.co.uk/*
Mercedes Benz	*http://www.mercedes-benz.com/*
MG	*http://www.mgcars.com/*
Mini	*http://www.mini.com/*

Mitsubishi	*http://www.mitsubishi-cars.co.uk/*
Morgan	*http://www.morgan-motor.co.uk/*
Nissan	*http://www.nissan-usa.com/*
Opel	*http://www.opel.com/*
Peugeot	*http://www.peugeot.com/*
Porsche	*http://www.porsche.com/*
Proton	*http://www.proton.co.uk/*
Renault	*http://www.renault.com/*

Rolls Royce	*http://www.rolls-royceandbentley.co.uk/*
Rover	*http://www.rovercars.com/*
Saab	*http://www.saab.com/*
SEAT	*http://www.seat.com/*
Skoda	*http://www.skoda-auto.com/*

Subaru	*http://www.subaru.com/*
Suzuki	*http://www.suzuki.co.uk/*
Toyota	*http://www.toyota.co.uk/*
TVR	*http:// www.tvr-eng.co.uk/*
Vauxhall	*http://www.vauxhall.co.uk/*
Volkswagon	*http://www.vw.com/*
Volvo	*http://www.car.volvo.se/*

Bike Manufacturers

Like cars, manufacturers of bikes also have their sites on the Internet.

BMW	*http://www.bmw.com/*
Ducati	*http://www.ducati.com/*
Harley Davidson	*http://www.harley-davidson.com/*
Honda	*http://www.honda.com/*
Kawasaki	*http://www.kawasaki.com/*

MOTORCYCLES | GUZZI WORLD | THE COMPANY | Site Map | Sales Network   MOTO GUZZI

Home | Motorcycles | Daytona

Daytona

▸ **Daytona RS**

Sometimes you want that little bit more from a sports motorcycle: thrills and passion - all those sensations that only a truly great Italian sports motorcycle can give. In other words, you want a Daytona.

Moto Guzzi	*http://www.motoguzzi.it/*
Suzuki	*http://www.suzukicycles.com/*
Triumph	*http://www.triumph.co.uk/*
Yamaha	*http://www.yamaha-motor.com/*

Auto Sites

There are many more auto sites run by enthusiasts, but the quality can vary enormously.

Auto Classic	*http://www.net.hu/autoclassic*
Autolink (UK) Limited - Links	*http://www.autolinkuk.co.uk/ clubs.htm*
Automobilia	*http://www.chycor.co.uk/tourism/cata/ automobilia/automobilia.htm*
Cars Classics	*http://www.cars.classics.co.uk/*
Classic Car Directory	*http://www.classicdirect.co.uk/*
Classic Motor Cars	*http://www.classic-motor-cars.co.uk/*

Classic Motor Monthly   *http://www.classicmotor.co.uk/*

Drive	*http://www.drive.com.au/*
iMotors.com	*http://www.imotors.com/*
Motor Trend	*http://www.motortrend.com/*
Motoring links	*http://www.spartan-oc.demon.co.uk/links.htm*
Net Car Links Page	*http://www.netcar.co.uk/links.html*
On Your Marques	*http://www.288online.co.uk/classiccars*

Team.Net
Automotive Webs

Welcome to the Team.Net
(the dot is not silent) World Wide Webs.

| Team Net | *http://www.team.net/* |
| Yahoo | *http://www.yahoo.com/recreation/automotive* |

Bike Sites

Bikers are a loyal bunch and this is reflected in their websites depicting their favourite bike.

All About Cycles   *http://www.allaboutcycles.com/*
AMA Superbike   *http://www.amasuperbike.com/*
Bike Net   *http://www.bikenet.com/*
Bikers Rights Online   *http://www.sasnet.com/bro*

The BMWSite

A Center for BMW Motorcycle Links

on the World Wide Web

Choose one of the following categories to view links:

- Dealers/Service
  Listing of dealerships, sales, service, and repair.
- Clubs
  Clubs to join and people to visit.
- Images
  Images of older and newer bikes.

Or you can:

- Submit your URL or a correction/suggestion
- Yahoo's BMW Motorcycle Collection
- Alta Vista search on BMW Motorcycles
- BMW NA's Motorcycle Homepage
- Go to the pages of our latest sponsor

BMW Bikes   *http://www2.tower.org/bmwsite*
Cycle Highway   *http://www.cyclehighway.com/*
Cycle News   *http://www.cyclenews.com/*
International Riders' Rights   *http://dredd.meng.ucl.ac.uk/www/mag*
    Directory

Longriders	*http://www.longriders.com/*
Motoplex	*http://www.motoplex.com/*
Motorcity.net	*http://www.motorcity.net/*
Motorcycle Online	*http://www.motorcycle.com/*
Motorcycle Travellers' Help	*http://members.tripod.com/*

Motorcycle USA	*http://www.motorcycle-usa.com/*
Motorcycle Web Index	*http://sepnet.com/cycle*
Motorcyclerow.com	*http://www.motorcyclerow.com/*
Motorsports Network	*http://www.motorsports-network.com/*
MotoWorld Network	*http://www.motoworld.net/*
Sidecar.com	*http://www.sidecar.com/*

In-Car Entertainment

I'm not sure whether it's a good idea to have all this gadgetery under the driver's nose. In most countries it is an offence to have a TV in the driver's view if the car is moving.

000 Audio	*http://www.000-audio.com/*
A Taste of Music	*http://www.tasteofmusic.com/*
Ace Electronics	*http://www.pathway.net/aceelectronics*
Ace Sound Designz	*http://www.acedesignz.com/*
Adler Audio	*http://www.adleraudio.com/*
Alien Audio	*http://www.alienaudio.com/*

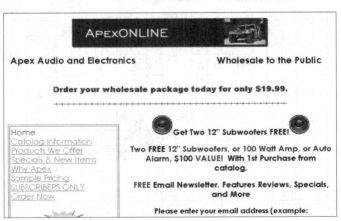

Apex Audio and Electronics	*http://www.apex-audio.com/*
Arocks Car Audio	*http://www.arocks.com/*
Audio Cyclone	*http://www.audiocyclone.com/*

Audio in Motion	*http://www.audioinmotion.com/*
Audio On Wheels	*http://www.audioonwheels.com/*
Audio Wizard	*http://www.theaudiowizard.com/*
Audiodiscounters	*http://www.audiodiscounters.com/*
Auto Sound Online	*http://www.autosoundonline.com/*
Auto Vibes	*http://www.autovibes.com/*
Balance Audio Systems	*http://www.balanceaudio* *.emerchantpro.com/*

Bass Car Audio	*http://www.basscaraudio.com/*
Bass Station 2000	*http://www.bass-station2000.com/*
Bass4Cars	*http://members.tripod.com/elmansa/*
Bllamb Car Audio	*http://www.bllamb.com/*
Car Audio Index	*http://caraudioindex.com/*
Car Audio Works	*http://www.caraudioworks.com/*

Car Stereo Outlet	*http://www.carstereooutlet.com/*
Car Stereo World	*http://www.carstereoworld.com/*
Caraudio1	*http://www.caraudio1.com/*
CarMedia1	*http://www.carmedia1.com/*
Cellbox Soundsystems	*http://www.cellboxsoundsystems.com/*
Continuous Audio	*http://continuousaudio.safeshopper.com/*
DC Car Audio	*http://www.flash.net/~caraudio*
Discount Auto Sound	*http://www.discountautosound.com/*
Discount Car Stereo	*http://www.audio-n-more.com/*
Discount Car Stereo Inc.	*http://www.discountcarstereo.com/*
Dynamic Auto Sounds	*http://www.dynamicautosounds.com/*
Ejde Audio	*http://www.ejdeaudio.com/*
ElectronicsHeadquarter	*http://www.electronicsheadquarter.com/*
Endless Audio	*http://www.endlessaudio.com/*
Full Line Audio	*http://www.full-line-audio.com/*
GLM Mobile Audio	*http://www.glm-online.com/indexaudio.html*
Graded-Ice.Com	*http://www.graded-ice.com/*
High Voltage Car Audio	*http://www.hvcamn.com/*
HQAudio.com	*http://hqaudio.com/*
Hurricane Sound Labs	*http://www.hurricanesoundlabs.com/*
J M Electronics	*http://www.jmelectronix.com/*
Just Car Audio	*http://www.justcaraudio.com/*
Logjam Electronics	*http://www.logjamelectronics.com/*
M-Customs Car Audio	*http://www.mcustoms.com/*
MMXpress.com	*http://www.mmxpress.com/*

Okada Audio	*http://www.okada-audio.com/*
Omegacomm Car Audio	*http://www.audiomegacom.net/*
OnLine Car Stereo	*http://www.onlinecarstereo.com/*
Outlaw Audio	*http://www.outlawaudio.net/*

Car stereo faces, faceplates
Used Stereos, Stereo faces and Amplifiers
(Pioneer cable boxes wanted)

Play It Again Audio	*http://www.playitagainaudio.com/*
Precise Audio	*http://www.preciseaudio.net/*
Radios and More	*http://www.radiosandmore.com/*
RPM Industries	*http://caraudio.rpmindustries.com/*
Sound Creations	*http://www.sound-creations.com/*
SoundDomain.com	*http://www.sounddomain.com/*
Sounds Great	*http://www.soundsgreat.net/*
Stereo Direct	*http://www.stereodirect.com/*
Stereo Liquidators	*http://www.stereoliquidators.com/*
Sweet Audio	*http://www.sweetaudio.com/*

The Best Guys	*http://thebestguys.com/*
The Car Stereo Connection	*http://www.carstereoconnection.com/*
The Wood Shop	*http://www.the-woodshop.com/*
Tune-Town	*http://www.tune-town.com/*
Ultimate Sounds	*http://www.ultimate-sounds.com/*
Wholesale Sounds Car Audio	*http://www.wholesalesounds.com/*

Insurance

Whether you're driving a car or a bike, third-party liability is a requirement. Phoning around insurance companies to get the best quote is an annual drudge, but the Internet can make it a little more pleasant. Some companies offer online quotations.

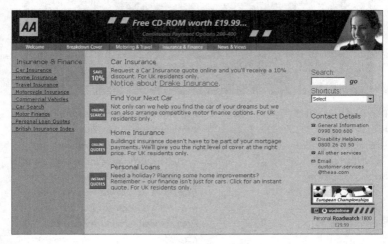

AA   *http://www.aainsurance.co.uk/*

Admiral	*http://www.admiral.uk.com/*
Bell Direct	*http://www.belldirect.co.uk/*
Car Quote	*http://www.carquote.co.uk/*
CGU	*http://www.cgudirect.co.uk/*
Direct Line	*http://www.directline.com/*
Diamond	*http://www.diamond.uk.com/*

Eagle Star Direct	*http://www.eaglestardirect.co.uk/*
Ironsure	*http://www.ironsure.com/*
Norwich Union Direct	*http://www.norwichuniondirect.co.uk/*
Quoteline Direct	*http://www.nwnet.co.uk/wilsons*
Screentrade	*http://www.screentrade.com/*
Sun Alliance	*http:/www.sunalliance.co.uk/*

Leasing

The cost doesn't end when you've bought a car. There's servicing and repairs, and finally you've got the hassle of selling it when you need/like something different. Leasing a car overcomes all of this.

AMA	*http://www.vehiclecontracts.co.uk/*
AVC Rent-A-Car	*http://www.all-vehicles.co.uk/*
Brooklands	*http://www.brooklands-group.co.uk/*
Car Myke	*http://www.carmyke.co.uk/*
City Contracts	*http://www.citycontracts.co.uk/*

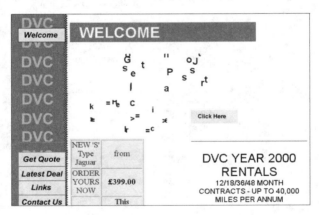

DVC	*http://www.dvc-contracthire.co.uk/*
Fairway	*http://www.fairway-leasing.com/*
Fleetlease	*http://www.fleetlease.co.uk/*
Fulton	*http://www.fultonnetwork.co.uk/*
West Midlands Vehicles	*http://www.westmidvehicles.co.uk/*

Motoring Organisations

In case of breakdown, it's advisable to belong to an organisation which will recover your car and get you to your destination.

AAA   *http://www.aaa.com/*
Automobile Association   *http://www.theaa.co.uk/*
BSM   *http://www.bsm.co.uk/*
Green Flag   *http://www.greenflag.co.uk/*

Institute of Advanced Motorists   *http://www.iam.org.uk/*
RAC   *http://www.rac.co.uk/*

News

To keep abreast of all the motoring news and views, there is a plethora of magazines and papers, many of which are now on the web.

Auto Channel	*http://www.theautochannel.com/*
Auto Express	*http://www.autoexpress.co.uk/*
Auto.com	*http://www.auto.com/*
Autovantage	*http://www.autovantage.com/*
Autoweb	*http://www.autoweb.com/*
BBC Top Gear	*http://www.topgear.com/*

BMW Car Magazine	*http://www.bmwcarmagazine.com/*
Car and Driver Magazine Online	*http://www.caranddriver.com/*
Car Connection	*http://www.thecarconnection.com/*
Car Magazine	*http://www.carmagazine.co.uk/*

Cartalk	*http://www.cartalk.com/*
Classic Car World	*http://www.classiccarworld.co.uk/*
Classic Motor	*http://www.classicmotor.co.uk/*
Final Lap	*http://www.finallap.com/*
Microsoft Carpoint	*http://carpoint.msn.com/*
Motor Cycle World Magazine	*http://www.motorcycleworld.co.uk/*
Motorsports Journal Online	*http://www.motorsportsjournal.com/*

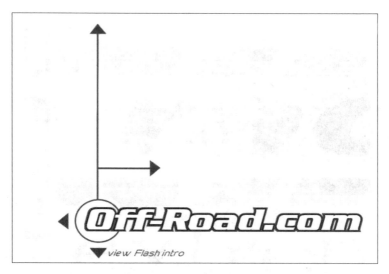

Off-Road.com	*http://www.off-road.com/*
Victory Lane Magazine	*http://www.victorylane.com/*
Wrenchead	*http://www.wrenchead.com/*
Xtra Motoring Network	*http://www.autonews.co.nz/*

Owners' Clubs

Owners of classic cars frequently can't get spares from the usual sources and some spares are all but impossible to buy. This is where a club dedicated to a particular model can be invaluable.

Aston Martin Owners Club *http://www.amoc.org/*
BMC Car Parts *http://www.cars.classics.co.uk/adverts/ car/bmc.html*
Classic Car Owner's Clubs *http://www.288online.co.uk/ classiccars/clubs.htm*

At DeLorean One, the difference is in the details.

If you respect your DeLorean and you want the very best, DeLorean One is the source for you. We will provide you with the highest level of service and the finest parts available anywhere.

If, on the other hand, you are simply looking for the cheapest way out, please look elsewhere. You can always find someone to do it cheaper. Never someone to do it better.

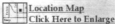

Location Map
Click Here to Enlarge

Home | Order Parts and Accessories | About DeLorean One | Pickup Service | Repair, Service and Body Work | Refurbished DeLoreans

DeLorean One *http://www.deloreanone.com/*

Ford Classic and Capri Owners
    Club

http://www.mistral.co.uk/pipes/
fccoc.html

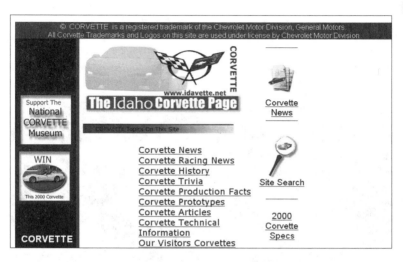

Idaho Corvette Page — *http://www.idavette.net/*
Jensen Owners — *http://www.british-steel.org/*
Memphis British Sports Car Club — *http://www.memphisbritcars.tn.org/*
North West Italian Car Owners
    Club — *http://www.provider.co.uk/users/*
hystericsoft/nw-italian-owners
Norton Owners Club — *http://www.noc.co.uk/*
Old English Car Club — *http://www.islandnet.com/~oecc/*
oecc.htm

Rolls Royce - Owners Club — *http://www.rroc.org/*
Rolls Royce and Bentley — *http://www.rrab.com/*

Rolls Royce Facts	*http://www.darkforce.com/royce/facts.htm/*
Sunbeam - Sunbeam Rapier Owners' Club	*http://www.wskisoft.co.uk/sroc/magtitle.htm*
Sunbeam Tiger Owner Association	*http://www.engravers.com/tiger*
The MG Cars Webring	*http://www.mgcars.org.uk/webring*
The UK Motor Sport Index	*http://www.ukmotorsport.com/groups.html*

Triumph Owners	*http://www.harding.co.uk/triumph*
UK Car Owners Clubs	*http://www.ukmotorsport.com/uk_car_clubs.html*

Parts and Accessories

All cars need spares and third parties frequently produce parts which are as good as the manufacturer's original equipment, but a lot cheaper. There's also a big market in accessories.

Auto Vogue	*http://www.autovogue.com/*
Beltronics	*http://www.beltronics.com/*
Carbug	*http://www.carbug.co.uk/*
Euro Car Parts	*http://www.eurocarparts.com/*

Haynes Manuals	*http://www.haynes.co.uk/*
Kenwood	*http://www.kenwood-electronics.co.uk/*

Kwik-Fit	*http://www.kwik-fit.com/*
National Tyres	*http://www.national.co.uk/*
Navtrak	*http://www.navtrak.com/*

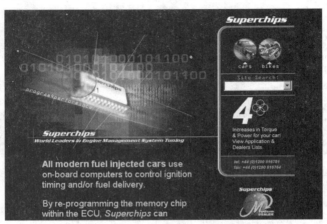

Superchips	*http://www.superchips.co.uk/*
Tire Rack	*http://www.tirerack.com/*
Trackstar	*http://ractrackstar.co.uk/*
VDO Dayton	*http://www.vdodayton.com/*
Vehix	*http://www.vehix.com/*

Petrol

To find out more about the stuff that propels your car or bike, visit one of these sites.

Amoco/BP	*http://www.bpamoco.com/*

Esso	*http://www.esso.co.uk/eaff/essouk*
Shell	*http://www.shell.com/*
Texaco	*http://www.texaco.com/*
Total/Fina/Elf	*http://www.totalfinaelf.com/fr/html*

Registration Plates

It's a peculiarly British thing: getting a registration plate that reads something
– the name of the driver or car. The costs can be very high.

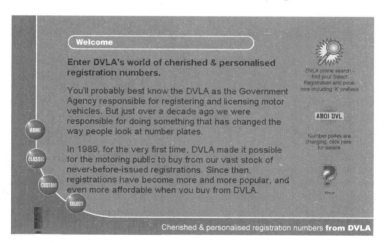

DVLA	*http://www.dvla-som.co.uk/*
Ne-Numbers	*http://www.ne-numbers.co.uk/*
Registration Plates	*http://www.regplate.com/*
Registration Transfers	*http://www.regtransfers.co.uk/*
Speedy Registrations	*http://www.speedyregistrations.co.uk/*

Rental

For the odd occasion, a hired car is the answer.

Avis Rent A Car   *http://www.avis.com/*
BCR Car and Van Rental   *http://www.bcvr.co.uk/*
Classic Car Hire   *http://www.classic-car-hire.co.uk/*
Craven Classic Car Hire   *http://www.yorkshirenet.co.uk/visinfo/*
                                  ccch/

Easy Rentacar   *http://www.easyrentacar.com/*
Hertz Rent A Car   *http://www.hertz.com/*

Trading Autos

Buying and selling cars either privately or through dealers is the theme of this section.

Auto Trader	*http://www.autotrader.co.uk/*
Autobytel	*http://www.autobytel.com/*
Autoexchange	*http://www.autoexchange.co.uk/*
Autohit	*http://www.autohit.com/*
Autohunter	*http://www.autohunter.co.uk/*
Autopig	*http://www.autopig.com/*

Autotrader	*http://www.autotrader.com/*
Best Offer	*http://www.bestoffer.com/*
Blue Chip Motors	*http://www.bluechipmotors.co.uk/*
Bristol Street Motors	*http://www.bristolstreet.co.uk/*
Burbank	*http://www.burbankautomotive.com/*
Buy a BMW	*http://www.buyabmw.co.uk/*
Buy a Mercedes	*http://www.buyamercedes.co.uk/*

Car Credit	*http://www.yescarcredit.net/*
Car Prices	*http://www.carprices.com/*
Car Sauce	*http://www.carsauce.co.uk/*
Carbusters	*http://www.carbusters.com/*
Carclub.com	*http://www.carclub.com/*

Cars.com	*http://www.cars.com/*
Carsdirect	*http://www.carsdirect.com/*
Carshop	*http://www.carshop.co.uk/*
Continent Vehicles	*http://www.continent-vehicles.com/*
Daily Telegraph	*http://www.motoring.ads*
	@telegraph.co.uk/
Dixon Motors	*http://www.dixonmotors.co.uk/*
Economy Cars	*http://www.ecomcars.co.uk/*
Elite Classics	*http://www.elite.co.uk/*

Euro Car Consultants	*http://www.eurocar.uk.com/*
Fish 4 Cars	*http://www.fish4cars.co.uk/*
Go Brussels	*http://www.gobrussels.com/*
IntelliChoice Car Center	*http://www.intellichoice.com/*
KSB	*http://www.ksb.co.uk/*

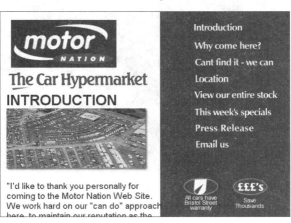

"I'd like to thank you personally for coming to the Motor Nation Web Site. We work hard on our "can do" approach here, to maintain our reputation as the

Motor Nation	*http://www.motornation.co.uk/*
Motorpoint	*http://www.motorpoint.co.uk/*
P&O	*http://www.posl.com/*
Parkers Guide	*http://www.parkers.co.uk/*
Planet Moto	*http://www.planetmoto.co.uk/*
Signature	*http://www.signature.uk.com/*
Sussex Imports	*http://www.sussex-imports.co.uk/*
Sytner	*http://www.sytner.co.uk/*
Tom Hartley	*http://www.tomhartley.com/*

Trade Sales	*http://www.trade-sales.co.uk/*
What Car	*http://www.whatcar.co.uk/*
Wundercars	*http://www.wundercars.co.uk/*

| Wykehams | *http://www.wykehams.com/* |

Trading Bikes

Buying and selling bikes is just as popular as buying and selling cars. There's no shortage of websites around the world and it's a great deal more pleasurable than visiting each store in person.

Auto Parts Superstore	*http://www.apss.com/*
Bike Trader	*http://www.biketrader.co.uk/*
Biker Mart	*http://www.bikermart.com/*
Cyber Cycles	*http://www.cybercycles.co.uk/*
Motor City	*http://www.motorcity.net/*
Motor Cycle City	*http://www.motorcycle-city.co.uk/*

Music

Whether you play an instrument or press the button of a CD player, there is plenty of scope on the Internet to pursue your hobby.

CD, Vinyl and Minidisc

The number of websites selling CDs seem to come second only to those selling books. There are some excellent deals to be had and the delivery is frequently very fast.

101CD	*http://www.101cd.com/*
13th Floor Company	*http://www.13thfloorcompany.com/*
Abbey Records	*http://www.abbeyrecords.com/*
ABC Music	*http://www.abcmusic.co.uk/*
Action Records	*http://www.action-records.co.uk/*
Amazon	*http://www.amazon.com/*
Audiostreet	*http://www.audiostreet.com/*
Beat Museum	*http://www.thebeatmuseum.com/*
Black Music	*http://www.blackmail.com/*
Blockbuster	*http://www.blockbuster.co.uk/*
Blues & Rhythm	*http://www.bluesworld.com/BnR*
BOL	*http://www.bol.com/*
Borrow Or Rob	*http://shop.borroworrob.com*
Boxman	*http://www.boxman.co.uk/*

Britannia Music and Video	*http://www.britanniamusic.co.uk/*
CD Now	http://www.cdnow.com/
CD Paradise	*http://www.cdparadise.com/*
CD-Wow	*http://www.cd-wow.com/*

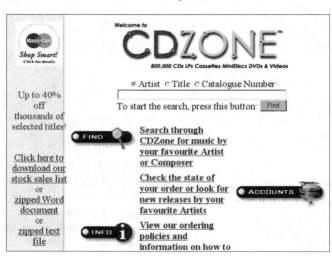

CD Zone	*http://www.cdzone.co.uk/*
Chart CD	*http://www.chartcd.com/*
Cheap or What!	*http://www.cow.co.uk/*
Classical Choice	*http://www.cdchoice.com/*
Classical Insites	*http://www.classicalinsites.com/*
CMS Music	*http://www.cmsmusic.co.uk/*
Compact Classics	*http://www.compactclassics.co.uk/*
Crotchet	*http://www.crotchet.co.uk/*

Dalriada	*http://www.argyllweb.com/dalriada*
Dotmusic	*http://www.dotmusic.com/*
E-Dance	*http://www.e-dance.co.uk/*
Entertainment Express	*http://www.entexpress.com/*
Fusion Records	*http://www.fusionrecords.co.uk/*

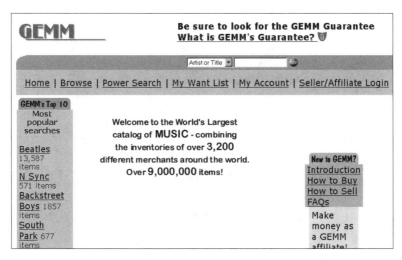

GEMM	*http://www.gemm.com/*
Global Groove Records	*http://www.globalgroove.co.uk/*
Hard To Find Records	*http://www.htfr.co.uk/*
Heyday Mail Order	*http://www.heyday-mo.com/*
HMV	*http://www.hmv.co.uk/*
Interactive Music & Video Shop	*http://www.musicshop.co.uk/*
Internet Music Shop	*http://www.musicsales.co.uk*

Jungle.com	*http://www.jungle.com/*
Kode	*http://www.kode.co.uk/*
Littlestar Music CD Shop	*http://www.littlestar.co.uk/*
Look Music	*http://www.lookmusic.com/*
Magpie Direct	*http://www.magpiedirect.com/*
MDC Classic	*http://www.mdcmusic.co.uk/*

Mello Yello	*http://www.melloyello.co.uk/*
Ministry of Sound	*http://www.ministryofsound.co.uk/*
Moving Music	*http://www.movingmusic.co.uk/*
Music 365	*http://www.music365.com/*
Music Box	*http://www.musicbox.uk.com/*
Music Capital	*http://www.musiccapital.com/*
Musicmania	*http://www.musicmania.co.uk/*

Music Metropolis	*http://www.musicmetropolis.com/*
Music Stop	*http://www.music-stop.co.uk/*
Net Megastore	*http://www.internet-shopping.uk.com/*
New World Music	*http://www.newworldmusic.com/*
NME	*http://www.nme.com/*
Online Records	*http://www.onlinerecords.co.uk/*

Past Perfect	*http://www.pastperfect.com/*
Plantagenet Music	*http://www.plantagenetmusic.co.uk/*
Psappha	*http://www.nwnet.co.uk/psappha*
Recollections	*http://www.recollections.co.uk/*
Record Store	*http://www.recordstore.co.uk/*
Riffage	*http://www.riffage.com/*
Seaford Music	*http://www.seaford-music.co.uk/*

Sentimental Records	*http://www.sentimentalrecords.com/*
Shop DVD	*http://www.shopdvd.co.uk/*
Sounds Great Music	*http://www.soundsgreatmusic.com/*
The Lobby	*http://www.thelobby.co.uk/*
The Muse	*http://www.themuse.co.uk/*
Timewarp Records	*http://www.tunes.co.uk/timewarp*
Tower Records UK	*http://www.towerrecords.co.uk/*

Uptown Records	*http://www.uptownrecords.com/*
VCI	*http://www.vci.co.uk/*
Vinyl Tap Records	*http://www.vinyltap.co.uk/*
Virgin Megastore	*http://www.virginmega.com/*
WH Smith Online - CD Channel	*http://cds.whsmithonline.co.uk/*
Y2K Music	*http://www.y2k-music.co.uk/*
Yalplay	*http://www.yalplay.com/welcome.htm*
Ynot Music	*http://www.ynotmusic.co.uk/*

Musical Instruments

If it's a musical instrument you're after, or you want some help with playing, try visiting one of these sites.

2000 Gibson   *http://www.gibson.com/products/ gibson/*

ABC Music   *http://www.abcmusic.co.uk/*

Aboriginal Art of Australia   *http://www.ozemail.com.au/~hallpa/*

Action Guitar   *http://www.actionguitar.com/*

Al Brisco's Steel Guitars   *http://www.steelguitarcanada.com/*

Alamo Music Center   *http://www.alamomusic.com/*

Bill's Music House   *http://www.billsmusic.com/*

Bluegrass in Scotland   *http://www.ednet.co.uk/~russell/*

BPM Music Express   *http://www.bpmmusic.com/*
Canada - Maestronet   *http://www.maestronet.com/*
Carter Steel Guitars   *http://www.steelguitar.com/*
Caruso Music Online   *http://www.caruso.net/*
Chamberlain Music   *http://www.chamberlainmusic.com/*
Churchill's Music   *http://www.churchills-music.co.uk/*

Conway Music Company   *http://www.conwaymusic.com/*
Dietze Music House   *http://www.dietze.com/*
Elderly Instruments   *http://www.elderly.com/*
FolkCraft Instruments   *http://www.folkcraft.com/*
Fred's Music Shop   *http://www.fredsmusic.com/*
Freehold Music Center   *http://www.freeholdmusic.com/*

General Music	*http://www.generalmusic.com/*
Giardinelli	*http://www.giardinelli.com*

Guitar	*http://www.guitar.com/*
Guitar (Bob's)	*http://www.guitarbob.com*
Guitar Chords	*http://www.ws64.com/guitarchords/*
Guitar World Online	*http://www.guitarworld.com*
Harmony Central	*http://www.harmony-central.com*
Harry Kolbe Soundsmith	*http://www.soundsmith.com/*
Hart Dynamics	*http://www.hartdynamics.com/*
Hubbard Harpsichords	*http://www.hubbard.qds.com*
Hurdygurdy	*http://www.hurdygurdy.com/*
International Saxophone	*http://www.saxophone.org*

K&K Music	*http://www.kandkmusic.com/*
King Music Inc.	*http://www.kingmusic.com/*
Lone Star Percussion	*http://www.lonestarpercussion.com/*

Long & McQuade Musical Instruments

ABOUT L&M | LOCATIONS | DEPARTMENTS | THIS MONTH | TIPS & TRICKS | HOT GEAR

About L&M | Location Maps | Departments | This Month at L&M | Tips & Tricks | Hot Gear

Original design & authoring: Art & Soul. Site maintained & updated by: re·site·solutions·ltd
Contact the Webmaster

Long & McQuade	*http://www.long-mcquade.com/*
Maitland Music	*http://www.cali.co.uk/mait*
Mandala - Beyond A Lucid State	*http://www.progressive-music.com/*
Marsha Taylor Oboe Products	*http://www.oboe.or/g*
McCabe's Guitar Shop	*http://www.mccabesguitar.com/*
MIDI Wind Controllers FAQ	*http://www.harmony-central.com/*
	midi/doc/wind-controllers.txt
Midi.com	*http://www.midi.com/*
Midwest Musical Imports	*http://www.mmimports.com/*

Music and Audio Connection	*http://www.musicandaudio.com/*
Music Connection	*http://www.the-music-connection.com/*
Music Industries	*http://www.musicindustries.com/*
Music Resources - Sibelius Academy	*http://www.siba.fi/Kulttuuripalvelut/music.html*

Musician's Friend	*http://www.musiciansfriend.com/*
Musician's Swap Shop	*http://www.swap-shop.com/*
National Educational Music Company	*http://www.nemc.com/*
Optek Music Systems, Inc.	*http://www.optekmusic.com/*
Organ Supply Industries	*http://www.organsupply.com/*
Paul Reed Smith Guitars	*http://www.prsguitars.com/*
Pensa Custom Guitars	*http://www.pensaguitars.com/*

Percussive Arts Society	*http://www.pas.org/*
Powell Flutes	*http://www.powellflutes.com/*
RNCM Instruments Collection	*http://www.library.rncm.ac.uk/*
	libhwm.htm
Rocky Mountain Music	*http://www.rockymountainmusic.com/*

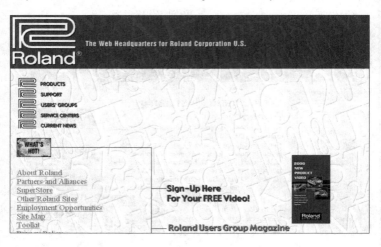

Roland US	*http://www.rolandus.com/*
Rose-Morris Music Store	*http://www.rose-morris.co.uk/*
Santa Cruz Guitar Company	*http://www.santacruzguitar.com/*
Selmer Musical Instruments	*http://www.selmer.com/*
Smith-Watkins Brass	*http://www.rsmi.u-net.com/*
Sound Beat UK	*http://www.soundbeat.mcmail.com/*
Sound Club	*http://www.springsoft.com/sclub.htm*
Studio Instrument Rentals	*http://www.sirny.com/*

The Piano Page	*http://www.ptg.org/*
The Recorder	*http://www.iinet.net.au/~nickl/ recorder.html*
The Theremin Home Page	*http://www.nashville.net/~theremin*
Trumpet Player Online	*http://www.v-zone.com/tpo*
Tutti	*http://www.tutti.co.uk/*
Uilleann.com	*http://www.uilleann.com/*
Used Guitar	*http://www.usedguitar.com/*

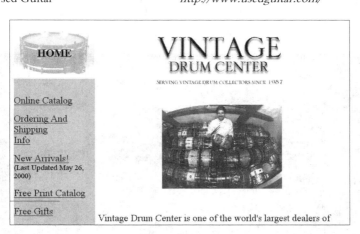

Vintage Drum Center	*http://www.vintagedrum.com/*
Viola da Gamba Society	*http://www.vdgs.demon.co.uk/*
Washington Music Center	*http://www.wmcworld.com/*
West Music	*http://www.westmusic.com/*
Wichita Band Instrument Co.	*http://www.wichitaband.com/*
Wink Music World Sounds	*http://www.winkworldsounds.com/*

MP3

MP3 is a file format for compressed digital music files. You need an MP3 player for your PC and then you can download digital music from the Internet and play it on your computer. If you want to play it on something rather more portable than your computer, you can buy a battery powered portable MP3 player.

MP3 Players

MP3 Players & Tools *http://www.mysharewarepage.com/ mp3.htm*

Sonique *http://www.sonique.com/*
Xing *http://www.xingtech.com/*

MP3 Music Files

Abstract MP3	*http://www.abstractmp3s.com/*
Access Music Network	*http://www.a-m-n.com/index.asp*
Audio Find	*http://www.audiofind.com/*
Audio Grab	*http://www.audiograb.com/*
BURBs	*http://www.burbs.co.uk/*
Crunch	*http://www.crunch.co.uk/*
Fast MP3 Search	*http://mp3.lycos.com/*
Hot MP3s	*http://members.xoom.com/mp3_suite/*
Hungry Bands	*http://www.hungrybands.com/*
MP3 Bot Search Engine	*http://www.informatch.com/mediabot/*

MP3 Central	*http://music.lycos.com/mp3*

MP3 MTV Hits	*http://come.to/mp3mtvhits*
MP3 Now	*http://www.mp3now.com/*

MP3.com	*http://www.MP3.com/*
MP4 music	*http://www.mp4music.com/*
Music Match	*http://www.musicmatch.com/*
Palavista Digital Music Metacrawler	*http://www.palavista.com/*
RioPort	*http://www.rioport.com/*
Technomusic	*http://www.technomusic.com/*
Tony's International MP3	*http://www.funaki.com/Tony/mp3/*
Vitaminic	*http://www.vitaminic.com/*

Orchestras

Adelaide Symphony Orch.	*http://www.aso.com.au/*
Association of British Orch.	*http://www.orchestranet.co.uk/ abo.html*
BBC Philharmonic Orch.	*http://www.bbc.co.uk/orchestras/ philharmonic/*

BBC Symphony Orchestra	*http://www.bbc.co.uk/orchestras*
Bristol Concert Orchestra	*http://www.ellwoodmail.freeserve .co.uk/bco/bco.html*
Cyber Symphony Orchestra	*http://www.nettaxi.com/citizens/jgriff/ music/cyberorch.*
Edinburgh Symphony Orchestra	*http://www.geocities.com/Vienna/ Strasse/4779/*

Glasgow Chamber Orch.	*http://gco.freeservers.com/*
Irish Chamber Orchestra	*http://www.ul.ie/~iwmc/ico/home.html*
Kensington Symphony Orchestra	*http://ds.dial.pipex.com/town/close/yl32/*
London Metropolitan Orch.	*http://www.lmo.co.uk/*
London Philharmonic Orch.	*http://www.lpo.co.uk/*
London Symphony Orch.	*http://www.lso.co.uk/*

Metropolitan Symphony Orch.	*http://www.mtn.org/~mso*
National Assoc. of Youth Orchestras	*http://www.nayo.org.uk/*
National Youth Orchestra of Great Britain	*http://www.btinternet.com/~nyo/*
New Edinburgh Orchestra	*http://www.ndirect.co.uk/~williams/neo/*

New Zealand Symphony Orchestra	*http://www.nzso.co.nz/*
Oxford University Orchestra	*http://users.ox.ac.uk/~orch/*
Philadelphia Orchestra	*http://www.philorch.org/*
Philharmonia Orchestra	*http://www.philharmonia.co.uk/*
Royal Liverpool Philharmonic Orchestra	*http://rlps.merseyworld.com/*
Royal Orchestra	*http://www.royalopera.org/orchestra/ orchestra1.htm*
Royal Philharmonic Orch.	*http://www.orchestranet.co.uk/ rpo.html*
Royal Scottish National Orchestra	*http://www.scot-art.org/rsno/*
Seattle Symphony Orchestra	*http://www.seattlesymphony.org/*
Studio Symphony Orchestra	*http://www.users.globalnet.co.uk/ ~asg/*

Stars' Web Sites

Fanclubs can be very lucrative for the stars, but most are there just to keep fans up-to-date with the singer of the group, forthcoming concerts and record releases.

ABBA *http://www.polydor.com/polydor/artists/abba/*

Bread *http://www.ktb.net/~insync/breadtitle.html*

Britney Spears *http://www.britneyspears.org/*

Bryan Adams *http://members.tripod.com/~agk*

Cyndi Lauper *http://www.epiccenter.com/epiccenter/cyndilauper/*

Elton John	*http://www.eltonjohn.com/*
Find a Fanclub	*http://fanclubs.eonline.com/*
Geri Halliwell	*http://www.geri-halliwell.com/*
Janet Jackson	*http://www.janet-online.com/*
Joan Baez	*http://www.baez.woz.org/*
Lisa Stansfield	*http://www.aristarec.com/aristaweb/ lisastansfield/main.html*
Madonna	*http://www.madonnafanclub.com/*
Mariah Carey	*http://www.mariahcarey-fanclub.com/*
Martine McCutcheon	*http://www.martinemccutcheon.com/*
Michael Bolton	*http://www.michaelbolton-fanclub.com/*
Michael Jackson	*http://www.epiccenter.com/epiccenter/ custom/artistfan.taf?artistid=86*

Roy Wood	*http://www.roywood.com/*

Simon & Garfunkel   *http://www.sonymusic.com/artists/ simonandgarfunkel/*

Simply Red   *http://www.simplyred.co.uk/*

Status Quo   *http://www.statusquo.co.uk/*

Tears For Fears   *http://www.sonymusic.com/artists/ tearsforfears/*

The Hollies   *http://www.cae.wisc.edu/~gansler/ hollies/hollies.htm*

Tina Turner   *http://www.virginrecords.com/artists/ vr.cgi?artist_name=tina_turner*

Unofficial Sites

In addition to the 'official' websites of the stars, there are also many unofficial ones which have been put together by loyal fans.

ABBA   *http://mercury.beseen.com/chat/*
                               rooms/g/4896/avatar

Artist Information   *http://www.artistinformation.com/*

Badfinger   *http://hjem.get2net.dk/Badfinger*
Black Sabbath   *http://www.inx.de/~arack/bsfcd.html*
Britney Spears   *http://www.artistinformation.com/*
                               britney_spears.html
Cyndi Lauper   *http://members.aol.com/goldust14/*
                               cyndipage.htm

343

David Bowie	*http://www.nj.com/spotlight/bowie/*
Duran Duran	*http://www.geocities.com/hollywood/ mansion/1332/*
Electric Light Orchestra	*http://clix.to/elo*
Eric Clapton Fanzine	*http://www.xs4all.nl/~slowhand*
Kylie Minogue	*http://www.kylie.com/*
Linda Wong	*http://members.aol.com/bearpage/ linda/*

Olivia Photos

Click on the photo's to enlarge them.

Olivia Newton-John	*http://www.geocities.com/rainforest/ vines/5945/oliviahighlights.htm*
Online Talent	*http://www.onlinetalent.com/*
Robbie Williams Internet-ional	*http://nettrash.com/users/tt/rw.htm*
Spice Girls	*http://degrees.simplenet.com/spice100/*

News

The Internet can provide all the news you want to keep abreast of the latest worldwide developments.

Magazines

There are countless magazines and periodicals published throughout the world and many of them are also available on the Internet.

BMJ Medical Journal   *http://www.bmj.com/*

Car and Driver   *http://www.caranddriver.com/*

Career Magazine	*http://www.careermag.com/*
Data Communications Magazine	*http://www.data.com/*
Economist, The	*http://www.economist.com/*
Feed Magazine	*http://www.feedmag.com/*
Men's Health	*http://www.menshealth.com/*
Motor Cycle Online	*http://www.motorcycle.com/*
Motor Trend Online	*http://www.motortrend.com/*
National Enquirer Online	*http://www.nationalenquirer.com/*

National Geographic	*http://www.nationalgeographic.com/*
Nature	*http://www.nature.com/*
New Scientist Planet Science	*http://www.newscientist.com/*
Science Daily Magazine	*http://www.sciencedaily.com/*
Scientific American	*http://www.sciam.com/*
TIME.com	*http://www.time.com/*

Newspapers

Instead of reading the news on paper, you can log onto the newspaper's website. It's all very clever, but I still think paper is easier to read than a screen.

ABC Rural Bush Telegraph (AU)   *http://www.abc.net.au/rural/*

Aberdeen Independent (UK)	*http://www.aberdeen-indy.co.uk/*
Age, The (AU)	*http://www.theage.com.au/*
An Phoblacht / Republican News (UK)	*http://www.irlnet.com/aprn/*
Andersonstown News (UK)	*http://www.belfast-news.ie/*
Arizona Republic and Phoenix Gazette (US)	http://www.azcentral.com/
Athlone Observer (IE)	*http://ireland.iol.ie/littlebug/athobs*
Atlanta Journal-Constitution (US)	*http://www.accessatlanta.com/ajc*

Newspapers

Aucklandlive News (NZ)   *http://www.aucklandlive.co.nz/news*

Augusta-Margaret River Mail (AU)   *http://www.margaret-river-online.com.au/amrmail*

AustralAsian (AU)   *http://www.theaustralasian.com/*

Australia Daily (AU)   *http://www.ausdaily.net.au/*

Australian Financial Review (AU)   *http://www.afr.com.au/*

Australian News Network (AU)   *http://www.news.com.au/*

Baltimore Sun (US)   *http://www.sunspot.net/*

Barnsley Chronicle (UK)   *http://www.barnsley-chronicle.co.uk/*

Belfast Telegraph (UK)   *http://www.belfasttelegraph.co.uk/*

Bendigo Advertiser (AU)   *http://www.bendigoaddy.com.au/*

Big Issue, The (UK)   *http://www.bigissue.com/*

Bolton Evening News (UK)   *http://www.thisislancashire.co.uk/lancashire/bolton/index.html*

Boston Globe (US)   *http://www.boston.com/globe/*
Brighton Evening Argus (UK)   *http://www.thisisbrighton.co.uk/*
Bristol Evening Post (UK)   *http://www.epost.co.uk/*
Burnley Express (UK)   *http://www.eastlancsnews.co.uk/*
                               behome.html
Bury Free Press (UK)   *http://www.buryfreepress.co.uk/*

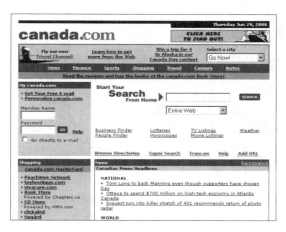

Canada.com (CA)   *http://www.canada.com/*
Canadian Jewish News (CA)   *http://www.cjnews.com/*
Canberra Times (AU)   *http://www.canberratimes.com.au/*
Capital Q Weekly (AU)   *http://www.capitalq.com.au/*
Charlotte Observer (US)   *http://www.charlotte.com/*
Chicago Sun-Times (US)   *http://www.suntimes.com/index*
Chicago Tribune (US)   *http://www.chicagotribune.com/*
Chichester Observer (UK)   *http://www.chiobserver.co.uk/*

Christchurch Press Online (NZ)   *http://www.press.co.nz/*
Christian Science Monitor (US)   *http://www.csmonitor.com/*
Cincinnati Enquirer (US)   *http://enquirer.com/today/*
Cincinnati Post (US)   *http://www.cincypost.com/*
Clare Champion (IE)   *http://www.clarechampion.ie/*

Cleveland Plain Dealer (US)   *http://www.cleveland.com/*
Clitheroe Advertiser and   *http://www.eastlancsnews.co.uk/*
   Times (UK)   *clithhome.html*
Colne Times (UK)   *http://www.eastlancsnews.co.uk/*
                  colnehome.html
Columbus Dispatch (US)   *http://www.dispatch.com/*
Congleton Chronicle (UK)   *http://www.beartown.co.uk/*
Connaught Telegraph (IE)   *http://www.mayo-ireland.ie/Mayo/*
                  News/ConnTel/ConnTel.htm

County Times (UK)	*http://www.nwn.co.uk/ nwninternetpages/ countytimesnews.html*
Courier Mail (AU)	*http://www.thecouriermail.com.au/*
Courier On-line (UK)	*http://www.dcthomson.co.uk/courier/*

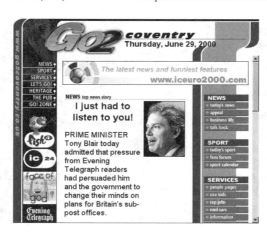

Coventry Evening Telegraph (UK)	*http://www.go2coventry.co.uk/*
Daily Express (UK)	*http://express.lineone.net/*
Daily Record and Sunday Mail (UK)	*http://www.record-mail.co.uk/rm/*
Dallas Morning News (US)	*http://www.dallasnews.com/*
Denver Post (US)	*http://www.denverpost.com/*
Denver Rocky Mountain News (US)	*http://www.rockymountainnews.com/*
Derry People and Donegal News (IE)	*http://www.donegalnews.com/*

351

Detroit Free Press (US) *http://www.freep.com/*
Detroit News (US) *http://www.detnews.com/*
East Lancashire Newspapers (UK) *http://www.eastlancsnews.co.uk/*
Eastern Counties Network (UK) *http://www.ecn.co.uk/*
Edmonton Journal Extra (CA) *http://www.edmontonjournal.com/*

Electronic Telegraph (UK) *http://www.telegraph.co.uk/*
Evening Chronicle (UK) *http://www.evening-chronicle.co.uk/*
Evening Gazette (UK) *http://www.eveninggazette.co.uk/*
Evening Telegraph (UK) *http://www.dcthomson.co.uk/mags/*
tele

Examiner, The (IE) *http://www.examiner.ie/*
Falkirk Herald (UK) *http://www.falkirkherald.co.uk/*
Financial Times (UK) *http://www.ft.com/*
Foinse (IE) *http://www.foinse.ie/*

Fort Lauderdale Sun-Sentinel (US)	*http://www.sun-sentinel.com/*
Fort Worth Star-Telegram (US)	*http://www.star-telegram.com/*
Globe and Mail (CA)	*http://www.globeandmail.ca/*
Grimsby Evening Telegraph (UK)	*http://www.grimsby-online.co.uk/*
Guardian, The (UK)	*http://www.guardian.co.uk/*
Harrogate Advertiser Online (UK)	*http://www.harrogate-advertiser-series.co.uk/*
Hartford Courant (US)	*http://www.ctnow.com/*
Herald, The (UK)	*http://www.theherald.co.uk/*
Hexham Courant Newspaper (UK)	*http://www.hexham-courant.co.uk/*
Holyport Examiner (UK)	*http://www.richardw.clara.net/*
Houston Chronicle (US)	*http://www.chron.com/*
Hucknall Dispatch (UK)	*http://www.hucknall-dispatch.co.uk/*

Hull Daily Mail (UK)	*http://www.thisishull.co.uk/*

Independence Avenue (UK) *http://www.independenceavenue.com/*

Independent Newsgroup (AU) *http://www.independentnewsgroup*
.com.au/

Independent, The (UK) *http://www.independent.co.uk/*

Ireland on Sunday (IE) *http://www.irelandonsunday.com/*

Ireland Today (IE) *http://www.ireland-today.ie/*

Irish Echo (IE) *http://www.irishecho.com/index.cfm*

Irish Independent (IE) *http://www.independent.ie/*

Irish News (IE) *http://www.irishnews.com/*

Irish News (UK) *http://www.irishnews.com/*

Irish Post (UK) *http://www.irishpost.co.uk/*

Irish Regional Newspapers *http://www.rmbi.ie/*
Online (IE)

Irish Times (IE) *http://www.ireland.com/*

Irish Voice Online (IE) *http://www.irishvoice.com/*

Irish World (IE)	*http://www.theirishworld.com/*
Irish X-Press (IE)	*http://www.adnet.ie/xpress/*
Isle of Wight County (UK)	*http://www.iwcp.co.uk/*
Jacksonville Florida Times(US)	*http://jacksonville.com/*
Journal, The (UK)	*http://www.the-journal.co.uk/*
Kansas City Star (US)	*http://www.kcstar.com/*
Kerry's Eye Online (IE)	*http://www.iol.ie/kerryseye*
Lancashire Evening Post (UK)	*http://www.lep.co.uk/*
Leicester Mercury (UK)	*http://www.leicestermercury.co.uk/*
Leinster Times and The Nationalist (IE)	*http://www.lowwwe.com/nationalist/index.html*
Limerick Leader Online (IE)	*http://www.limerick-leader.ie/*
Limerick Post (IE)	*http://www.limerickpost.ie/*

Llangollen Courier (UK) *http://www.courier-llan.u-net.com/*
London Daily (UK) *http://www.london-daily.com/*
London Evening Standard (UK) *http://www.thisislondon.com/*

Los Angeles Times (US) *http://www.latimes.com/*
Malvern Gazette (UK) *http://www.newsquestmidlands.co.uk/*
 malvern
Mayo Gazette (IE) *http://www.mayogazette.com/*
Mayo News (IE) *http://www.mayonews.ie/*
MegaStar (UK) *http://www.megastar.co.uk/*
Miami Herald (US) *http://www.herald.com/*
Milwaukee Journal Sentinel (US) *http://www.onwis.com/*
Minneapolis Star Tribune (US) *http://www.startribune.com/*
Mirror Online (UK) *http://www.mirror.co.uk/*
Montreal Gazette (CA) *http://www.montrealgazette.com/*

Munster Express (IE)	*http://www.munster-express.ie/*
Nando Times (US)	*http://www.nando.net/*
National Post Online (CA)	*http://www.nationalpost.com/*

Nelson Leader (UK)	*http://www.eastlancsnews.co.uk/nelshome.html*
Netreader (CA)	*http://www.netreader.com/*
New York Daily News (US)	*http://www.nydailynews.com/*
New York Newsday (US)	*http://www.newsday.com/*
New York Post (US)	*http://www.nypostonline.com/*
New York Times (US)	*http://www.nytimes.com/*
Newark Advertiser (UK)	*http://www.newarkadvertiser.co.uk/*
Newark Star-Ledger (US)	*http://www.nj.com/news/ledger/index.html*
News Corporation Limited (AU)	*http://www.news.com.au/*

News Group (UK)   *http://www.newsquestmidlands.co.uk/newsgrp*

News Online (UK)   *http://www.thenews.co.uk/*
News Unlimited   *http://www.newsunlimited.co.uk/*
Norfolk Virginian-Pilot (US)   *http://www.pilotonline.com/*
North Devon Journal (UK)   *http://www.northdevonjournal.co.uk/*

Northland Age Ltd (NZ)   *http://www.northnz.co.nz/*
Northside People (IE)   *http://www.northsidepeople.ie/*
Oakland Tribune (US)   *http://www.newschoice.com/newspapers/alameda/tribune*

Odsal Times (UK)   *http://www.users.globalnet.co.uk/~odsal*

Orlando Sentinel (US)   *http://www.orlandosentinel.com/*
Otago Daily Times (NZ)   *http://www.odt.co.nz/*

Ottawa Citizen (CA)	*http://www.ottawacitizen.com/*
Oundle Chronicle Online (UK)	*http://www.tulley.co.uk/chronicle*
People Newspapers (IE)	*http://www.peoplenews.ie/*
Philadelphia Inquirer (US)	*http://www.phillynews.com/inq*
Phoenix: Arizona Republic (US)	*http://www.azcentral.com/*
Pittsburgh Tribune-Review (US)	*http://triblive.com/*

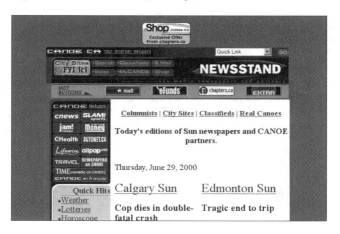

Planet Sun (CA)	*http://www.canoe.ca/planetsun*
Portland Oregonian (US)	*http://www.oregonian.com/*
Press and Journal (UK)	*http://www.pressandjournal.co.uk/*
Private Eye (UK)	*http://www.private-eye.co.uk/*
Providence Journal-Bulletin (US)	*http://www.projo.com/*
Racing Post Online (UK)	*http://www.racingpost.co.uk/*
Rochester Democrat and Chronicle (US)	*http://www.democratandchronicle.com/*

Sacramento Bee (US)	*http://www.sacbee.com/*
Salt Lake Deseret News (US)	*http://www.desnews.com/*
Salt Lake Tribune (US)	*http://www.sltrib.com/*
San Antonio Express-News (US)	*http://www.expressnews.com/*
San Diego Union-Tribune (US)	*http://www.signonsandiego.com/*
San Francisco Chronicle (US)	*http://www.sfgate.com/chronicle*
San Francisco Examiner (US)	*http://www.examiner.com/*
Saoirse (IE)	*http://ireland.iol.ie/~saoirse/*
Scotland on Sunday (UK)	*http://www.scotlandonsunday.com/*

Scotsman, The (UK)	*http://www.scotsman.com/*
Scottish and Universal Newspapers (UK)	*http://www.inside-scotland.co.uk/*
Seattle Times (US)	*http://www.seattletimes.com/*
Sentinel, The (UK)	*http://www.thesentinel.co.uk/*

Sheffield Star & Telegraph (UK)	*http://www.sheffweb.co.uk/*
Shepparton News (AU)	*http://www.shepparton.net.au/*
Shetland Times (UK)	*http://www.shetland-times.co.uk/*
Shields Gazette (UK)	*http://www.shields-gazette.co.uk/*
Shropshire Star (UK)	*http://www.shropshirestar.com/*
Skerries News (IE)	*http://www.cognition.ie/skerries_news*
South East Newspapers (AU)	*http://www.senews.com.au/*
Southern Cross Newspaper (UK)	*http://www.southerncross.co.uk/*
Southern Daily Echo (UK)	*http://www.dailyecho.co.uk/*
Sporting Life (UK)	*http://www.sportinglife.co.uk/*
St. Helens Star (UK)	*http://www.thisislancashire.co.uk/ lancashire/sthelens*
St. Louis Post-Dispatch (US)	*http://www.postnet.com/*
St. Petersburg Times (US)	*http://www.sptimes.com/*
Sun Herald, The (AU)	*http://www.sunherald.com.au/*
Sun, The (UK)	*http://www.the-sun.co.uk/*
Sunday Business Post (IE)	*http://www.sbpost.ie/newspaper/ current*
Sunday Herald (UK)	*http://www.sundayherald.com/*
Sunday Mirror (UK)	*http://www.sundaymirror.co.uk/*
Sunday People (UK)	*http://www.people.co.uk/*
Sunday Post (UK)	*http://www.sundaypost.com/*
Sunday Sun (UK)	*http://www.sundaysun.co.uk/*
Sunday Times (UK)	*http://www.sunday-times.co.uk/*
Sunday Tribune (IE)	*http://www.tribune.ie/*
Sunderland Echo (UK)	*http://www.sunderland-echo.co.uk/*
Sunny Daze (IE)	*http://www.iol.ie/~moranp/sunny/ index.html*

Newspapers

Vancouver Sun (CA)	*http://www.vancouversun.com/*
Voice, The (UK)	*http://www.voice-online.co.uk/*
Wairarapa Times-Age (NZ)	*http://times-age.co.nz/*
Wall Street Journal (US)	*http://www.wsj.com/*
Warrandyte Diary (AU)	*http://home.vicnet.net.au/~warrandy*
Washington Post (US)	*http://www.washingtonpost.com/*
Washington Times (US)	*http://www.washtimes.com/*
Waterford Today (IE)	*http://www.waterford-today.ie/*
Week, The (UK)	*http://www.theweek.co.uk/*
Weekend Independent (AU)	*http://www.uq.oz.au/jrn/twi/twi.html*
West Australian News Review (AU)	*http://www.perth-wa.com/*
Western Australian Business News (AU)	*http://www.businessnews.com.au/*
Western Morning News (UK)	*http://www.westernmorningnews .co.uk/*
Westmeath Examiner (IE)	*http://www.westmeath-examiner.ie/*
Wharf, The (UK)	*http://www.wharf.co.uk/*
Worcester Evening News (UK	*http://www.thisisworcestershire.co.uk/ worcs/wen/index.htm*
Worthing Herald (UK)	*http://www.worthingherald.co.uk/*
XTRA Today News (NZ)	*http://www.xtra.co.nz/news/index.html*
Yorkshire Evening Post (UK)	*http://www.yorkshire-evening- post.co.uk/*

YORKSHIRE POST YORKSHIRE POST *interactive*

Yorkshire Post (UK)	*http://www.ypn.co.uk/*

News

There are several other sources of news, including TV websites.

CNN Interactive	*http://www.cnn.com/*
Electronic Newsstand	*http://www.enews.com/*
ESPNet SportsZone	*http://espnet.sportszone.com/*
Excite Live!	*http://live.excite.com/*
Journalism UK	*http://www.octopod.demon.co.uk/ journ_uk.htm*
London News Network Online	*http://www.lnn-tv.co.uk/*
Lycos News	http://news.lycos.de/news/uk/
Mercury Center (San Jose Mercury News)	*http://www.sjmercury.com/*
MSN News	*http://www.msnbc.com/news*

News Bytes	*http://www.nbnn.com/*
NewsPage	*http://www.newpage.com/*
NPR on the Web	*http://npr.org/*
PoliticsNow	*http://www.politicsnow.com/*
PopSci.com	*http://www.popsci.com/*
Press Association	*http://www.pa.press.net/*
Reuters	*http://www.reuters.com/*
Suck	*http://www.suck.com/*
USA Today	*http://www.usatoday.com/*

Weather

For some people the weather is a matter of extreme importance. Up-to-the-minute weather details are available round-the-clock, worldwide, from numerous Internet websites.

Airport Information & Weather	*http://www.avnet.co.uk/tmdg/weather*
Ant Veal's UK Weather Centre	*http://web.bham.ac.uk/ggy4atv3/weather.htm*

BBC Weather Centre	*http://www.bbc.co.uk/weather*

CNN.com	*http://www.cnn.co.uk/*
Intellicast - Europe Local Weather	*http://www.intellicast.com/ localweather/world/europe*
Medium-Range Weather Forecasts	*http://www.ecmwf.int/*
Meterology Office	*http://www.meto.gov.uk/*
Online Weather (UK)	*http://www.onlineweather.com/ britishisles/britishisles.html*
PA News Centre - Weather	*http://www.pa.press.net/weather/ main.html*
Snow Sport World	*http://www.snowsportworld.com/*
The Weather Channel	*http://www.weather.com/*
Today's Weather Forecast	*http://www.msn.co.uk/page/2-12.asp*
UK Aviation Weather	*http://www.pilotweb.co.uk/pwx.htm*
UK Weather	*http://www.pa.press.net/weather*
UK Weather	*http://www.uk-weather.co.uk/*
UK Weather Links	*http://www.greasby.demon.co.uk/ weather/pages*
Weather	*http://uk.multimap.com/map/ weather.cgi*
Weather	*http://www.guardianunlimited.co.uk/ weather*
Weather Glossary	*http://www.geocities.com/heartland/ 1102/wxdefs.html*
Weather Reports From Around the UK	*http://www.meto.gov.uk/datafiles/ wx_uk.html*
Weather.com	*http://www.weather.com/intl/*
Yahoo! Weather	*http://uk.weather.yahoo.com/*
Yellow Pages Weather	*http://www.yell.co.uk/travel/ worldweather.html*

Pets

It has been proven that owning a pet, in particular a cat or a dog, is very beneficial. Dog and cat owners seem to live longer and are less stressed.

Pet Care

These sites deal in general pet supplies and pet issues. There are also a few which specialise in particular types of animals.

Acme Pet   *http://www.acmepet.com/*

AKC   *http://www.akc.org/*

Animail	*http://www.animail.co.uk/*
Animal Network	*http://www.animalnetwork.com/*
Animal People	*http://www.animalpeople.com/*
Complete Hamster Guide	*http://www.hamsters.co.uk/*
Hartz	*http://www.hartz.com/*
Healthy Pet	*http://www.healthypet.com/*
High Hopes for Pets	*http://www.highhopes4pets.com/*

Welcome to the site for dedicated pet owners and pet fans! This is the place to look when you need the latest info on pet diets, health care, fun and games. Enter our photo contest, ask our vet a question, check out our online catalogue or join Paws and Claws on their cyber adventures! There is plenty to do and see here so have fun and let us know what you think!

 You're in Good Hands

Company History
New Products
Guestbook

I Love My Pet	*http://www.ilovemypet.com/*
Iams	*http://www.iams.com/*
In Memory of Pets	*http://www.in-memory-of-pets.com/*
Kingsnake	*http://www.kingsnake.com/*

Pet Net	*http://www.pet-net.net/*
Pet of the Day	*http://www.petoftheday.com/*
Pet Planet	*http://www.petplanet.co.uk/*
Pet Quarters	*http://www.petquarters.com/*
Pet Shelter	*http://www.petshelter.org/*
Pet Station	*http://www.petstation.com/*
Pet Store	*http://www.petstore.com/*
Pet Unlimited	*http://www.petsunlimited.com/*
Pet Vacations	*http://www.petvacations.com/*

Pet's Pyjamas	*http://www.petspyjamas.com/*
Petfinder	*http://www.petfinder.org/*

Petmarket	*http://www.petmarket.com/*
Petopia	*http://www.petopia.com/*
Petplan	*http://www.petplan.co.uk/*
Pets and People	*http://www.petsandpeople.com/*
Pets in Need	*http://www.petsinneed.org/*
Pets Part of the Family	*http://www.petspartofthefamily.com/*

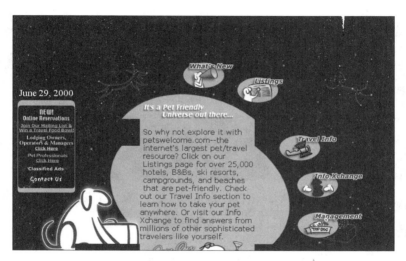

Pets Welcome	*http://www.petswelcome.com/*
Pets.com	*http://www.pets.com/*
Petsmart	*http://www.petsmart.com/*
Petz	*http://www.petz.co.uk/*
Poozle Animus	*http://www.poozleanimus.com/*
Power Paws	*http://www.powerpaws.com/*

SFB	*http://www.sfb.com/*
That Pet Place	*http://www.thatpetplace.com/*
The Pet Channel	*http://www.thepetchannel.com/*
Travel Pets	*http://www.travelpets.com/*

These sites deal specifically in one particular type of animal:

Birds

Birds n Ways Guide to Parrots & Exotic Pet Birds

Complete Guide to Pet Birds, Pet Parrots & Exotic Birds

**Birds n Ways for pet parrots, exotic birds, birds supplies
& pet bird information. Your complete guide to
pet parrots & exotic birds on the NET!**

**Finches, budgies, conures, amazons, african greys, cockatoos,
macaws, lovebirds, lories, parrots, cockatiels, parakeets,
parrotlets, pionus, eclectus, senegals, meyers, etc**

Birds 'N' Ways	*http://www.birdsnways.com/*
Fanciers	*http://www.fanciers.com/*
FC Aviary	*http://www.fcaviary.com/*
Parrot Parrot	*http://www.parrotparrot.com/*

Parrot Sanctuary	*http://www.parrot-sanctuary.org/*
Parrots and Company	*http://www.parrotsandcompany.com/*
Pet Parrot	*http://www.petparrot.com/*
Quaket Parrots	*http://www.quakerparrots.com/*

Cats

Cats	*http://www.cats.org/*
Cat Care Society	*http://www.catcaresociety.org/*
Cat Claws	*http://www.catclaws.com/*

The Cat Company™ & Veterinary HouseCalls for Cats

The Cat Company offers a unique approach to a total care system for you and your cat. Because we specialize in cats only, we can provide a more focused experience of the joy of living with a feline friend.

Cat Company, The	*http://www.thecatcompany.com/*
Cat Faeries	*http://www.catfaeries.com/*
Cats and Kittens	*http://www.catsandkittens.com/*
Cats and Rabbits and more	*http://www.catsandrabbitsandmore.com/*

Cats Magazine	*http://www.catsmag.com/*
Cat Treasures	*http://www.cattreasures.com/*
Cute Cats	*http://www.cutecats.com/*

Dreamcats	*http://www.dreamcats.com/*
Feral Cat	*http://www.feralcat.com/*
I Love Cats	*http://www.i-love-cats.com/*

Dogs
| A Dog Net | *http://www.adognet.com/* |
| Aaarf | *http://www.aaarf.org/* |

| Canismajor | *http://www.canismajor.com/* |

Digital Dog

Home

Dog Tales

Breeding

Behavior

Our Trainer

Dedicated to teaching everyone about "The Dog Within Us"

Welcome to the new Digital Dog site. This month marks our fifth anniversary and we want to thank you, our dog-loving audience, for your support, comments and contributions over these past five years. We will continue with dog training, dog breeds, dog adoption and dog stories as well as expanding the breed sections to allow for more user contributions (especially when you disagree with our comments).

A new service we have just added is a customized printing service that features a wide array of <u>customizable products</u> to celebrate your dog. Whether you want a

Current Features

<u>Rudi, a new story from</u>
Charles Ruckstuhl

<u>Letters to the Dog</u>
<u>Dog Stories</u>
<u>Old Ottis - one family's greatest dog</u>
<u>Adopting from an Animal Shelter-A Rags to Riches Tale</u>
<u>Mixed Breeds</u>
<u>Dog Rescue Drives</u>

Digital Dog	*http://www.digitaldog.com/*
Dog Breed Info	*http://www.dogbreedinfo.com/*
Dog.com	*http://www.dog.com/*
Dog Info	*http://www.doginfo.com/*
Dog-On-It	*http://www.dog-on-it.com/*
Dog Play	*http://www.dog-play.com/*
Dog Pro	*http://www.dogpro.com/*
Dogs Top	*http://www.dogstop.com/*
Dogs Friend	*http://www.dogsfriend.com/*
Dog World Magazine	*http://www.dogworldmag.com/*
Dog Zone	*http://www.dogzone.com/*
i-Dog	*http://www.i-dog.com/*

Infodog	*http://www.infodog.com/*
Pugs	*http://www.pugs.com/*
Sled Dog	*http://www.sleddogcentral.com/*
Travel Dog	*http://www.traveldog.com/*
Woofs - magazine	*http://www.woofs.org/*

 WorkingDogWeb©

Working Dog   *http://www.workingdogweb.com/*

Welcome to WorldClassDogs.com!
Our goal is to provide in-depth information, entertaining
features, and unique products and services of interes
dog enthusiasts the world over.

The Day of the Basset!

Click here to
join our online
Breeder Directory.
It's fast, easy and free!

J. Alfred Prufrock revisited.

World Class Dogs   *http://www.worldclassdogs.com/*

Fish

Evolve Fish   *http://www.evolvefish.com/*
Fishlink Central   *http://www.fishlinkcentral.com/*

FishTalk   *http://www.fishtalk.com/*
Pet Fish   *http://www.petfish.com/*

Rabbits

Bunny Luv   *http://www.bunnyluv.com/*
Cats and Rabbits and more   *http://www.catsandrabbitsandmore
.com/*

House Rabbit	*http://www.houserabbit.org/*
Rabbit	*http://www.rabbit.org/*
Rabbit	*http://www.rabbits.com/*

HOUSE RABBIT SOCIETY

June 29, 2000

House Rabbit Society is an all-volunteer, non-profit organization that <u>rescues</u> rabbits and educates the public on rabbit <u>care</u>.

First Time Visitor?
We've put together <u>FAQs</u> on all the important areas including <u>litter-training</u>, <u>diet</u>, <u>housing</u>, <u>chewing</u>, and <u>aggression</u>.

What's New?
Fun: <u>A Random Bunny Picture</u>
Medical Alert: <u>Problems Reported With Topical Flea Products</u>
Tip of the Month: <u>Annual Checkup</u>
<u>Sign up</u> to be notified of site and journal updates.
True or False? A baby rabbit is called a kit.   (<u>answer</u>)

Wild Bunnies May Not Need Your Help!
Wild rabbits only nurse for 5 minutes during the night, and moms vanish the rest of the day. Lookout for nests when mowing or gardening. If you've disturbed a nest, put the babies back, restore the fur/grass covering and leave them alone. The mother will move them over the next 48 hours. <u>More info...</u>

Most Popular Articles
<u>Spaying & Neutering</u>, <u>Article Index</u>, <u>Mail Order Sources</u>, <u>Cute Quotes & Pictures</u>, <u>Medical Concerns</u>, <u>Toys</u>, <u>Recommended Vets</u>.

Read a Good Book Lately?
Hop on over to the <u>rabbit reading room</u> for reviews and recommendations. You can even purchase titles online.

The HRS Adoption and Education Center
This summer, House Rabbit Society will open an <u>adoption and education center</u> in the San Francisco Bay Area. <u>We need your support!</u> Please <u>join</u> today and <u>get involved</u> in our rescue and education efforts.

| Rabbit Web | *http://www.rabbitweb.net/* |
| Show Bunny | *http://www.showbunny.com/* |

Recruitment

Searching for a job can be a sole-destroying activity. The Internet can speed things up by allowing you to search for specific types of jobs.

1 Jobs	*http://www.1-jobs.com/*
100s Au Pairs	*http://www.100s-aupairs.co.uk/*
Antal International	*http://www.antal-int.com/*
APN Development Training	*http://www.apn.co.uk/*
Aupairs	*http://www.aupairs.co.uk/*

Big Blue Dog   *http://www.bigbluedog.com/*

Brainbench.com	*http://www.brainbench.com/*
Brassring	*http://www.brassring.com/*
BUNAC	*http://www.bunac.org.uk/*
Byron	*http://www.byron.com.au/*
Career Builder	*http://www.careerbuilder.com/*
Career Connections	*http://www.career.com/*
Career Exchange	*http://www.careerexchange.com/*
Career Magazine Online	*http://www.careermag.com/*

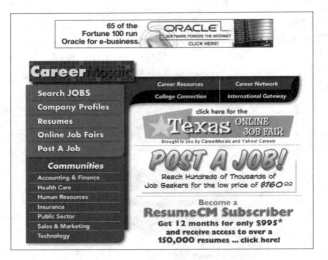

Career Mosaic	*http://www.careermosaic.com/*
Career Path	*http://www.careerpath.com/*
Careerlab.com	*http://www.careerlab.com/*
College Graduate Job Hunter	*http://www.collegegrad.com/*

Computer Jobs.com	*http://www.computerjobs.com/*
Cool Works	*http://www.coolworks.com/*
CT International	*http://www.aupairetc.co.uk/*
CV Search	*http://www.cvsearch.net/*
DICE	*http://www.dice.com/*
E-mum	*http://www.e-mum.com/*

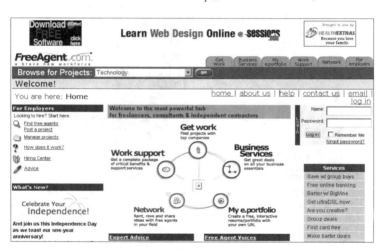

Free agent.com	*http://www.freeagent.com/*
Freetimejobs.com	*http://www.freetimejobs.com/*
Guru.com	*http://www.guru.com/*
Head Hunter	*http://www.headhunter.net/*
Hot Jobs	*http://www.hotjobs.com/*
Job Options	*http://www.joboptions.com/*
Job.com	*http://www.job.com/*

Jobasia.com	http://www.jobasia.com/
JobDirect	http://www.jobdirect.com
Jobs at HP	http://www.jobs.hp.com/

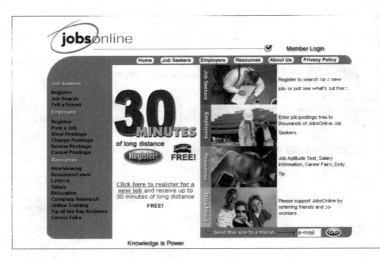

Jobs Online	http://www.jobsonline.com/
Jobs UK	http://www.topjobs.net/
Jobs.com	http://www.jobs.com/
Jobsdb.com	http://www.jobsdb.com/
Jobsearch	http://www.jobsearch.gov.au/
JobServe	http://www.jobserve.com/
JobTrak	http://www.jobtrak.com/
JobWeb	http://www.jobweb.com/
London Careers	http://www.londoncareers.net/

| Manpower | *http://www.manpower.com/* |
| Monster.com | *http://www.monster.com/* |

My Career	*http://www.mycareer.com.au/*
Nation Job Online	*http://www.nationjob.com/*
Net-temps	*http://www.net-temps.com/*
New Scientist Jobs.com	*http://www.newscientistjobs.com/*
Overseas Jobs Web	*http://www.overseasjobs.com/*
People Bank	*http://www.peoplebank.co.uk/*
Planet Recruit.com	*http://www.planetrecruit.com/*
Recruitability	*http://www.recruitability.com/*
Reed	*http://www.reed.co.uk/*
Retail Careers	*http://www.retailcareers.co.uk/*

| Seek | *http://www.seek.com.au/* |
| Six Figure Income | *http://www.sixfigureincome.com/* |

Summer Jobs	*http://www.summerjobs.com/*
Talent 2000	*http://www.bbc.co.uk/education/lzone/*
	talent2000/index.shtml
Techies.com	*http://www.techies.com/*
Top Jobs	*http://www.topjobs.net/*
Total Jobs	*http://www.totaljobs.com/*
UK Recruiters	*http://www.nmib.com/*
Vault.com	*http://www.vault.com/*
Wet Feet	*http://www.wetfeet.com/*

Reference

The Internet is a tremendous source of information about anything and everything. Because of the powerful search features, information can be located very quickly.

Encyclopedia

I can't imagine there's much that the average person would want to know that isn't here.

Bartleby.com   *http://www.bartleby.com/65*

Comptons Home Library   *http://www.comptons.com/*

Conflict World Encyclopedia   *http://www.emulateme.com/*
Encarta Online   *http://encarta.msn.com/*
Encyberpedia   *http://www.encyberpedia.com/*

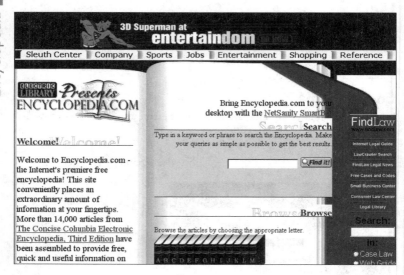

Encyclopedia   *http://www.encyclopedia.com/*
Encyclopedia Britannica   *http://www.britannica.com/*
Encyclopedia Britannica Online   *http://www.eb.com*
Encyclopedia Smithsonian   *http://www.si.edu/resource/faq/*
     start.htm

EncycloZine   *http://encyclozine.com/*
Expert Central   *http://www.expertcentral.com/*
FAQ Finder   *http://ps.superb.net/faq/main.shtml*

Free Internet Encyclopedia	*http://www.clever.net/cam/ encyclopedia.html*
Free Online Encyclopedia	*http://www.theinfosphere.com/*
Funk and Wagnalls	*http://www.funkandwagnalls.com/*
Grup Encyclopedia Catalana	*http://www.grec.net/home/grec/ english/index.htm*
Nolos Legal Encyclopedia	*http://www.nolo.com/briefs.html*
Nupedia	*http://www.nupedia.com/*
The Archive of Useless Facts and Trivia	*http://www.funtrivia.com/trivia.html*
Virtual Encyclopedia	*http://www.abp1.com/1getsmrt/ index.html*

World Book	*http://www.worldbookonline.com/*

General Knowledge

More information can be gleaned from these dictionaries, atlases and other sites of knowledge.

A Man's Life   *http://www.manslife.com/*
Acronyms   *http://www.acronymfinder.com/*
American Medical Association   *http://www.ama-assn.org/*
Big Book   *http://www.bigbook.com/*

Biography Online   *http://www.biography.com/*
City.Net   *http://www.city.net/*
City Search   *http://www.citysearch.com/*
Dictionary   *http://www.dictionary.com/*
Ditto   *http://www.ditto.com/*

eHow	*http://www.ehow.com/*
Electric Library	*http://www.elibrary.com/*
Flags	*http://www.fotw.net/flags*
Four11	*http://www.four11.com/*
Funk and Wagnall	*http://www.funkandwagnalls.com/*
Getty Thesaurus	*http://shiva.pub.getty.edu/tgn_browser*
Grammar	*http://www.edunet.com/english/ grammar*
Grove Dictionary of Art	*http://www.groveart.com/*

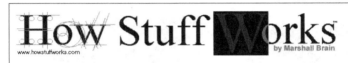

Search How Stuff Works

Enter 1 or 2 Keywords

Search | Instructions

Win a Free T-Shirt!

The HSW Registration System lets you sign up for the free HSW newsletter, control how often

Welcome to How Stuff Works!

Have you ever wondered how the engine in your car works or what makes the inside of your refrigerator cold? Then **How Stuff Works** is the place for you! Click on the categories below to see hundreds of cool articles!

How Fireworks Work!

Fireworks -- especially the aerial kind -- are incredibly popular around the 4th of July in the U.S. -- Click here to learn exactly how fireworks work, and also to see a great field guide to

Check These Out!

· Question of the Day!
· Huge Question Archive!
· Link of the Day!
· Link Archive!
· Book of the Day!
· Book Archive!
· Survey Archive!
· News Archive!
· Super Useful Links!
· Amazing Factory Tours!
· The BIG List!

How Stuff Works	*http://www.howstuffworks.com/*

Internet FAQs	*http://www.faqs.org/*
Learn 2	*http://www.learn2.com/*
Look Smart	*http://www.looksmart.com/*
Map Quest	*http://www.mapquest.com/*
Merrium-Webster	*http://www.m-w.com/*
Mythology	*http://www.pantheon.org/mythica*
NASA	*http://www.nasa.gov/*
National Geographic	*http://www.nationalgeographic.com/*
One Look Dictionary	*http://www.onelook.com/*
Scholastic Network	*http://www.scholastic.com/*

Scientific American	*http://www.sciam.com/*

The Why Files	*http://whyfiles.news.wisc.edu/*
Thomas:Legislation Info on the Internet	*http://thomas.loc.gov/*
World CIA Factbook	*http://www.odci.gov/cia/publications/factbook*
World of Flags	*http://www.flagwire.com/*

Libraries

If you want a book for reference, use a library.

British Library	*http://www.bl.uk/*
Library of Congress	*http://www.loc.gov/*
New York Public library	*http://www.nypl.org/*

Finding Out

There is a great deal of information which can be tracked down on the Internet, from train times to the whereabouts of your local plumber.

Allexperts.com	*http://www.allexperts.com/*
Info Please	*http://www.infoplease.com/*
Post Office Counters Ltd	*http://www.postoffice-counters.co.uk/*
Railtrack: Travel Information	*http://www.railtrack.co.uk/travel*
Scoot	*http://www.scoot.co.uk/*
TheTrainline.com	*http://www.thetrainline.com/*
The Weather Channel	*http://www.weather.com/*
The Yellow Pages (UK)	*http://www.yell.co.uk/*
The Yellow Pages (US)	*http://www.yell.com/*
Timetables	*http://www.rail.co.uk/ukrail/planner/planner.htm*

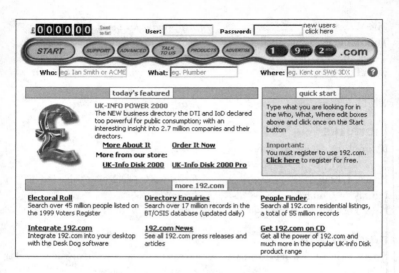

UK Directory Enquiries   *http://www.192.com/*
UK Public Transport Information   *http://www.pti.org.uk/*

Maps

If you want to find out where you are, or where you'd like to be, use the Internet to look it up. Just about every square inch of the planet is covered.

Absolute Authority on Cartography   *http://www.absoluteauthority.com/
                                      cartography*
Amazing Picture Machine   *http://www.ncrtec.org/picture.htm*
Artique   *http://www.articque.com/*
Atlantic Ocean   *http://geography.miningco.com/library/
                                      maps/blatlantic.htm*

Atlapedia Online   *http://www.atlapedia.com/*
Atlas of the World   *http://cliffie.nosc.mil/~natlas/*
Carta-Graphics   *http://www.carta-graphics.com/*

For Cartesia Software's line of digital maps used in graphic design follow the links below:

For MapArt Publishing's line of maps, quides, and software follow the links below:

CARTESIA

MAPArt.

(map resources)

Cartesia Software

Publishes a line of digital maps for use in graphic design. It is now marketed under the brand name Map Resources.

MapArt Publishing

Canada's largest map publisher, sets coast-to-coast quality benchmarks with its best-selling maps, guides, and software.

Cartesia MapResources   *http://www.map-art.com/*
Cartographic Resources   *http://130.166.124.2/cart.html*
Clover Point Cartographics   *http://www.cloverpoint.com/*
Creative Force Inc   *http://www.creativeforceinc.com/*
Cyber Atlas   *http://www.cyberatlas.com/*
DeLorme   *http://www.delorme.com/*
Digital Cartographics   *http://www.digitalcarto.com/*
Digital Cartography   *http://www.digiatlas.com/ang*

Digital City   *http://home.digitalcity.com/maps/*
Digital Data Services   *http://ddsllc.com/gis.htm*
Digital Wisdom   *http://www.digital-wisdom.org/*
Dreamline Cartography   *http://pw2.netcom.com/~animated/*
                                               main.html
Earth Resources Observation   *http://edcwww.cr.usgs.gov/*
    Systems

The Electronic Map Library

Department of Geography
CALIFORNIA STATE UNIVERSITY, NORTHRIDGE

The Electronic Map Library includes a series of atlases currently being produced by individual
authors or project groups. The majority of these volumes are being frequently enlarged and
modified in response to the changing instructional needs of the Department of Geography.
Questions and comments should be directed to the authors, who will respond by email as their
other commitments allow. Individual maps are most commonly stored in GIF format. In some
cases, EPS and TIFF images are also archived. Those wishing to download and otherwise
manipulate individual files should honor copyright restrictions and the wishes of the authors.

- **United States Atlas**   - **New York City Atlas**
- **California Atlas**   - **Seattle, Washington and Vicinity Atlas**
- **Los Angeles Region Atlas**   - **Washington D.C.Atlas**
- **San Francisco Bay Area Atlas**   - **Boston, Massachusetts Atlas**
- **San Diego, California Atlas**   - **Chicago and Cook County, Illinois Atlas**
- **Sacramento, California Atlas**   - **Honolulu and Oahu, Hawaii Atlas**

Electronic Map Library   *http://130.166.124.2/library.html*
ESRI   *http://www.esri.com/*
Eureka Cartography   *http://www.maps-eureka.com/*
Freelance Cartography   *http://www.flcartography.com/*
Frog Heaven Maps   *http://www.frogheaven.com/*

GeoCommunity   *http://www.geocomm.com/*
GeoMapping   *http://www.geomapping.com/*
GeoPlace   *http://www.geoplace.net/*
Geoplaning   *http://www.geoplaning.com/*
Graphic Maps   *http://www.graphicmaps.com/aatlas/*
                                     world.htm
Great Globe Gallery   *http://main.amu.edu.pl/~zbzw/glob/*
                                     glob1.htm
Imagemaps from Wildgoose   *http://www.imagemapuk.com/*
International Cartographic   *http://www.geog.psu.edu/ica/*
   Association   *icavis.html*
International Map Trade   *http://maptrade.org/*
   Association
KennKart Digital Mapping   *http://www3.sympatico.ca/kennkart*
Kingfisher Maps and Charts   *http://www.kfmaps.com/*
Location Maps   *http://www.finders-uk.co.uk/*
Map History and Cartography   *http://mypage.bluewin.ch/duerst/*
Map Machine   *http://www.nationalgeographic.com/*
                                     maps/
Map World   *http://www.mapworld.com/*
Mapcraft Custom Cartography   *http://www.mapcraft.com/*
MapFinder   *http://maps-online.net/*
MapHist Discussion Group   *http://www.maphist.nl/*
MapMart   *http://www.mapmart.com/*
MapQuest!   *http://www.mapquest.com/*
Maps of the Solar System   *http://maps.jpl.nasa.gov/*
Maps of the States   *http://welcome.to/states_maps*
Maps.com   *http://www.maps.com/*

Mercator's World	*http://www.mercatormag.com/*
National Geographic Society	*http://www.nationalgeographic.com/*
National Imagery and Mapping Agency	*http://www.nima.mil/*
NewsMaps	*http://www.newsmaps.com/*
Quick Maps	*http://www.theodora.com/maps/ abc_world_maps.html*
Rustbelt Cartography	*http://www.rustbelt.com/*
Scale Finder	*http://www.onthelimit.freeuk.com/*
Solid Terrain Modeling	*http://www.solidterrainmodeling.com/*
Spellex Geographical Dictionary Software	*http://www.spellex.com/geo1.htm*
Streetmap UK	*http://www.streetmap.co.uk/*

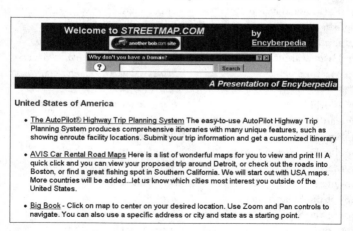

Streetmap USA   *http://www.streetmap.com/*

Survair	*http://www.laseroptronix.com/geo/ survair/survairinshort.html*
Tercomp	*http://www.tercomp.it/*
TerraServer	*http://www.terraserver.com/*
U.S. Geological Survey	*http://www.usgs.gov/*
United States Army Corps of Engineers	*http://www.usace.army.mil/*
USGS National Mapping Information	*http://mapping.usgs.gov/*
Versamap Digital Mapping	*http://www.versamap.com/*
Washington Map Society	*http://users.supernet.com/pages/ jdocktor/washmap.htm*

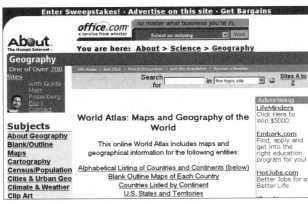

World Atlas	*http://geography.about.com/library/ maps/blindex.htm*
World Atlas	*http://www.sitesatlas.com/atlas/polatlas/ polatlas.htm*

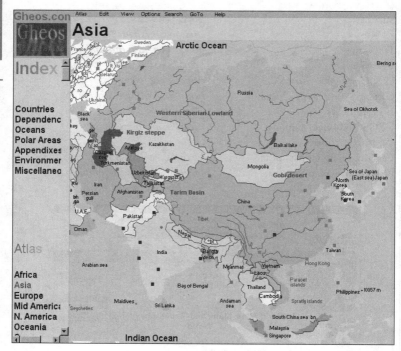

World Atlas 2000	*http://thedeejays.com/atlas*
World Maps for Web Sites	*http://www.theodora.com/maps/new2/more_world_maps.html*
World Maps from Map Marketing	*http://www.mapmarketing.com/indexse.asp*
Xerox PARC MapWeb Server	*http://mapweb.xerox.com/*

Shopping

There are thousands of shopping sites on the Internet which allow you to choose a product and then pay for it online.

Auctions

Selling and buying at an auction is great fun, I'm assured. Using an Internet auction is just as much fun and you can bid across the world. Some auction sites actually own the stock themselves whilst others are merely brokers for third parties to sell.

Able Auctions	*http://www.ableauctions.com/*
Adventurebid	*http://www.adventurebid.com/*
Afternic	*http://www.afternic.com/*
Allegro Auction	*http://www.allegro.com.sg/*
AltaVista	*http://auction.shopping.com/*
Amazon Auctions	*http://www.amazon.com/*
Antiquorum	*http://www.antiquorum.com/*
Aucland	*http://www.aucland.co.uk/*
Auction Addict	*http://www.auctionaddict.com/*
Auction Classifieds	*http://www.cityauction.com/*
Auction Depot	*http://www.auctiondepot.com/*
Auction Guide	*http://www.auctionguide.com/*
Auction HK	*http://www.auctionhk.com/*
Auction Hunter	*http://www.auctionhunter.com/*

Auction IT   *http://www.auction-it.net/*
Auction Port   *http://www.auctionport.com/*

Auction Sales   *http://www.auction-sales.com/*

Auction Watch	*http://www.auctionwatch.com/*
Auction World	*http://www.a-world.com/*
Auctionet	*http://www.auctionet.com/*
Auction-Land	*http://www.auction-land.com/*
Auctionrover	*http://www.auctionrover.com/*
Auctions.com	*http://www.auctions.com/*
Auctiontrader	*http://www.auctiontrader.com.au/*
Auction-Warehouse	*http://www.auction-warehouse.com/*
B Squared Coins	*http://www.stratamar.com/bsquared/*
Bestads	*http://www.bestads.com/*
Bid 4 It	*http://www.bid4it.com/*

Bid Bonanza	*http://www.bidbonanza.com/*

Bid Now	http://www.bidnow.com/
Bid.com	http://www.bid.com/
BidAway	http://www.bidaway.com/
Bidder Suite	http://www.biddersuite.com/
Biddington's	http://www.biddingtons.com/
Bidhit	http://www.bidhit.com/
Bidn4it	http://www.bidn4it.com/
Blasfer	http://www.blasfer.com/
Blue Cycle	http://www.bluecycle.com/
Boston.com	http://auctions.boston.com/
Boxlot Auction	http://www.boxlot.com/
Bullnet online auctions	http://www.bullnet.co.uk/auctions/
Buy Bid Win	http://www.buybidwin.com/

Buy it	*http://www.buyit.com/*
CDSeek	*http://www.cdseek.com/*
Click-a-Bid	*http://www.clickabid.com/*
Collecting Nation	*http://www.collectingnation.com/*
Deal Deal	*http://www.dealdeal.com/*
DealerNet.com	*http://www.dealernet.com/*
Dupont Registry	*http://www.dupontregistry.com/*
e Hammer	*http://www.ehammer.com/*
Easy Auction	*http://www.easyauction.com/*

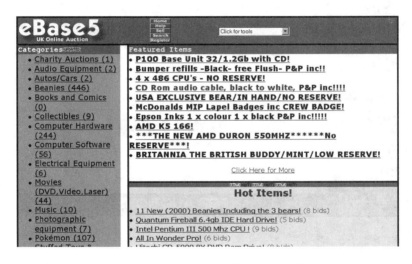

eBase5	*http://www.ebase5.com/*
eBay	*http://www.ebay.com/*
eBid	*http://www.ebid.co.uk/*

eGuide2000	*http://www.eguide2000.com/*
Elance	*http://www.elance.com/*
EP	*http://www.ep.com/*
Excite Auctions	*http://auctions.excite.com/*

EZ bid	*http://www.ezbid.com/*
Free Forum	*http://www.freeforum.com/*
Freemarkets	*http://www.freemarkets.com/*
Gavelnet	*http://www.gavelnet.com/*
Gibson	*http://www.gibson.com/*

GM bid	*http://www.gmbid.com/*
Go Ricardo	*http://www.goricardo.com/*
Goldsauction	*http://www.goldsauction.com/*
Grupo Control	*http://www.grupocontrol.com/*
GunBroker	*http://www.gunbroker.com/*
Heffel.com	*http://www.heffel.com/*

Heritage Coin	*http://www.heritagecoin.com/*

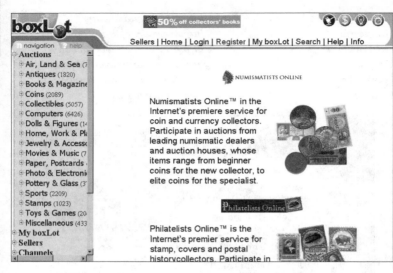

Hobby Markets	*http://www.hobbymarkets.com/*
Holiday Auctions	*http://www.holidayauctions.net/*
Honesty	*http://www.honesty.com/*
iCollector	*http://www.icollector.com/*
iCollector	*http://www.icollector.co.uk/*
Imandi	*http://www.imandi.com/*
Infinite Horizon	*http://www.infinitehorizon.com/auctions.htm*
Interactive Auction Online	*http://www.iaoauction.com/*
Internet Auction List	*http://www.internetauctionlist.com/*
Jewelnet Auctions	*http://www.jewelnetauctions.com/*

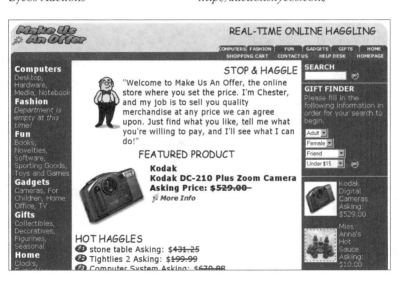

Nationwide Equine Auction	*http://www.equineauction.com/*
Net Auction	*http://www.netauction.com/*
Onsale Auction Supersite	*http://www.onsale.com/*
Polar Auctions	*http://www.polarauctions.com/*
Pottery Auction	*http://www.potteryauction.com/*
Prints	*http://www.prints.com/*
QXL	*http://www.qxl.com/*

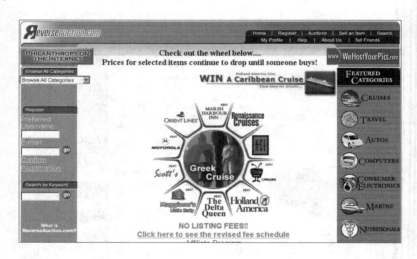

ReverseAuction.com	*http://www.reverseauction.com/*
Rocket8	*http://www.rocket8.com/*
Rotman Auction	*http://www.rotmanauction.com/*
Sell and Trade	*http://www.sellandtrade.com/*
Shopnow	*http://www.shopnow.com/*

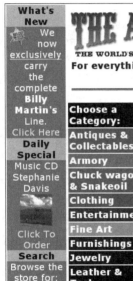

THE WORLD'S LARGEST WESTERN MERCHANDISE SITE
For everything from early 1800's through the Hollywood West.

Auction
Postcards
Weather
Movies
Radio

What's New
We now *exclusively* carry the complete **Billy Martin's** Line. Click Here

Daily Special
Music CD Stephanie Davis

Click To Order

Search
Browse the store for:

Choose a Category:
Antiques & Collectables
Armory
Chuck wagon & Snakeoil
Clothing
Entertainment
Fine Art
Furnishings
Jewelry
Leather & Tack

Welcome to TheAmericanWest.Com.

You can search the store at the left, or browse by category.

We pride ourselves on bringing quality western merchandise to the web. Everything from replica badges, to a fully functional stage coach. We carry a vast amount of items including: Holsters, Saddles, Native American Jewelry, Boots, Spurs, Shirts, Vests, and more! Plus name brands you're familiar with: Stetson, Wah-Maker, Buffalo Runner, Resistol, Four Winds and more. If you have something western in mind and you can't find it, please feel free to contact us.

Trade Me	*http://www.trademe.co.nz/*
Travel Auction	*http://www.travelbreak.com/ostrbr.html*
Travelbids	*http://www.travelbids.com/*
U Auction it	*http://www.uauction.com/*
U Bid 4 it	*http://www.ubid4it.com/*
U Bid Online Auction	*http://www.ubid.com/*
Up 4 Sale	*http://www.up4sale.com/*
URU link	*http://www.urulink.com/*
Webswap	*http://www.webswap.com/*
What the heck is that	*http://www.whattheheckisthat.com/*
WhatAmIBid Online Auctions	*http://www.whatamibid.com/*
Wine Bid	*http://www.winebid.com/*
Yahoo auctions	*http://auctions.yahoo.com/*

ZDNet	*http://auctions.zdnet.com/*

Shopping Malls

A virtual shopping mall is designed to work in a similar way to a real shopping mall – the mall itself sells nothing, but houses stores which do.

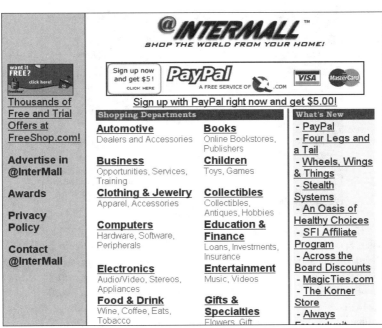

@InterMall   *http://iaswww.com/mall*
African-American Shopping Mall   *http://www.bnl.com/aasm/*
All-Internet Shopping Directory   *http://www.all-internet.com/*
Antique Alley   *http://bmark.com/aa*

Click here!

Welcome to AsianMall...

... the ultimate online Asian shopping experience!

Japanimation novelties, the latest Hongkong movies, medicinal herbs, unique gifts from the Orient, delicious Asian food items, Taylor & Ng cookware, financial services, job agencies, and much much more!

Asian Mall	*http://www.asianmall.com/*
Classic England Shopping Mall	*http://www.classicengland.co.uk/*
Clothesnet.Com	*http://www.clothesnet.com/*
Cowboy Mall	*http://www.cowboymall.com/*
Ecomall	*http://www.ecomall.com/*
EduMart	*http://www.edumart.com/*
eSmarts	*http://www.esmarts.com/*
Fashion Mall	*http://www.fashionmall.com/*
Fisher Scientific	*http://www.fisher1.com/*
Hotnew.com	*http://www.hotnew.com/*

International Mall	*http://www.nativecreations.com/*
NetMarket	*http://www.netmarket.com/*
Planet Shopping Network	*http://www.planetshopping.com/*
SafeStreet Shopping Centre	*http://www.safestreet.co.uk/*
ShopGuide	*ttp://www.shopguide.com/*
ShopperConnection.com	*http://www.shopperconnection.com/*
Shopping Network	*http://www.planetshopping.com/*
Shopping.com	*http://www.shopping.com/ibuy*

SkyMall   *http://www.skymall.com/*

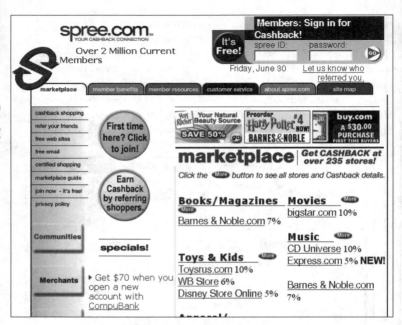

More Bargains

These sites offer a wide range of products and many of the goods are significantly lower than high street prices.

Alta Vista   *http://shopping.altavista.com/home.sdc*

Bigsave.com   *http://www.bigsave.com/*
British Shopping Links   *http://www.british-shopping.com/*
Consumer Gateway   *http://www.consumer.gov.uk/*
Egg Shopping   *http://shopping.egg.com/shopping*
Fish4 Online Shopping   *http://www.fish4.co.uk/category/*
                              shopping/
Freeserve – Shopping   *http://www.freeserve.com/shopping/*
Gus Home Shopping   *http://www.gus.co.uk/*

415

Homefree Shopping · *http://homefree.co.uk/*
LetsBuyIt.com · *http://www.letsbuyit.com/*
Online Shopping UK · *http://www.internetics.co.uk/shop/*

PriceWonders.com · *http://www.pricewonders.com/
main.asp*
Shop Guide · *http://www.shopguide.co.uk/*
Shop TV · *http://www.shop-tv.co.uk/*
Shop! · *http://www.shop-i.co.uk/*
Shopping Center.net · *http://www.shoppingcenter.net/*

Shopping from Yell	*http://www.shopyell.co.uk/*
Shopping On The Net	*http://www.shoppingonthenet.co.uk/*
Shopping Unlimited	*http://shoppingunlimited.co.uk/*
ShopSmart.com	*http://www.shopsmart.com/*
UK Online Shopping	*http://www.ukonlineshopping.com/*
UK Shopping City	*http://www.ukshops.co.uk/*
Virtual Store	*http://www.thevirtualstore.co.uk/*
WebMarket	*http://www.webmarket.com/*

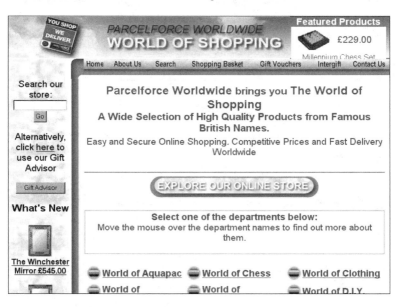

World of Shopping	*http://www.worldofshopping.com/*

Compare Prices

You can ensure you get the best deal by comparing prices.

Bottom Dollar   *http://www.bottomdollar.com/*

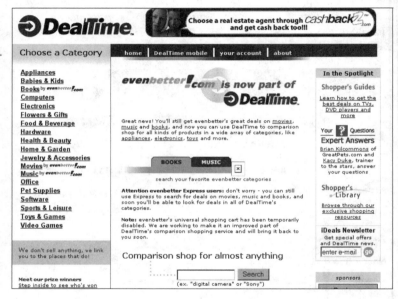

Deal Time   *http://www.dealtime.com/*
Price Checker   *http://www.pricechecker.co.uk/*
Price Offers   *http://www.priceoffers.co.uk/*
Price Scan   *http://www.pricescan.com/*
Shop Genie   *http://www.shopgenie.com/*

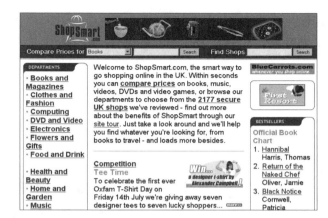

ShopSmart   http://www.shopsmart.com/

Smartshop   http://www.smartshop.com/

Consumer Advice

There are some rogue traders on the Internet, just as there are in everyday life. If you should fall foul of one, get some advice.

Online Shopping   *http://www.oft.gov.uk/html/shopping/*

WHICH@nline

What's New
Forums
Shopping ▶
Campaigns

Product Testing
Food and Drink
Gardening
Health
Holiday
Legal
Money
Motoring
Public Interest

Search the Site

Help
Sitemap
Homepage
Email this page

Shopping

Importing a car?
Visit **Carbusters**
for Internet car
savings from
Europe

Carbusters.com

Guaranteed low prices
for subscribers in our
Shopping Centre.

**Choose your
own best buy**
with **Product Picker**

PRODUCTpicker

**Shop online with
confidence** with over
650 **Which? Web
Traders**.

Buy Which? books

Free trial
CLICK HERE

Our **Online Shopping
Guide** looks at the tax,
legal and safety
implications of online
shopping.

Problems with your
online shopping? Use
**Which? Legal
Service** advice lines.

Tips and advice about
Internet shopping from
the **Office of Fair**

Which? – Shopping   *http://www.which.net/shopping/*
                                   contents.html

Special Occasions

We all have occasions which are special for one reason or another. The Internet can provide help for all special times.

Flowers

Sending flowers is a great way to demonstrate that you are thinking of someone, be it your Mum, spouse or 'friend'. Most of these sites will allow you to order online and specify where they are to be delivered. Some even offer a reminder service which will automatically email you to remind you of an approaching occassion for which flowers would be deemed highly appropriate.

101 Flowers   *http://www.101flowers.net/*

1-800 Flowers   *http://www.1800flowers.com/*

1-800 I Love You	*http://www.800iloveyou.com/*
1-800-SendMaui	*http://www.sendmaui.com/*
4Florist	*http://www.4florist.com/*
4Flowers	*http://www.4flowers.com/*
911Florist	*http://www.911florist.com/*
Axelrod and Bennet	*http://www.flowers-florist.com/*

Bamboo Green Florist	*http://www.bambooflorist.com.my/*
Beautiful Bouquet Florist	*http://www.beautifulbouquet.com/*
BestFlowers.com	*http://www.bestflowers.com/*
Brecka's Floral and Gifts Company	*http://www.breckasfloral.com/*
Calyx and Corolla	*http://www.calyxandcorolla.com/*

Cyberflowers	*http://www.cyberflowers.com/*
Expressions In Bloom	*http://www.teleflora-flowers.com/*
Find Flowers	*http://www.findflowers.com/*
Floral Alliance	*http://www.floralalliance.com/*
Floresnaweb.com	*http://floresnaweb.com/*

Florist Directory	*http://www.florist-directory.com/*
Flower Korea	*http://www.flowerkorea.com/*
Flowerbud.com	*http://www.flowerbud.com/*
FlowerFocus.com	*http://www.flowerfocus.com/*
Flowers Etc	*http://www.ftd.com/flowers*

Flowers NZ	*http://www.downtown.co.nz/flowers-nz/international.shtml*
Flowers: The Shopping Guide	*http://shoppingguide.hypermart.net/flowers.html*
Flowers-4-You	*http://www.flowers-4-you.com/index1.htm*
Flower Web	*http://www.flowerweb.nl/*
Flower Wire	*http://www.flowerwire.com/*
Funeral Flowers	*http://www.funeralflowers.com/*
Great Flowers	*http://www.greatflowers.com/*
Interflora	*http://www.interflora.co.uk/*
Israel Flowers	*http://www.flowers.co.il/*
Lee Flower	*http://www.leeflower.com/*

My Flowers	*http://www.myflowers.com.sg/*

Wholesale Flowers   *http://www.sdflowers.com/*

Worldwide Florist   *http://worldwide-florist.com/*

Gifts

It's great to receive presents but it's even better to give. Except that it can take an inordinate amount of time to find and send a present.

Alternative Gift Company   *http://www.alt-gifts.com/*
Country Homes Collectables   *http://www.collectible-gifts.com/*
   & Gifts
Dial A Basket Gift Service   *http://www.heartphelt.co.uk/*
Dome Shopping   *http://www.shopping.dome2000.co.uk/*

EasyJet Gifts   *http://www.easyjetgifts.com/*
Gift Box   *http://www.gotogifts.co.uk/for/silver*
Gift Bureau Ideas and Information   *http://www.loud-n-clear.com/gifts*

The Gift Delivery Co. Ltd

"The Gift Delivery Company" is here to make the art of giving as easy and personal as possible. Please **ENTER** our **SECURE** webstore to make your gift giving even easier.

enter here

We have a varied and ever changing selection of gifts for all occasions. Each item will be individually gift wrapped free of charge and your message hand-written on a card and sent to the recipient or to you, to give to the recipient personally.

We provide a free reminder service which means never again will you forget that special day.

Freephone: 08 0800 GIFTS (08 0800 44387)
Tel: +44 (0)1483 267577
Fax: +44 (0)171 681 2619
Email address info@giftdeliveryco.com

24 Smithbrook
Kilns,
Cranleigh
Surrey, GU6 8JJ
United Kingdom

Gift Delivery   *http://www.city2000.com/giftdelivery*
Gift Delivery Company   *http://www.giftdeliveryco.com/*
Gift Ideas   *http://www.gotogifts.co.uk/*
Gift Selection Online   *http://www.giftselection.co.uk/*
Gift Time   *http://www.gifttime.co.uk/*
Goldfoiled Promotion Gifts   *http://www.lifestyle.demon.co.uk/gold*
Goodies – Gifts for all Occasions *http://www.interdart.co.uk/goodies*
Internet Gift Store   *http://www.internetgiftstore.com/*
Kaven – Essentials for Women   *http://www.gifts-for-women.co.uk/*

Lastminute.com Love Gifts	*http://www.lastminute.com/lmn/ lmn_valentines_lover.asp*
MacGillivrays Scottish Gifts	*http://www.freeshop.co.uk/front/ macgillivray*
More Gifts	*http://www.more-gifts.co.uk/*
Owl Barn Gift Catalogue	*http://www.the-owl-barn.com/*
Promark Business Gifts	*http://www.promark.demon.co.uk/*
Quality Gifts	*http://www.quality-gifts.co.uk/*
R & D Gifts & Woodcraft	*http://www.gotogifts.co.uk/for/ woodcrafts*

Scottish Gifts	*http://www.scotch-corner.co.uk/*

Sherlock Holmes Gift Shop	*http://www.sherlockholmes.meteor.co.uk/*
Shop for Gifts	*http://msn.co.uk/page/14-134.asp*
Star Names	*http://www.starnames.co.uk/*
Stork Express Baby Gifts	*http://www.storkexpress.co.uk/*
Tartan Gift	*http://www.tartangift.co.uk/*
Thorntons Online Store	*http://www.thorntons.co.uk/*

Valentine's Day

The day that lovers remember each other seems to take more and more planning each year.

Amore' on the Net
  Valentines Day

http://www.holidays.net/amore

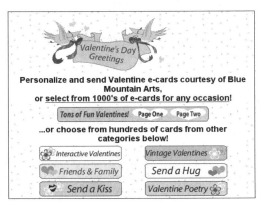

Blue Mountain Valentines

http://www1.bluemountain.com/eng/valentine

Confetti Valentines	*http://www.confetti.co.uk/valentines/default.asp*
Egreetings – Who do you love?	*http://www.egreetings.com/*
Epicurious – Valentine's Day	*http://epicurious.com/e_eating/e04_valentine/valentine.html*
Lastminute.com Love Gifts	*http://www.lastminute.com/lmn/lmn_valentines_lover.asp*
Love Is All You Need	*http://msn.co.uk/page/11-210.asp*
Lovingyou.com's Valentine's Day Guide	*http://holidays.lovingyou.com/february*
Remember Valentine's Day	*http://orders.mkn.co.uk/valentin/.en*
Sugarplums	*http://www.w2.com/docs2/act/food/sugarplums/holidays.html*
Valentine's Day Links	*http://orders.mkn.co.uk/valentin/links.en*
Valentine's Love Messages	*http://www.123greetings.com/events/valentinesday*
Valentines.com	*http://www.valentines.com/*

Weddings

The day when two people publicly declare their commitment to each other needs to go without a hitch. Whether it be advice, presents, etiquette or hiring the dress, the Internet can help.

Absolutely Wedding Crackers	*http://mkn.co.uk/help/cracker/wedding*
Accent Bridal Accessories	*http://www.directproducts.com/accent*
Advantage Discount Bridal	*http://www.advantagebridal.com/*
BestBridesmaid.com	*http://www.bestbridesmaid.com/*

Bridal Creations	*http://www.bridalcreations.com/*
Bridal Info	*http://www.bridalinfo.co.uk/*
Bridal Marketplace	*http://www.bridalmarketplace.com/*
Bridemaids.com	*http://www.bridesmaids.com/*
Chris Peake Wedding Stationery	*http://www.weddingstationery*
	.freeserve.co.uk/

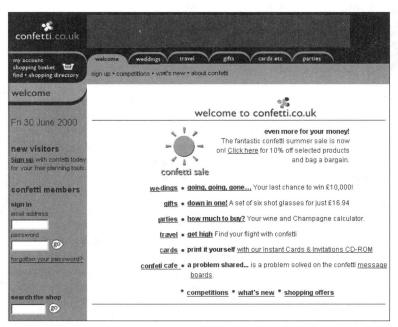

Confetti   *http://www.confetti.co.uk/*

Demetrios Wedding Gowns	*http://www.weddingguide.co.uk/demetrios.html*
Distinctive Designs	*http://ajs.weddingdirectory.co.uk/*
Guild of Wedding Photographers	*http://www.gwp-uk.co.uk/*
Planning Your Wedding	*http://members.tripod.com/pollyc/wedding.html*
Romance and Valentino	*http://www.msn.co.uk/page/13-104.asp*
Web Wedding	*http://www.webwedding.co.uk/*
Wedding Belles	*http://www.wedding-belles.co.uk/*
Wedding City	*http://www.wedding-city.co.uk/*
Wedding Design Studio	*http://www.weddingdesignstudio.co.uk/*
Wedding Gift List Manager	*http://www.servcon.co.uk/*
Wedding Guide UK	*http://www.weddingguide.co.uk/*
Wedding Information Service	*http://www.wedding.demon.co.uk/*
Wedding Pages	*http://www.wedding-pages.co.uk/*
Wedding Present	*http://www.westnet.com/weddoes/*
Wedding Services	*http://www.wedding-services.demon.co.uk/*
Wedding Stationery	*http://www.wedding-stationery.com/*
Wedding-day.co.uk	*http://www.wedding-day.co.uk/*
Weddings & Brides (UK)	*http://www.weddings-and-brides.co.uk/*
Weddings in Scotland by Sheena	*http://dialspace.dial.pipex.com/town/avenue/zn69*
Wedding Jokes	*http://www.weddingjokes.com/*
Weddings UK	*http://www.weddings.co.uk/*

Sport

Sport is probably the most popular free-time pursuit. For every sport you can think off, and most of those you can't, there are dozens of websites produced by both the governing body and by supporters.

Assorted Sports

Most of these sites comment on sport in general although some are dedicated to a specific sport.

AFL   *http://www.afl.com.au/*

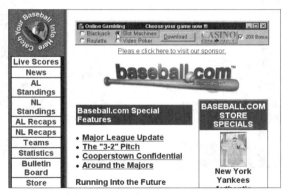

Baseball   *http://www.baseball.com/*

Canoe	*http://www.canoe.ca/*
CBS SportsLine	*http://www.sportsline.com/*
CNN – Sports Illustrated	*http://www.cnnsi.com/*
ESPN.com	*http://espn.sportszone.com/*
Fast Ball	*http://www.fastball.smallworld.com/*
Fogdog	*http://www.fogdog.com/*
Fox Sports	*http://www.foxsports.com/*
Headbone	*http://www.headbone.com/*

LiveScore	*http://www.livescore.com/*
Major League Baseball	*http://www.majorleaguebaseball.com/*

NBA.com	*http://www.nba.com/*
NFL.com	*http://www.nfl.com/*
Sandbox	*http://www.sandbox.com/*
Small World Sports	*http://sports.smallworld.com/*
Sporting Life	*http://www.sporting-life.com/*
Sports	*http://www.sports.com/*
Sportstalk	*http://www.sportstalk.com/*
That's Racin'	*http://www.thatsracin.com/*

The Mountain Zone   *http://www.mountainzone.com/*

The Sporting News   *http://www.sportingnews.com/*

The Sports Network   *http://www.sportsnetwork.com/*

Times Mirror Interzines   *http://www.tminterzines.com/*

Extreme Sports

For some people, gentle sports like tiddlewinks is not enough. They need to go bungie-jumping or free-falling out of an aeroplane at 10,000ft with a surfboard.

Adrenalin Sports   *http://www.adren-a-line.com/*

Adventure Time Magazine   *http://www.adventuretime.com/*

Break the Limits   *http://student.hivolda.no/brandan/*
                                       sport.htm

Classic Ski Tours   *http://www.classicskitours.com/*

Gravity Games   *http://www.gravitygames.com/*

Gravity Graphics	*http://gravitygraphics.com/*
Motocross	*http://www.motocross.com/*
Mountain Zone	*http://www.mountainzone.com/ski/*
MX World	*http://www.mxworld.com/docs/*
New Zealand Boarder Zone	*http://www.boarderzone.co.nz/*
Off-Road	*http://www.off-road.com/*

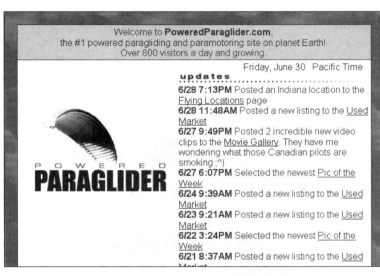

Welcome to **PoweredParaglider.com**,
the #1 powered paragliding and paramotoring site on planet Earth!
Over 800 visitors a day and growing.

Friday, June 30 Pacific Time

updates

6/28 7:13PM Posted an Indiana location to the Flying Locations page

6/28 11:48AM Posted a new listing to the Used Market

6/27 9:49PM Posted 2 incredible new video clips to the Movie Gallery. They have me wondering what those Canadian pilots are smoking ;^)

6/27 6:07PM Selected the newest Pic of the Week

6/24 9:39AM Posted a new listing to the Used Market

6/23 9:21AM Posted a new listing to the Used Market

6/22 3:24PM Selected the newest Pic of the Week

6/21 8:37AM Posted a new listing to the Used Market

POWERED
PARAGLIDER

Paraglider	*http://www.poweredparaglider.com/*
Pirates of the Rubicon 4WD Club	*http://www.pirate4x4.com/*
Radical Motor Sport	*http://www.radicalms.co.uk/*
Sierra Rock Crawlers	*http://www.sierrarockcrawlers.com/*
Ski Central	*http://skicentral.com/*

Top Rusty Surfboards	*http://www.rusty.com/*
Top Skateboard Science	*http://www.exploratorium.edu/ skateboarding/*
Top Snowboarding Online	*http://www.twsnow.com/*
Wake World	*http://www.wakeworld.com/*
Xtreme Scene	*http://www.xtremescene.com/*

Cricket

There are two sides – one's in the clubhouse, the other's out in the field. The side that's in is out, and the side that's out are trying to get all those in, out. Very confusing.

| CricInfo | *http://www.cricket.org/* |
| Cricket Direct | *http://www.cricketdirect.co.uk/* |

| Cricket Unlimited | *http://www.cricketunlimited.co.uk/* |

Cricket World Monthly	*http://www.cricketworld.com/*
Cricketer International	*http://www.cricketer.co.uk/asp/ homepage.asp*
Express Sport Live	*http://cricket.express-sport.co.uk/*
Lord's – English & Welsh Cricket Board	*http://www.lords.org/*
Sky Sports – Cricket	*http://www.sky.co.uk/sports/cricket/*
Sporting Life – Cricket	*http://www.sporting-life.com/cricket/ news/*
Women's Cricket Association	*http://users.ox.ac.uk/~beth/wca.htm*

Equestrian

This is all about trying to steer a horse around a course, of course.

Latest News

Ti Papa Winter Series coming soon!

We have set dates for our Winter Show Jumping series, sponsored by Stirrups Equestrian Supplies and HR Fisken & Sons Ltd. Entries close Tuesday prior to the day, and late entries will only be accepted subject to available space. Check out our new pages that give conditions of the series, the entry form, and the great prizes up for grabs.

Auckland Show Jumping Group	*http://www.auckland.jumper.com/*

British Show Jumping Association	*http://www.bsja.co.uk/*
eQuestrian	*http://equest.remus.com/*
Jump! Magazine	*http://jumpmagazine.com/*
Olympia Show Jumping Championships	*http://www.olympia-show-jumping.co.uk/*
Olympic Games Equestrian Three Day	*http://www.orbital.co.za/olympic/eqsttred.htm*
Show Jumping	*http://www.expage.com/page/sj*
The Equestrian Times	*http://www.horsenews.com/live/showjump.htm*
UAE Equestrian and Racing Federation	*http://www.smartvision.ch/uae/*
Welcome to Equiweb.co.uk	*http://www.equiweb.co.uk/*

Football

Bill Shankley once said, "Some people think football is a matter of life and death. They're wrong, it's much more important than that." 'Nuff said.

BBC Online – Football	*http://www.bbc.co.uk/sport/football/*
Daily Soccer	*http://www.dailysoccer.com/*
English Football Association	*http://www.the-fa.org/*
FIFA.com	*http://www.fifa.com*
Football	*http://www.football.smallworld.com/*
Football Supporters' Assoc.	*http://www.fsa.org.uk/*
Football Unlimited	*http://www.footballunlimited.co.uk/*
Football365	*http://www.football365.co.uk/*
FootballNews	*http://www.footballnews.co.uk/*
Professional Footballers Assoc.	*http://www.thepfa.co.uk/*

Sky Sports – Football	*http://www.sky.co.uk/sports/football*
Soccernet	*http://www.soccernet.com/*
Sportal	*http://www.sportal.co.uk/*

The Football League	*http://www.football-league.co.uk/*
UAFA	*http://www.uefa.com/*

Formula 1

Isn't it ironic that Formula 1 motor races, with enormously fast and powerful cars, are frequently decided when the cars are in the pits, stationary and on jacks!

Atlas F1	*http://www.atlasf1.com/*
Autosport	*http://www.autosport.com/*
Daily F1	*http://www.DailyF1.com/*
Express Sport Live – Formula One	*http://formula1.express-sport.com/*

F1 Live	*http://www.f1-live.com/GB*
F1 Merchandise	*http://www.f1merchandise.co.uk/*
F1 Online	*http://www.f1online.de/international*

F1 Picture Net	*http://www.f1picturenet.com/*
F1 Racing	*http://www.f1racing.co.uk/*
F1 Instinct	*http://www.f1-instinct.com/*
Formula 1.co.uk	*http://www.formula-1.co.uk/*
Formula 1.com	*http://www.formula1.com/*
Formula 1 World	*http://www.formulaoneworld.co.uk/*
Formula One Supporters Association	*http://www.fosa.org/*
Gale Force F1	*http://www.galeforcef1.com/*

Grand Prix History	*http://www.ddavid.com/formula1*
ITV – Formula One	*http://www.itv-f1.com/*
Jordan F1	*http://www.jordangp.com/*

McLaren Magazine	*http://www.mclaren.co.uk/*
Mercedes-Benz	*http://www.mercedes-benz.com/e/ msports/formula1*
Sky Sports – Formula One	*http://www.sky.co.uk/sports/center/ formula1.htm*
Sporting Life – Formula One	*http://www.sporting-life.com/ formula1/news/*
Web – F1	*http://www.web-f1.com/agfa.html*

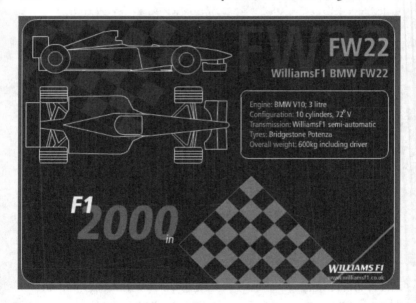

Williams F1	*http://www.williamsf1.co.uk/*

Golf

A good walk spoiled, until you reach the 19th hole, that is.

English Golf Union	*http://www.englishgolfunion.org/*
Express Sport Live	*http://golf.express-sport.co.uk/*
Golf History	*http://www.golf-historian.co.uk/*
Golf Reservations	*http://www.golf-reservations.co.uk/*
Golf Today	*http://www.golftoday.co.uk/*

Golf UK	*http://www.golfzone.co.uk/*
Golf.com	*http://www.golf.com/*
Golf Web	*http://www.golfweb.com/*
PGA.com	*http://www.pga.com/*
Scottish Golf	*http://www.scottishgolf.com/*
Slazenger Golf UK	*http://www.slazengergolf.co.uk/*
Sporting Life – Golf	*http://www.sporting-life.com/golf/ news/*
UK Golf	*http://www.uk-golf.com/*

Motor Sport

If it's got more than one wheel, you can bet there is a race somewhere for it.

About.com – Auto Racing   *http://autoracing.about.com/*
Best in British Motor Sport   *http://www.btcc.co.uk/*
CART   *http://www.cart.com/*
CBS SportsLine – Auto Racing   *http://www.sportsline.com/u/racing/
                                       auto/*
CNN/SI – Motor Sports   *http://www.cnnsi.com/motorsports*
FIA   *http://www.fia.com/*
Grassroots Motorsports   *http://www.grmotorsports.com/*
Motor Sports Association   *http://www.ukmotorsport.com/racmsa*
Motorsport News International   *http://www.motorsport.com/*

MotorSports (Bikes)   *http://www.sportbikes.net/*

Motorsports Weekly Online	*http://www.motorsportsweekly.com/*
NASCAR Online	*http://www.nascar.com/*

NHRA Online	*http://www.nhra.com/*
North American Motorsports Pages	*http://www.na-motorsports.com/*
Race Net International Motorsports	*http://www.nerc.com/~pcs/racenet.html*
Race Net International Motorsports	*http://www.tao.com/racenet.html*
Rally Zone	*http://www.rallyzone.co.uk/*
RSAC – Motor Sport	*http://www.motorsport.co.uk/rsacms.html*
The Score! – Motor Sport	*http://www.topgear.beeb.com/news/news_on_wheels_frameset.html*
UK Motor Sport Index	*http://www.ukmotorsport.com/*

Rugby

This very popular European game is played by 22 men with odd-shaped balls.

Allied Dunbar Premiership Rugby	*http://www.rugbyclub.co.uk/*
International Rugby Board	*http://www.irfb.com/*
ITV Rugby World Cup	*http://www.itv-rugby.co.uk/*
Planet Rugby	*http://www.planetrugby.co.uk/*
Rugby Football Union	*http://www.rfu.com/nf_frm.html*

Rugby Heaven	*http://www.rugbyheaven.com/*
Rugby Leaguer	*http://www.rugbyleaguer.co.uk/*
Rugby Network	*http://jjpayne.co.uk/rugbynet/*
Rugby News	*http://www.rugbynews.net/*
Scrum.com	*http://www.scrum.com/*
Sporting Life – Rugby League	*http://www.sporting-life.com/rleague/news/*
Sporting Life – Rugby Union	*http://www.sporting-life.com/rugby/news/*
The Score!	*http://www.thescore.beeb.com/*

Snooker

At one stage during the 1980's it seemed that snooker was on every night. You could watch a few frames in one tournament, change channels and see the same players in a different tournament.

Australian Billiards & Snooker	*http://www.billsnook.com.au/*
Embassy World Snooker Championship	*http://www.embassysnooker.com/*

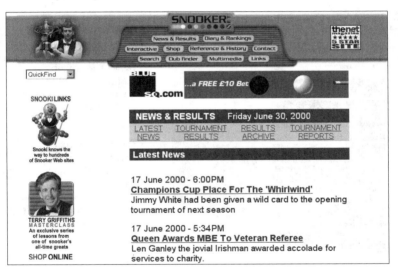

Snookernet	*http://www.snookernet.com/*
WWW Snooker	*http://www.ifi.uio.no/~hermunda/ Snooker/*

Table Tennis

It's always worth seeing the Chinese national team playing Ping-Pong. Do they still throw the ball into the rafters when they serve and hold the bat upside down?

British Olympic Association –
Table Tennis
Table Tennis

*http://www.olympics.org.uk/
tabletennis.htm*
http://tabletennis.about.com/

Table Tennis – USA
WorldSport.com – Table Tennis

http://www.usatt.org/
*http://looksmart.remarq.com/
discussions/C0909*

Tennis

Not to be confused with Real Tennis, this version of bat 'n' ball has a huge following and some very skillful players who hand rocket the ball at frightning speeds.

ATP Tour Tennis Online	*http://www.atptour.com/*
British Olympic Association – Tennis	*http://www.olympics.org.uk/ tennis.htm*
International Tennis Federation	*http://www.itftennis.com/ fl_index.html*
Lawn Tennis Association	*http://www.lta.org.uk/lta.htm*

Royal Tennis Court	*http://www.realtennis.gbrit.com/*

Sky Sports – Tennis	*http://www.sky.co.uk/sports/tennis/*
Sporting Life – Tennis	*http://www.sporting-life.com/tennis/news/*
Tennis Net	*http://www.btinternet.com/~tennis.net/*
Tennis Org UK	*http://www.tennis.org.uk/*
Tennis Wales	*http://www.tennis.wales.org/*
Tennis Worldwide Chat	*http://www.tennisw.com/chat.html*

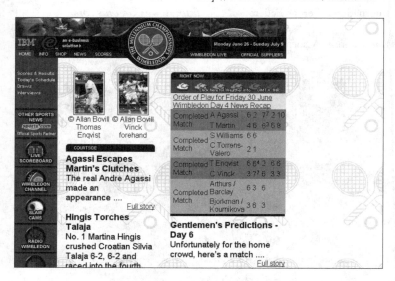

Wimbledon.com	*http://www.wimbledon.com/*
Worldsport.com – Tennis	*http://www.sportlive.com/ws/allsports/home/*

Wrestling

Once the preserve of the Saturday afternoon TV sports show, the participants never seemed to have much regard for the rules, and the referee didn't seem to be able to do much about it. Now it's undergone a re-birth, there seems even less regard for rules and absolutely no consideration to fair play.

BAWA   *http://www.homeusers.prestel.co.uk/*
                                          bawa/

British Internet Wrestling   *http://members.xoom.com/biwf*
    Federation UK

British Wrestling   *http://www.britishwrestling.cwc.net/*

Technology

During the last 50 years there has been a headlong rush of new sophisticated technology that previously couldn't even have been dreamed about. What is more incredible is that this technology is affordable by almost everyone.

Cameras and Photography

I've never owned a good camera other than a digital one. The reason is that when I embark on something new I like to do it wholly. That would mean a darkroom, developing equipment and all the paraphernalia that goes with it. I've never had the space to get into that. One day maybe.

1st Cameras   *http://www.1stcameras.co.uk/*

20-20Consumer	*http://www.20-20consumer.com/*
4 Cameras	*http://www.4cameras.com/*
888-camcorder	*http://www.888camcorder.com/*
AAA Camera	*http://www.aaacamera.com/*
AAAnet	*http://www.aaanet-inc.com/*

Abbey Camera	*http://abbeycamera.com/*
Abe's Of Maine	*http://www.abesofmaine.com/*
Abes Camera and Video	*http://www.abescamera.com/*
Abolins Inc	*http://www.abolins.com/*
Access Cameras and Film	*http://www.123-cameras.com/*
Access Discount Camera	*http://www.accesscamera.com/*
Adolph Gasser Inc	*http://www.gassers.com/*

Adorama Camera	*http://www.adorama.net/*
Albany Photographic Center	*http://www.albanyphoto.com/*
Amazing Holga	*http://www.holgacamera.com/*
Apex Photo	*http://www.apexphoto.net/*
Apogee Photography Guide	*http://www.apogeephoto.com/*

Art's Cameras Plus	*http://www.artscamera.com/*
B&H Photo-Video-Pro Audio	*http://www.bhphotovideo.com/*
Ball Photo Supply	*http://www.ballphoto.com/*
Beach Camera	*http://beachcamera.com/*
Beach Photo and Video	*http://beachphoto.com/*
Bel Air Camera	*http://www.belaircam.com/*
Bender Photographic Inc	*http://www.benderphoto.com/*

Best Photo Video	*http://www.bestphotovideo.com/*
Bob Davis Camera	*http://www.bobdaviscamera.com/*
Bridge Net	*http://www.bridgenet.com.tw/*
Broadway Camera	*http://www.broadwaycamera.com/*
Bromwell Marketing	*http://www.bromwell.com/*
Buy with a Group	*http://www.buywithagroup.com/*

Calumet Photographic	*http://www.calumetphoto.com/*
Cambridge Camera Exchange	*http://www.cambridgeworld.com/*
Camera Barn	*http://www.camerabarn.com/*
Camera Corner	*http://www.camcor.com/*
Camera Craft Shop Online	*http://www.cameracraft.com/*
Camera Depot	*http://www.cameradepot.co.uk/*

Camera Direct	*http://www.camera-direct.com/*
Camera House	*http://www.camerahouse.com.au/*
Camera People	*http://www.camerapeople.net/*
Camera Sphere	*http://www.camerasphere.com/*
Camera Store	*http://www.camerastore.com.au/*
Camera Store	*http://www.thecamerastore.net/*

Cameras Brookwood	*http://www.camerasbrookwood.com/*
Cameras Direct	*http://www.camerasdirect.co.uk/*
Cameras Plus	*http://www.camerasplus.com/*
Cameraworld.com	*http://www.cameraworld.com/*
Cannon Camera Center	*http://www.mall21.com/camera*
Charlotte Camera	*http://charlottecamera.com/*

CoCam Photo	*http://www.cocam.co.uk/*
Community Camera Center	*http://www.communitycamera.com/*
D.L. Accents	*http://www.dlaccents.com/*
Dale Photographic Services	*http://www.dalephotographic.co.uk/*
Dan's Camera City	*http://www.danscamera.com/*
Digital Distributors	*http://www.digitaletc.com/*
Discount Camera	*http://www.discountcamera.com/*
E.P.Levine Inc	*http://www.cameras.com/*
Eaglecameraone.com	*http://www.eaglecameraone.com/*
Euro Foto Centre	*http://www.euro-foto.com/*
European Camera Specialists	*http://sites.netscape.net/eurocameras/*
F/Stop Camera Corporation	*http://www.f-stopcamera.com/*
Ffordes Photographic Ltd	*http://www.ffordes.co.uk/*
Fife Foto Centre	*http://www.fifefotocentre.co.uk/*
Flashcube	*http://www.flashcube.com/*
Ginfax Development Limited	*http://www.ginfax.com/*
Glazer's Camera Supply	*http://www.glazerscamera.com/*
Goodwin Photo Inc	*http://www.goodwinphotoinc.com/*
Harry Pro Shop	*http://harrysproshop.com/*
Harvard Camera	*http://www.harvardcamera.com/*
Hawaiian Camera Supply	*http://www.hassy.com/*
Henrys Cameras and Electronics	*http://www.henrys.com/*
Igor's Camera Exchange	*http://www.igorcamera.com/*
JCR Cameras	*http://www.jcr-cameras.com/*
Jens Madsen Cameras and Imaging	*http://www.madsens.com.au/*
Jessops	*http://www.jessops.com/*
Karl Heitz Service	*http://www.karlheitz.com/*
Kenmore Camera	*http://www.kcamera.com/*

Leica Store   *http://www.theleicastore.com/*
Lotts Photo   *http://www.lottsphoto.com/*
LR Mansley Ltd   *http://www.camera-centre.co.uk/*
Lumière Shop   *http://www.fotolaborgeraete.de/*
Main Street .   *http://www.ashlandcamera.com/*

CAMERAS
QUALITY USED
PHOTOGRAPHIC EQUIPMENT
BUY · SELL · TRADE

DICK McRILL
EUGENE, OR 97404

SLR 35 mm
Canon
  EOS Auto Focus
  Manual-FD
Contax
Leica
Minolta
  Manual-MC &
  MD
  Maxxum Auto
  Focus
Nikon
  Manual &3 Auto
  Focus
Olympus

Be sure to bookmark our site. Our inventory changes daily so be sure to check often.

Specializing in exceptional quality used cameras and photographic equipment, 9.7 and above, from beginner to pro and collector. We listen first and then recommend the best equipment to meet your specific photographic needs within your budget. All brands, all formats, systems or just the hard to find items you need. Hundreds to choose from, all with

90 Day Warranty (except collectibles)

McRill's Cameras   *http://www.cameraguy.com/*
Morris Photographic Centre   *http://www.morrisphoto.co.uk/*
National Camera and Video   *http://www.nationalcamera.com/*
  Exchange
Northern Photographics   *http://www.northernphotographics
                                .com/*

Oakdale-Bohemia Camera Inc	*http://www.obcameras.com/*
Patience Photographic Co Ltd	*http://www.patience-photographic* *.co.uk/*
Photo Alley	*http://www.photoalley.com/*
Photo Factory	*http://www.photofactory.com.au/*
Photo Shopping Guide	*http://www.photomagazines.com/*
Photo Source	*http://www.mmphoto.com/*
Photoco	*http://www.photococan.com/*
Photographx Unlimited	*http://www.photographxunlimited* *.com/*
Photomall.com	*http://www.photomall.com/*

Photorama	*http://www.photorama.com/*

Photoshopper	*http://www.photoshopper.com/*
Porter's Camera Store	*http://www.porters.com/*
Precision Camera and Video	*http://www.precision-camera.com/*
Prime Direct	*http://www.primedirect.com/*
ProCam Online	*http://www.procam.com/*
Ritz Camera Centers	*http://www.ritzcamera.com/*
Roberts Imaging	*http://www.robertsimaging.com/*
Rockbrook Camera	*http://www.rockbrookcamera.com/ docs/*
Russian Camera Exchange	*http://www.gkweb.com/rcx/*
Studio Outlet	*http://www.studio-outlet.com/*
Sussex Camera Centre	*http://www.tradecameras.co.uk/*
Technik Camera	*http://www.technikcamera.com/*
Terry's Camera	*http://www.terryscamera.com/*
Thompson Photo Products	*http://www.thompsonphoto.com/*
Travel Guides for Photographers	*http://phototravel.com/*
UK Camera Shops	*http://www.ukcamera.co.uk/*
Unique Photo	*http://www.netphotostore.com/*
Unruh Photography Shop	*http://www.flashcube.com/*
Vistek	*http://www.vistek.net/*
Wall Street Camera	*http://www.wallstreetcamera.com/*
Walters Photo-Video	*http://www.photo-video.u-net.com/*
Warehouse Photographic	*http://www.warehousephoto.com/*
Wolf Camera	*http://www.wolfcamera.com/*
Wolfe's	*http://www.wolfes.com/*
WolfXpress	*http://www.wolfxpress.com/*
World Wide Camera	*http://www.worldwidecamera.com/*

Consumer Electronics

There is a bewildering array of HiFi, TV and VCR readily available from countless outlets. Use the Internet to compare different models before buying.

1 Cache	*http://www.1cache.com/*
1st Manufacturers Outlet	*http://www.1stmfroutlet.com/*
220 volt appliances	*http://www.astrointl.com/*
42 St. Photo	*http://www.42photo.com/*
4Electronics	*http://www.4electronics.com/*
800.com	*http://www.800.com/*
A Plus Digital	*http://www.aplusdigital.com/*

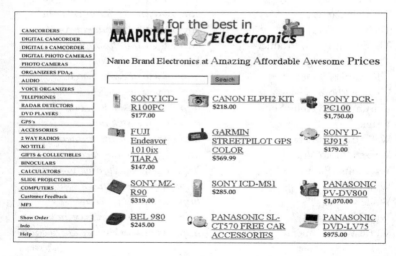

AAA price   *http://aaaprice.com/*

ABT Electronics	*http://www.abtelectronics.com/*
Access Electronics	*http://www.123-electronics.com/*
ALightning Audio Video	*http://www.lightav.com/*
Audio Warehouse Express	*http://www.audio-warehouse.com/*
Barrel of Monkeys	*http://www.barrel-of-monkeys.com/*
Best Buy Co Inc	*http://www.bestbuy.com/*
BestPriceAudioVideo.com	*http://www.bestpriceaudiovideo.com/*
Beststopdigital.com	*http://www.beststopdigital.com/*
Big Apple Company	*http://www.bigapplecompany.com/*
BlueLight.com	*http://store.bluelight.com/ electronics.html*

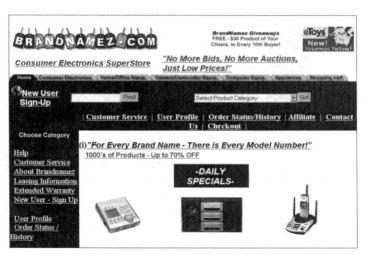

BrandNamez.com	*http://www.brandnamez.com/*

Creative.com	*http://www.hifi.com/*
Earthstations.com	*http://www.earthstations.com/*
Electro Buy	*http://www.1-800-electro.com/*
Electroland	*http://www.electroland.com/*

Electronic Explosion	*http://www.electronicexplosion.com/*
Electronic Express	*http://www.electronicexpress.com/*
Electronic Zone	*http://www.electronic-zone.com/*
Electronicaccessory.com	*http://www.electronicaccessory.com/*
Electronics Paradise	*http://www.electronicparadise.com/*
Electronics.net	*http://electronics.net/*
Electronics4Sale	*http://www.electronics4sale.com/*
Electronicsgallery.com	*http://www.electronicsgallery.com/*

Electro Shops	*http://www.electroshops.com/*
ESM	*http://www.e-s-m.com/*
eTown.com	*http://www.etown.com/*
Etronixs.com	*http://www.etronixs.com/*
Everyday Comfort	*http://www.everydaycomfort.com/*
e-Widgets.com	*http://www.e-widgets.com/*
Export Masters	*http://emcdepot.com/*
EZ Electronics	*http://www.ez.com/*
FINDIT	*http://www.finditanytime.com/*

Future Shop Canada   *http://www.futureshop.ca/*

G&G Electronics	*http://ggelectronics.com/*
Global Mart	*http://www.globe-mart.com/*
Goodguys	*http://www.thegoodguys.com/*

Goody Gadgets	*http://www.goodygadgets.com/*
Helpful Home Shopping Co	*http://www.helpful.co.uk/*
HiFi Buys	*http://www.hifibuys.com/*
HomeTicket.com	*http://www.hometicket.com/*
HTS Systems	*http://www.htssystems.com/*
IBS Electronics	*http://www.ibsstore.com/*
Internet Ontime.com	*http://www.internetontime.com/*
ItsoCool Products	*http://www.itsocool.com/*

J&R Music and Computer World	*http://www.jandr.com/*
Lee Electronics	*http://www.leeselect.com/*
LiquidPrice.com	*http://www.liquidprice.com/*
Luketech	*http://buy.at/luketech*
McNo Ltd	*http://www.mcno.com/*
MsMart.com	*http://www.msmart.com/*
MSN Guide	*http://national.sidewalk.msn.com/ buyersguide/electronics*
Netmarket	*http://www.netmarket.com/*
NextPurchase.Com	*http://www.nextpurchase.com/*
Nu-Visions Appliance Co.	*http://www.nu-visions.com/*
One Stop Home Technologies	*http://www.osht.com/*

| Pace Electronics | *http://www.paceworld.com/main.htm* |

Panasonic Family Dealer	*http://www.panwebi.com/*
PCseller.com	*http://www.pcseller.com/*
Photo Systems	*http://www.photo-systems.com/*
Planet3000	*http://www.planet3000.com/*
Primefocus.com	*http://www.primefocus.com/*
ProActive Electronics	*http://www.proactiveelectronics.com/*
QualityMark.net	*http://qualitymark.net/*
QVC	*http://www.qvc.com/*

Radio Shack	*http://www.radioshack.com/*
RCA	*http://www.rca.com/*
Sales Circular.com	*http://www.salescircular.com/*

The Video Doctor II	*http://www.thevideodoctor.com/*
Turbo Price	*http://www.turboprice.com/*
Tweeter etc.	*http://www.tweeter.com/*
Ugonet Photo and Electronics	*http://www.ugonet.com/*
Valco Electronics	*http://www.valcoelectronics.com/*
Wacko Deals	*http://www.wackodeals.com/*
Watchman Electronics Products	*http://www.watchmanproducts.com/*

Wholesale Connection	*http://www.wholesaleconnection.com/*
Wholesale Electronics	*http://www.electronicgear.com/*
Wholesale Products	*http://www.wholesaleproducts.com/*
Wireless Toys.com	*http://www.wirelesstoys.com/*
Worldwide Electronics	*http://www.welectronics.com/*

Mobile Phones

I'm not convinced that 90% of the people who own a mobile phone actually need one or even use one enough to justify its cost. Mobile phones are, in fact, little more than fashion accessories but why should I complain. The more people that buy them, the cheaper they become.

Access Telephones and Pagers   *http://www.123-phones.com/*

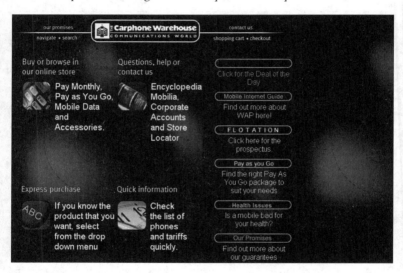

Carphone Warehouse   *http://www.carphonewarehouse.com/*
Ham Mall Amateur Radio   *http://www.hammall.com/*
Hello Direct.com   *http://www.hellodirect.com/*
Independent Technologies   *http://www.independenttech.com/*

Interzone UK	*http://www.interzone-uk.com/*
Just Call Me	*http://www.justcallme.com/*
Mobile Fun	*http://www.mobilefun.co.uk/*
Mobile Melodies	*http://www.mobile-melodies.com/*
Mobile Phone Store	*http://www.themobilephonestore.com/*
Mobiles Phones	*http://www.buy.co.uk/moneysm/ mobiles.asp*
Mobilize Now	*http://www.mobilizenow.com/*
National Cell Phone Rentals	*http://www.dwellings.com/cell*
Nokia	*http://www.nokia.com/*
Pocket Phone Shop	*http://www.pocketphone.co.uk/*
Phone Center	*http://www.aphone.com/*
Phonecity	*http://www.phonecity.co.uk/*
Phonethings.com	*http://www.phonethings.com/*
Point.com	*http://www.point.com/*
Polar Communications Ltd	*http://www.polarcommunications .com/*
Portable Concepts	*http://portableconcepts.com/*
Prime Page & Cellular	*http://primepage.net/*
Quantometrix	*http://www.quantometrix.com/ Ultim_Lis.htm*
Radios Plus.com	*http://radiosplus.com/*
Ringtones Direct	*http://www.ringtones-direct.com/*
Roy's Phones	*http://www.roysphones.com/*
SamsonWeb eStore	*http://www.samsonweb.com/estore*
Satellite Warehouse	*http://www.satphone.net/*
SaveOnCellular.com	*http://www.saveoncellular.com/*
Sezz	*http://www.sezz.at/*

Shop Cordless	*http://www.shopcordless.com/*
Shop Wireless	*http://www.shopwireless.com/*
Smart Hook	*http://www.singnet.com.sg/~smarthk*
Sundial.com	*http://www.sundial.com/*
SWS Communications	*http://www.swscommunications.com/*
TeleCell	*http://www.telecell.com/*

Telephone Superstore	*http://www.telephonesuperstore.com/*
The Phone Source	*http://www.thephonesource.com/*
The Pocket Phone Shop	*http://www.pocketphone.co.uk/*
Ultra Phones	*http://www.ultraphones.com/*
World of Wireless	*http://www.worldofwireless.com/*

Travel

The Internet is a great way to book travel and holiday accommodation.

Airlines

Every airline has a website and many will allow you to book flights online. Look out for special bargains and take note of airport information including departure and arrival times.

AB Airlines   *http://www.abairlines.com/*
Aces Columbia Airlines   *http://www.acescolombia.com/*
Aer Lingus   *http://www.aerlingus.ie/*

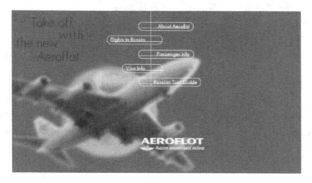

Aeroflot   *http://www.aeroflot.com/*

Aerolineas Argentinas	*http://www.aerolineas.com.ar/*
Air 2000	*http://www.air2000.co.uk/*
Air Atlanta Icelandic	*http://www.airatlanta.com/*
Air Baltic	*http://www.airbaltic.lv/*

Version française   **English version**

Air Caledonie	*http://www.air-caledonie.nc/*
Air Canada	*http://www.aircanada.ca/*
Air Caribbean	*http://www.sputnick.com/aircaribbean/*
Air Europa	*http://www.g-air-europa.es/linea-regular/*
Air Fiji	*http://airfiji.net/*
Air France	*http://www.airfrance.com/*
Air India	*http://www.airindia.com/*

Air Jamaica	*http://www.airjamaica.com/*
Air Macau	*http://www.airmacau.com.mo/*
Air Malta	*http://www.airmalta.com/*
Air Mauritius	*http://www.airmauritius.com/*

Air Moldova International	*http://www.ami.md/*
Air Nauru	*http://www.airnauru.com.au/*
Air New Zealand	*http://www.airnewzealand.co.nz/*
Air Niugini	*http://www.airniugini.com.pg/*
Air Philippines	*http://airphilippines.com/*
Aircalin	*http://www.aircalin.nc/*
Airlines of South Australia	*http://asa.mtx.net/*
Airlink	*http://www.airlink.com.pg/*

| Airtours | *http://www.airtours.com/* |
| Alaska Airlines & Horizon Air | *http://www.alaska-air.com/* |

Alitalia	*http://www.alitalia.it/*
All Nippon Airways	*http://www.ana.co.jp/index_e.html*
Aloha Air	*http://www.alohaair.com/*
America Trans Air (ATA)	*http://www.ata.com/*
American Airlines	*http://www.aa.com/*
American Airlines & American Eagle	*http://www.americanair.com/*
American World Airways	*http://welcome.to/ americanworldairways*
Ansett Australia	*http://www.ansett.com.au/*

Ansett New Zealand	*http://www.ansett.co.nz/*
Atlantic Airways	*http://www.atlantic.fo/*

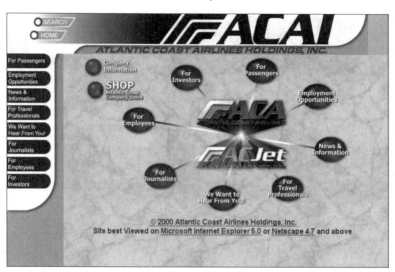

Atlantic Coast Airlines	*http://www.atlanticcoast.com/*
Austrian Airlines	*http://www.aua.com/*
Balkan Airlines	*http://www.balkan.com/*
Baltia Air Lines Inc	*http://www.iblf.com/baltia.htm*
Belau Air	*http://www.belauair.com/*
Britannia Airways	*http://www.britanniaairways.com/*
British Airways	*http://www.british-airways.com/*
British Midland	*http://www.iflybritishmidland.com/*
British Regional Airlines Limited	*http://www.british-regional.com/*

Canadian Airlines Intl. *http://www.cdnair.ca/*
Carnival Airlines *http://www.carnivalair.com/*

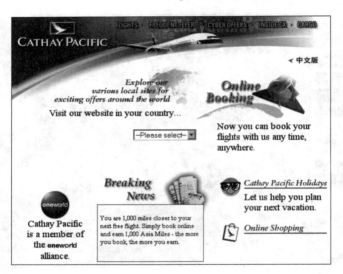

Cathay Pacific *http://www.cathaypacific-air.com/*
Cayman Airways *http://www.caymans.com/caymans/*
Cayman_Airways.html
China Airlines *http://www.china-airlines.com/*
Continental Airlines *http://www.continental.com/*
Cubana Air *http://www.cubana.cu/index.html*
Cyprus Airways *http://www.cyprusair.com.cy/*
Debonair Airways *http://www.debonair.co.uk/*
Delta Air Lines *http://www.delta-air.com/index.html*

Delta Express	*http://www.delta-air.com/express/index.html*
Dragon Air	*http://www.dragonair.com/*
EasyJet	*http://www.easyjet.com/*
Finnair	*http://www.finnair.com/*
First Air	*http://www.firstair.ca/*
Flight West Airlines	*http://www.fltwest.com.au/*
Go	*http://www.go-fly.com/*
Hawaiian Airlines	*http://www.hawaiianair.com/*

Iberia Airlines	*http://www.iberia.com/*
Icelandair	*http://www.icelandair.net/*

JAL Japan Airlines   *http://www.jal.co.jp/english/index_e.html*

JAT Yugoslav Airlines   *http://www.monarch-airlines.com/*

KLM UK   *http://www.klmuk.com/*

Korean Air   *http://www.koreanair.com/*

Lasca Airlines   *http://www.flylatinamerica.com/*

Lufthansa InfoFlyway   *http://www.lufthansa.co.uk/*

Malaysia Air   *http://www.malaysiaair.com/*

Manx Airlines   *http://www.manx-airlines.com/*

Mexicana Airlines   *http://www.mexicana.com/index.html*

Midway Airlines   *http://www.midwayair.com/*

Midwest Express Airlines	*http://www.midwestexpress.com/*
Monarch Airlines	*http://www.monarch-airlines.com/*
National Airlines	*http://www.nationalairlines.com/*
Necon Air	*http://www.neconair.com/necon/*

Welcome
to Olympic Airways' Web site

 Ελληνικά
ww2.olympic-airways.gr

TIMETABLE

ICARUS
Frequent Flyer

RESERVATIONS
 0801 - 444444
ONLY FOR CALLS

Flights
Inside OA
Passengers' Info
Programs &
Services
Press
Office/News
Contact us

Olympic Airways is pleased to see you and offer you its hospitality and service. As a successful airline we aim to please you and keep you flying with us.

We like to listen to what our customers say. That is why Olympic is spreading its wings. New services, new connections and new aircraft are all part of Olympic's effort to provide what our customers want.

Olympic Airways	*http://www.olympic-airways.gr/*
Orient Avia Airlines	*http://www.russia.net/home/orient/*
	index.html
Pacific Coastal Airlines	*http://www.pacific-coastal.com/*
Pacific Wings Hawaii	*http://www.pacificwings.com/*
Polynesian Airlines	*http://www.polynesianairlines.co.nz/*
Qantas Airlines	*http://www.qantas.com.au/*

Ryanair	*http://www.ryanair.ie/*
Sahara Airlines	*http://www.saharaairline.com/*
Scandanavian Airlines – SAS	*http://www.sas.se/*
Shuttle America	*http://www.shuttleamerica.com/*
Singapore Airlines	*http://www.singaporeair.com/*
Skyways	*http://www.skyways.se/*
Skywest Airlines	*http://www.skywest.com.au/*
Sobelair	*http://www.sobelair.com/*
Solomon Airlines	*http://www.solomonairlines.com.au/*
Southern Australia Airlines	*http://www.qantas.com.au/southern/ index.html*
Southwest Airlines	*http://www.iflyswa.com/*
Spanair	*http://www.spanair.com/*
Spirit Airlines	*http://www.spiritair.com/*
Star Airlines	*http://www.star-airlines.fr/*
Sunflower Airlines	*http://www.fiji.to/*
SwissAir	*http://www.swissair.com/*
SwissJet USA	*http://swissjet.com/*
Thai Airways International	*http://www.thaiair.com/*
Trans States Airlines	*http://www.transstates.net/*
TransBrasil	*http://www.transbrasil.com.br/*
Transmeridian Airlines	*http://www.transmeridian-airlines .com/*
TransWorld Airlines	*http://www.twa.com/*
Turkish Airlines	*http://www.turkishairlines.com/*
United Airlines	*http://www.ual.com/*
US Airways	*http://www.usairways.com/*
VARIG Airlines	*http://www.varig.com.br/*

VASP Airlines	*http://www.vasp.com.br/*
Virgin Atlantic Airways	*http://www.fly.virgin.com/*

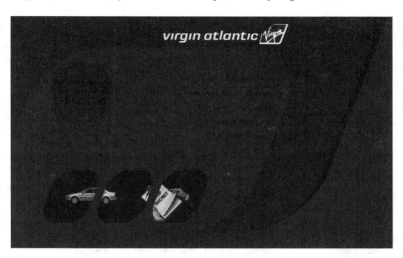

Virgin Atlantic UK	*http://www.virgin-atlantic.com/*
Volare Airlines	*http://www.volare-airlines.com/*
Vulcanair	*http://www.vulcanair.com/*
World Airways	*http://www.worldair.com/*
Yugoslav Airlines	*http://www.jat.com/*

Cheap/Late Flights

If you like booking at the last minute, or you just seem to end up booking at the last minute, try one of these sites to book a late flight. You can also book economy airfares through these sites.

Air Ticket Centre	*http://www.airticketcentre.co.uk/*
Bargain flights.com	*http://www.bargainflights.com/*
Bargain holidays.com	*http://www.bargainholidays.com/*

Cheap Flights	*http://www.cheapflights.co.uk/*
Deckchair.com	*http://www.deckchair.com/*
Discount Airfares	*http://www.etn.nl/discount*
Discount Holidays Flights	*http://www.dhf.co.uk/*
Flight Bookers	*http://www.flightbookers.co.uk/*
Flight Line	*http://www.flightline.co.uk/*
Last Minute	*http://www.lastminute.com/*
Netflights	*http://www.netflights.com/*
Web Holidays UK	*http://www.webholidays.co.uk/*

Boats

The alternative to an aeroplane is a boat, either a cruise liner or a ferry to get you across a particular stretch of water.

Adventuress River Cruises	*http://rivercruises.co.uk/*
Atlantis Cruising	*http://www.atlantistravel.co.uk/*
Chancery Cruising	*http://www.holborn-travel.co.uk/*

Cruise Holidays	*http://www.travelogue.co.uk/*
Cruise Transfers	*http://www.airport-transfers-uk.com/cruises.html*
Festival Cruises	*http://www.festival.gr/*
Fred Olsen Cruise Lines	*http://www.gbnet.co.uk/fred.olsen/*

Jacobite Cruises	*http://www.cali.co.uk/jacobite/*
Let's Cruise	*http://www.letscruise.co.uk/*
P&O Cruises	*http://www.pocruises.com/*
Peter Deilmann River Cruises	*http://www.european-waterways.co.uk/*
Royal Caribbean International	*http://www.rccl.com/1.0.3.html*
SeaView Cruise & Ferry Information	*http://www.seaview.co.uk/*

Swan Hellenic	*http://www.swan-hellenic.co.uk/*
The Cruise People	*http://members.aol.com/CruiseAZ*

Car Hire

Once you've arrived at your destination, you may need to book a car to enable you to explore further afield than the airport or ferry terminal.

Rates

Fleet

Reservation

Anniversary Specials

Los Angeles International Airport-LAX

This site has been created to help you learn about our Company and services we offer. You can find about our *Rate*. You will get information on our *Fleet*. You can easily get *Direction*, finally make a *Reservation* and avoid the hassle of looking for a car at Los Angeles International Airport (LAX).

For more Information call 1(800) 811-A-ONE or 1(310) 410-1414

Arriving at LAX, find our courtesy phone, near the baggage claim area/bulletin board.
Give us a call; we will pick you up.

 Info@aonerentacar.com

A One Rent-A-Car	*http://www.aonerentacar.com/*
Ace Rent-A-Car	*http://www.acerentacar.com/*
Advantage Rent-A-Car	*http://www.arac.com/*
Arriva Vehicle Rental	*http://www.cowie.co.uk/*
Autolease Rent-a-Car	*http://www.autolease-uae.com/*
Automotive Resources International	*http://www.arifleet.com/*
AutoNet International	*http://www.autonet-intl.com/*
Avcar Rental	*http://www.avcar.com/*
Avis Rent A Car	*http://www.avis.com/*
Beverly Hills Rent-A-Car	*http://www.bhrentacar.com/*

BreezeNet's Rental Car Guide — *http://www.bnm.com/miam.htm*
British Car Rental — *http://www.bcvr.co.uk/*
British Vehicle Rental & Leasing — *http://www.bvrla.co.uk/indextxt.html*

Crete Car Hire — *http://www.kalithea.demon.co.uk/*
Dollaro Express Rent-A-Car — *http://www.dollaroexpress.it/*
Eagle Rent A Car — *http://www.eagle-rent-a-car.com/*
Enterprise Rent-A-Car Co. — *http://www.pickenterprise.com/*
Eurodrive Car Rental — *http://www.eurodrive.com/*
Europa Rent-A-Car — *http://www.intercom.es/eurorent*
Europcar — *http://www.europcar.com/*

Eurostyle	*http://www.eurostyle.uk.com/*
Excellent Car Rental	*http://www.arweb.com/excellent*
Heiser Auto Group	*http://www.heiser.com/*

Hertz Rent A Car	*http://www.hertz.com/*
Holiday Cars Direct	*http://www.holidaycarsdirect.com/*
Kemwel Holiday Autos	*http://www.kemwel.com/*
Lowestfare.com	*http://www.lowestfare.com/*
Malone Car Rental Ireland	*http://www.clubi.ie/malone/*
National Car Rental	*http://www.nationalcar-europe.com/*
National Car Rental	*http://www.nationalcar.com/servlet/ DocHandler/*

Payless Car Rental	*http://www.paylesscar.com/*
Pegasus Rental Cars	*http://www.rentalcars.co.nz/*
Practical Car & Van Rental	*http://www.tsnxt.co.uk/practical/*
Practical Rent-A-Car Systems	*http://www.practical-rentacar.com/*
Ramniranjan Kedia Rent-A-Car	*http://www.rnk.com/*
Rent A Car UK	*http://www.rentacar-uk.com/*

Rent A Wreck	*http://www.rent-a-wreck.com/*
Rental Car Guide	*http://www.bnm.com/la.htm*
Specialty Car Rentals	*http://www.specialtyrentals.com/*
Sun Cars	*http://ds.dial.pipex.com/air-flights/ carhire.shtml*
Thrifty Car	*http://www.thrifty-wales.com/*

Thrifty Car Rental	*http://www.thrifty.co.uk/*
Trip.com	*http://www.thetrip.com/*
Vancouver's Lo-Cost Car Rental	*http://www.locost.com/*
West Coast Van Rental	*http://www.clearvista.com/ westcoastvan*
Woods Car Rental	*http://www.woods.co.uk/*
Yellow Pages Car Hire	*http://www.yell.co.uk/travel/ worldcarhire.html*

Coaches

If you want to take it slowly, and take in the scenery en route, try a coach. It's frequently the cheapest way to travel.

Astarea	*http://www.astarea.hr/*

Buses By Bill	*http://www.buscharters.net/*

Covered Wagon Travel Service *http://www.servtech.com/public/wagon/cwtravel.html*

Diethelm Travel *http://www.diethelm-travel.com/*

Eavesway Travel *http://www.eaveswaytravel.com/*

Evan Evans *http://www.evanevans.co.uk/*

Globe Treks *http://www.globetreks.com/*

Irish Travel *http://www.irishtravel.com.au/*

Luxury Travel Motor Coaches *http://www.luxurytravelcoaches.com/*

Mayflower Acme Tours *http://www.mayflower.com.my/*

National Express	*http://www.nationalexpress.co.uk/*
Nor-Way Bussekspress AS	*http://www.nbe.no/*
Nova Travel	*http://www.sleepercoaches.co.uk/*
Oz and Kiwi Experience	*http://www.ozex.com.au/*
Putnik Yugoslavia	*http://www.putnik.co.yu/*
Redwing	*http://www.redwing-coaches.co.uk/*
Scottish Highlands Travel	*http://www.host.co.uk/allareas/travel*
Selwyns Travel UK	*http://www.selwyns.co.uk/*
Sheppard Touring	*http://sheppard.touring.co.nz/*

Utopia Tours

Welcome to Utopia Tours!
We've been providing motorcoach tours for more than twenty-five years. Check out our tour schedule for a complete lineup of motorcoach, air, and cruise tours. Join us for an upcoming tour and see why Utopia Tours has become the trusted guide for thousands of travellers.

We'll take you there!

Most Utopia Tour package prices include trip cancellation and interruption coverage.   This is just one of the ways we'll make your travel experience worry-free.

Owners, Steve and Elaine Angen

Utopia Tours
4422 Utopia Drive NW
Garfield, MN 56332

Utopia Tours	*http://www.utopiatours.com/*

Trains

A train journey is generally the fastest way to move overland. It's safe and relatively cheap. These sites have information for tourists including timetables and prices. Some will allow you to book online.

Alaska Railroad   *http://www.akrr.com/*
Amtrak   *http://www.amtrak.com/*
Association of American Railroads   *http://www.aar.org/*
BritRail   *http://www.britrail.co.uk/*

Burlington Northern Santa Fe   *http://www.bnsf.com/*
Central Trains   *http://users.aol.com/walesrails/ct.htm*

CSX Transportation	*http://www.csxt.com/*
Delayed.net	*http://www.delayed.net/*
Deutsche Bahn AG	*http://www.bahn.de/home_e/f-engl.htm*
Eurostar	*http://mercurio.iet.unipi.it/eurostar/eurostar.html*
Eurostar Passenger Services	*http://www.railpass.com/eurostar/*
First Great Western	*http://www.great-western-trains.co.uk/*
Great Eastern Railway	*http://www.ger.co.uk/*

The Great Little Trains of Wales

The Great Little Trains of Wales are narrow gauge railways built through the beautiful scenery of north and west Wales. Built in a time less hasty than our own, most originally served to carry Welsh slate from hill to harbour.

Now tourists have replaced slate as the main traffic, and dedicated volunteers have joined the paid staff in the work of restoring and running these pretty little railways.

- **Bala Lake Railway**
- **Brecon Mountain Railway**
- **Frestiniog Railway**
- **Llanberis Lake railway**
- **Talyllyn Railway** and its **Narrow Gauge Railway Museum**

Great Little Trains of Wales	*http://www.whr.co.uk/gltw/*
High Speed Trains by Oliver Keating	*http://keating.ml.org/trains*

InterCityExpress (ICE)	*http://mercurio.iet.unipi.it/ice/ice.html*
Isles of Scilly Travel	*http://www.compulink.co.uk/issco*
Japan Railway	*http://www.ejrcf.or.jp/*
Llangollen Railway	*http://www.marl.com/lds/Lr/llan-railway.html*

Midland Mainline	*http://www.midlandmainline.com/*
National Rail Corporation	*http://www.nationalrail.com.au/*
North Western Trains	*http://nwt.rail.co.uk/*
Pikes Peak Cog Railway	*http://www.cograilway.com/*
Public Transit in British Columbia	*http://www.transitbc.com/*

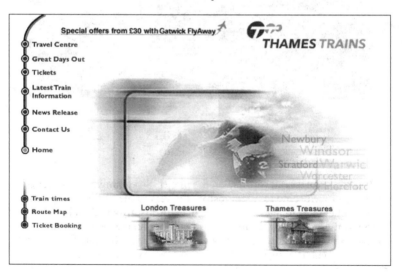

It is the greatest rail journey on the planet. Stretching almost 6,000 miles from Moscow to Vladivostok, the very name of this engineering marvel evokes images of exotic, adventurous, travel. As a leg of an around-the-world trip, I took the Trans-Siberian during the summer of 1994. Here I present my trip, as a guide for those who may follow, and entertainment for those who can't. Happy travels!

Tranz Rail	*http://www.tranzrail.co.nz/*
Travel Time	*http://www.vais.net/traveltime*
UK Railways	*http://www.rail.co.uk/*
Union Pacific Corp	*http://www.up.com/*
Union Pacific Railroad	*http://www.uprr.com/*
Virgin Trains	*http://www.virgintrains.co.uk/*

Welshpool and Llanfair Railway Society

The Station, Llanfair Caereinon, Powys, United Kingdom. SY21 0SF
Tel: +44 01938 810441 Fax: +44 01938 810861
Location: 52 39N 3 10W; UK National Grid reference: SJ218 075

Steep gradients and balcony saloon coaches from Austria feature on an eight-mile trip which starts a mile from Welshpool station on the national railway network. The Welshpool and Llanfair Railway is one of the eight <u>Great Little Trains of Wales</u>: narrow gauge railways located throughout the principality which have a combined marketing strategy giving bargain travel through purchase of a <u>Wanderer Ticket</u> valid either for eight days out of fifteen, or for four days out of eight.

| Welshpool & Llanfair Railway Society | *http://users.aol.com/walesrails/ wpool.htm* |
| West Coast Railway | *http://www.wcr.com.au/* |

Holidays

Some people prefer the 'all-in-one' approach and book a holiday that includes travel, accommodation, meals and even excursions.

A Travel Depot   *http://www.atraveldepot.com/*
Aerojets   *http://www.web-tech.co.uk/aerojets*
Amigo Travel & Tours   *http://www.usit.com/amigo*
B&B   *http://www.beduk.co.uk/*
Bargain Holidays   *http://www.bargainholidays.com/*

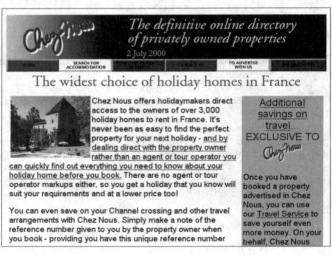

Chez Nous *The definitive online directory of privately owned properties* 2 July 2000

HOME | SEARCH FOR ACCOMMODATION | | CONTACT US | TO ADVERTISE WITH US |

The widest choice of holiday homes in France

Chez Nous offers holidaymakers direct access to the owners of over 3,000 holiday homes to rent in France. It's never been as easy to find the perfect property for your next holiday - <u>and by dealing direct with the property owner rather than an agent or tour operator you can quickly find out everything you need to know about your holiday home before you book.</u> There are no agent or tour operator markups either, so you get a holiday that you know will suit your requirements and at a lower price too!

You can even save on your Channel crossing and other travel arrangements with Chez Nous. Simply make a note of the reference number given to you by the property owner when you book - providing you have this unique reference number

<u>Additional savings on travel...</u> EXCLUSIVE TO Chez Nous

Once you have booked a property advertised in Chez Nous, you can use our <u>Travel Service</u> to save yourself even more money. On your behalf, Chez Nous

Chez Nous   *http://www.cheznous.com/*
Columbus Direct   *http://www.columbusdirect.com/*
Cornish Cottages   *http://www.corncott.com/*
Corsican Holidays   *http://www.corsica.co.uk/*

Country Holidays	*http://www.country-holidays.co.uk/*
Crystal	*http://www.crystal.co.uk/*
eBookers.com	*http://www.ebookers.com/*
Escaper Routes	*http://www.escaperoutes.com/*
Happy Time Tours and Travel	*http://www.httours.com/*

Internet Holidays	*http://www.holiday.co.uk/*
Internet Travel Services	*http://www.its.net/*
Ireland Travel	*http://www.12travel.com/*
James Villas	*http://www.jamesvillas.com/*
Jardine Travel Limited	*http://www.jardine-travel.com.hk/*
Last Stop	*http://www.laststop.co.uk/*

Magic Travel	*http://www.magictravelgroup.co.uk/*
Saga Holidays	*http://www.saga.co.uk/*
Scottish Travel	*http://www.travelscotland.co.uk/*
Simply Travel	*http://www.simply-travel.com/*
Thomas Cook	*http://www.thomascook.com/*
Ticket Anywhere	*http://www.ticketsanywhere.co.uk/*
Travel Bug	*http://www.flynow.com/*
Travel Bugs	*http://www.travel-bug.co.uk/*
Travel Select	*http://www.travelselect.com/*
Travel Travel	*http://www.travel-travel.co.uk/*
Travelstore.com	*http://www.travelstore.com/*
UK Hotels	*http://www.travellerschoice.net/*
Westravel	*http://www.westravel.co.uk/*
Worldtravelcenter.com	*http://www.worldtravelcenter.com/*
Worldwide Journeys	*http://www1a.btwebworld.com/ journeys*

Hotels

If you want to stop over for a night or two, or for whole weeks, there are lots of hotels on the web, many of which can be booked online, or reserved and confirmed by email.

A thru Z Hotel Finder	*http://www.from-a-z.com/*
All Hotels on the Web	*http://www.all-hotels.com/*
All Hotels on the Web - Scotland	*http://www.all-hotels.com/europe/ britisle/scotland*
All Hotels on the Web - UK	*http://www.all-hotels.com/europe/ britisle*

Best Hotel & Inn	*http://www.best-hotel.co.uk/*
Blackpool Hotels Directory	*http://www.blackpool-hotels.co.uk/*
British Hotel Reservation Centre	*http://www.bhrc.co.uk/londonhotels*
Country House Hotels Great Britain	*http://www.country-house-hotels.com/*
Creditview Bed and Breakfast	*http://www.bbcanada.com/*
Elegant English Hotels	*http://www.eeh.co.uk/eeh*

EVERYBODY .co.uk *incorporating*

* <u>Find hotels/services by County</u> or <u>Location</u> * <u>Hotel Central Res. Info</u> * <u>Airlines</u>
* <u>Forum</u> * <u>Shop</u>
* <u>About/How to Use</u> * <u>Pricing/Ratings Explained</u> * <u>Contact Us</u> * <u>Be Listed</u> *
<u>News</u> * <u>Links</u>

Welcome to the listings of World airlines, UK hotels and other travel related services which can all be used by anyone, disabled or able bodied

*** The world's ONLY accessible airline directory & the UK's most popular disability-friendly hotel directory! ***

- **Over 2000 mainstream, group and independently owned hotels assessed, listed & indexed by location**
- **Site listed in The Times' Top 50 Travel Sites on the Web : Over 100,000 visitors served to date!**
- **Not a hotelier or airline? - <u>Your service can still be listed here. How?</u>**

"Ideal for a family with a disabled member - you've probably never had such choice!"

Everybody's Hotel Directory	*http://www.everybody.co.uk/*
Expotel	*http://www.expotel.co.uk/*

Firmdale Hotels	*http://www.firmdale.com/*
Fodor's Hotel Index: London	*http://www.fodors.com/r*
Forte Hotels	*http://www.forte-hotels.com/*
Headwaters Hideaway Bed and Breakfast	*http://www.bbcanada.com/2121.html*
Holiday Inn London	*http://www.bookings.org/uk/html/ 30072.html*
Holiday Inns UK	*http://www.holidayinns.co.uk/*
Holiday Inns Worldwide	*http://www.basshotels.com/holiday-inn/*
Hotel Guide	*http://www.hotelguide.com/*
Hotels & Travel in the UK	*http://www.hotelstravel.com/uk.html*
Hotels Etcetera	*http://www.hotelsetc.com/d/905.htm*
Jarvis Hotels	*http://www.jarvis.co.uk/*
London Hotels	*http://www.demon.co.uk/hotel-net/ hotel.html*
London Hotels	*http://www.hotelsengland.com/*
London Hotels Reservation	*http://wkweb4.cableinet.co.uk/ ukhotels/ukhotels/*
Morton Hotels	*http://www.morton-hotels.com/*
Paramount Hotel Group	*http://www.paramount-hotels.co.uk/*
Posthouse Hotels	*http://www.posthouse-hotels.co.uk/*
Royal Glenn Hotel	*http://www.blackpool-hotels.com/*
Scenic Bed-and-Breakfast	*http://www.bbcanada.com/*
Scotland Hotels & Visitor Attractions	*http://www.freedomglen.co.uk/*
Smooth Hound: Hotels & Guesthouses	*http://www.s-h-systems.co.uk/*

Thistle Hotels	*http://www.thistlehotels.com/*
UK Hotels & Guest Houses	*http://www.smoothhound.co.uk/*
Virtual Hotels	*http://www.virtualhotels.com/*

Maps/Route Instructions

If you're touring the countryside you'll need to know where you're going and how to get there. These map sites should be very useful, especially if you can access the sites whilst you're on the move.

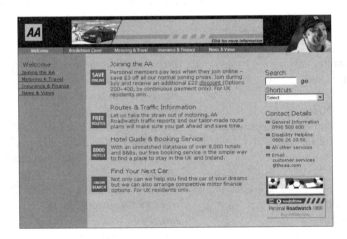

Automobile Association	*http://www.theaa.co.uk/*
Digital City	*http://home.digitalcity.com/maps*
EuroShell Route Planner	*http://www.shell.com/*
Michelin - Route planner, hotels and restaurants	*http://www.michelin-travel.com/*

RAC	*http://www.rac.co.uk/*
Railroad, Subway and Tram maps	*http://pavel.physics.sunysb.edu/RR/ maps.html*
United Kingdom Hotels & Maps	*http://www.guestaccom.co.uk/ mapuk.htm*

Travel Insurance

Insurance is something we all hope will never be needed, but accidents and mishaps do happen. If you arrive in San Fransisco and your baggage arrives in New York it will be reasurring to know that someone else can have the hassle while you just enjoy yourself.

1st Quote	*http://www.1stquote.co.uk/*
A1 Insurance	*http://www.a1insurance.co.uk/*
Bellevue Insurance	*http://www.bellevue-ins.co.uk/*
CGU Direct	*http://www.cgu-direct.co.uk/*
Champion Insurance Advantage	*http://www.charm.net/roy/*
Churchill Insurance	*http://www.churchill.co.uk/*
Clover Insurance	*http://www.clover-insurance.demon .co.uk/*
Columbus Direct Travel Insurance	*http://www.columbusdirect.co.uk/*
Cornhill	*http://www.cornhill.co.uk/*
Coversure	*http://www.coversure.co.uk/*
CSA Travel Protection	*http://www.travelsecure.com/*
Direct Insurance Group	*http://www.digs.co.uk/*
Eagle Star Direct	*http://www.eaglestardirect.co.uk/*
Endsleigh	*http://www.endsleigh.co.uk/protection/*
Global Travel Insurance	*http://www.globalholidays.co.uk/ intro.htm*

Halifax Travel — *http://www.halifax.co.uk/halifax-travel/*
Hamilton Fraser Insurance — *http://www.hamiltonfraser.co.uk/*
Hogg Robinson plc — *http://www.hoggrobinson.com/*
III Insurance Centre — *http://www.iii.co.uk/insurance/*
Insbuyer.com – Travel Insurance — *http://www.insbuyer.com/ travelinsurance.htm*

Insurance Centre — *http://www.theinsurancecentre.co.uk/*

Insurance Wide.com — *http://www.insurancewide.com/*
Insure Travel — *http://www.insuretravel.com/*
Int'l Student Travel Confederation — *http://www.istc.org/*
InterSure — *http://www.intersure.co.uk/cgi-bin/ nq_first*

Jacksons Insurance	*http://www.jacksons-insure.demon.co.uk/*
Leading Edge	*http://www.leadedge.co.uk/*
Livingstones Insurance	*http://www.livingstones-insurance.co.uk/*
Lombard Insurance Brokers Ltd	*http://www.lombardinsurance.co.uk/*
Midland Direct Travel Insurance	*http://www.midlanddirect.co.uk/docs*
Nomad Travel Insurance	*http://www.nomad-insurance.co.uk/*
Philip Everitt Insurance	*http://www.jca.co.uk/peveritt/*
Royal & Sun Alliance Insurance	*http://www.royal-and-sunalliance.com/*
Saga	*http://www.saga.co.uk/*
Simply Direct	*http://www.simplydirect.co.uk/sd_trav.htm*
SMS	*http://www.travelinsurance-sms.co.uk/*
SoreEyes – Insurance Quotes	*http://www.soreeyes.co.uk/*
SRI's Travel Medical Plans	*http://www.specialtyrisk.com/travel.htm*
St James Travel	*http://www.stjamestravel.co.uk/*
STA Travel	*http://www.statravel.co.uk/*
Tangent Insurance Brokers	*http://www.tangent-insurance.co.uk/*
TFG Global Travel Insurance	*http://www.globaltravelinsurance.com/*
TIA Travel Insurance	*http://www.travelinsurers.com/*
Travel Insurance Club Ltd	*http://www.travelinsuranceclub.co.uk/*
Travel Insurance Services	*http://www.travelinsure.com/*
Under The Sun Travel Insurance	*http://www.underthesun.co.uk/*
West Pennine Insurance	*http://www.westpennine.co.uk/*
Worldcare Travel Insurance	*http://www.worldcare.com.au/*
Worldcover Direct Limited	*http://www.worldcover.com/*
Worldwide Travel Insurance	*http://www.worldwideinsure.com/*